DEFINING DEMOCRACY

DEFINING DEMOCRACY

Electoral Reform and the Struggle
for Power in New York City

Daniel O. Prosterman

OXFORD
UNIVERSITY PRESS

OXFORD
UNIVERSITY PRESS

Oxford University Press is a department of the University of Oxford.
It furthers the University's objective of excellence in research, scholarship,
and education by publishing worldwide.

Oxford New York
Auckland Cape Town Dar es Salaam Hong Kong Karachi
Kuala Lumpur Madrid Melbourne Mexico City Nairobi
New Delhi Shanghai Taipei Toronto

With offices in
Argentina Austria Brazil Chile Czech Republic France Greece
Guatemala Hungary Italy Japan Poland Portugal Singapore
South Korea Switzerland Thailand Turkey Ukraine Vietnam

Oxford is a registered trade mark of Oxford University Press
in the UK and certain other countries.

Published in the United States of America by
Oxford University Press
198 Madison Avenue, New York, NY 10016

Library of Congress Cataloging-in-Publication Data
Prosterman, Daniel O.
  Defining democracy : electoral reform and the struggle for power in New York City /
Daniel O. Prosterman.
    p. cm.
  Includes bibliographical references and index.
  ISBN 978-0-19-537773-6 (hardback : alk. paper) 1. New York (N.Y.)—Politics and
government—1898–1951. 2. Elections—New York (State)—New York—History—20th century.
3. Municipal government—New York (State)—New York—History—20th century. 4. New York
(N.Y.). City Council—History—20th century.   I. Title.
JS1228.P76 2012
320.9747′109043—dc23

                                                                2012013156

9 8 7 6 5 4 3 2 1

Printed in the United States of America
on acid-free paper

To Megan

CONTENTS

ACKNOWLEDGMENTS

The saying goes that history is written by the winners. Nothing could be further from the truth according to the archival records of those who participated in the campaigns for proportional representation (PR) in New York City. Save for Robert Moses, the vast majority of PR's opponents within the Democratic and Republican parties did not leave their papers for public review. Pro-PR resources, however, remain abundant, with reform organizations and minority political parties providing a bounty of source material.

I would like to thank the many libraries and archives that allowed me access to their collections, in particular the Columbia University Rare Book and Manuscript Library. This library maintains the records of the Proportional Representation League, which served as the foundation for this study. Staffs provided invaluable assistance at so many other institutions, including (but certainly not limited to) the New York Public Library's Manuscripts and Archives Division, the Schomburg Center for Research in Black Culture, the Tamiment Library and Robert F. Wagner Labor Archives, the City Hall Library of New York City, the New York State Library, and the La Guardia and Wagner Archives at La Guardia Community College.

I thank the Trustees of the McDougall Trust Library for their generosity in providing a grant to supplement my research at the library and to deliver a presentation to individuals who currently advocate structural changes in democracy globally. The library shares offices with the Electoral Reform Society (ERS), several of whose members had recently returned from a campaign in Ohio when I arrived, demonstrating that an international struggle for electoral reform carries on in the twenty-first century. During my visits, Paul Wilder offered exquisite tea and hours of discussion concerning the history of proportional representation.

Funding from the Larry J. Hackman Research Residency Program, administered by the Archives Partnership Trust, enabled me to undertake research at the New York State Archives in Albany. Jim Folts helped me navigate the myriad resources available at the archives and never hesitated to suggest possible research strategies.

The Franklin and Eleanor Roosevelt Institute generously provided a grant for research at the Franklin D. Roosevelt Presidential Library. A fellowship with New York University's International Center for Advanced Studies created several opportunities for writing, research, and engaging scholars who participated in the interdisciplinary Project on the Cold War as Global Conflict.

I sincerely appreciate the commentaries of participants at the conferences where I delivered components of this project, including those at the University of London, the Museum of the City of New York, Columbia University, Wayne State University, Princeton University, University at Albany-SUNY, New York University, University College Dublin, Hamline University, and annual meetings of the American Historical Association in Atlanta and Philadelphia. I am especially obliged to the scholars who participated in the panel on democratic reform movements that I organized at the 2007 AHA Annual Meeting, including Elisabeth Israels Perry, Alexander Keyssar, and Robert Burnham.

During my graduate studies at New York University (NYU), my doctoral committee offered a stunning variety of perspectives that improved my understanding of the connections between electoral reform and broader historical movements. Ellen Schrecker, Robin D. G. Kelley, and Thomas Bender contributed their insight, while always prodding me to advance my own understanding of proportional representation's use and its implications for the study of urban political activism in a global context. Paul Mattingly helped create this project during my studies with him as a member of the Program in Public History at NYU. As my dissertation adviser, Marilyn Young offered seemingly endless encouragement through years of research and writing. Her perspectives on the Cold War spurred me to connect global processes and local events in ways I had never considered, and I remain indebted to her.

Gerald Leinwand and Louise Young graciously answered all my questions about life in academia and never failed to offer candid advice and support. For their thoughtful critiques and helpful recommendations, I also thank Rachel Bernstein, Martha Biondi, Neil Brenner, Linda Gordon, Greg Grandin, Steven Gregory, Allen Hunter, Walter Johnson, Rebecca Karl, Linda Kerber, Eric Klinenberg, Mary Nolan, Moss Roberts, Thomas Sugrue, and Daniel Walkowitz.

Graduate school can be a lonely place, and I am grateful to my peers at NYU for their advice and encouragement, including George Derek Musgrove,

Daniel Opler, David Kinkela, George Tomlinson, Erin McMurray, Suzanna Reiss, and Daniel Link.

As a Faculty Fellow in the College of Arts and Sciences at Syracuse University, I had the great fortune of working in a writing group with three superb colleagues: Jenna Loyd, Alicia DeNicola, and Judy Rohrer. Susan Wadley guided me through my early years out of graduate school with aplomb, and Vincent Stephens and William Robert provided wonderful camaraderie.

The Salem College community—colleagues and students—inspire me to always improve my teaching and scholarship. I am grateful to Susan Calovini and Ann McElaney-Johnson for their support in completing this book, as well as to the Committee on the Faculty. My department members—David Foley, Andrew Thomas, Tekla Ali Johnson, and Jennifer Piscopo—help make Salem a wonderful place to teach. For their years of mentoring, I thank Jo Dulan, Gary Ljungquist, Richard Vinson, Paula Young, and Janet Zehr. Elizabeth Novicki and the staff at the Dale H. Gramley Library never hesitated to provide assistance for any of my research quandaries. Julie Ann Bigsby, Sarah Abee, and Lindsey Dixon responded to my varied research queries with prompt, efficient assistance, and their work has been much appreciated. I single out the students in the 2010 Clio Colloquium for critiquing a presentation of this research.

The editorial and design staffs at Oxford University Press have been extraordinarily supportive and helpful through every stage of this book's development. My heartfelt gratitude goes especially to my editor, Nancy Toff, who has believed in this manuscript from its most embryonic stages, and Sonia Tycko, who has diligently facilitated all aspects of this project. Rick Stinson, production editor, and Patterson Lamb, copyeditor, offered critical feedback as the project neared publication. I also appreciate the comments provided by the press's two anonymous reviewers. I thank everyone at Oxford for their patience, enthusiasm, and encouragement, and for making me a better writer in the process of making this a better book.

I must offer my humble appreciation and love to my near and extended colleagues, friends, and families. Many thanks to Siobhan Ciminera, Kelli Chipponeri, Nova Ren Suma, and Lisa Mulligan, as well as Scott and Wendy. Chris, Sally, Judy, and Mike have welcomed me into their lives and this manuscript is better because of it. My brother, Jeff, and his wife, Karen, are always ready, willing, and able to aid in whatever ways they can. A big brother's advice is sometimes not fully recognized, much less followed. But Jeff has contributed to my intellectual and personal development since I can remember. I'm grateful that Vickie has joined our family, as we're all better off for her kindness. My parents, Louis and Dianne, always encouraged my studies and never wavered in their support. I hope they know how their words and thoughts continue to guide me. My daughter, Clara, showed endless patience for delayed playtime while I refined this manuscript. She is my reason for getting out of bed every morning (and several times during the night as well).

Finally, this manuscript is dedicated to the love of my life. My wife, Megan, has given more support to this project than I could have ever imagined. Our conversations and her witticisms both kept me on my toes and buttressed me in the most trying of circumstances. My dearest appreciation forms every word of this text.

INTRODUCTION

THE PERILS AND PROMISE OF DEMOCRATIC REFORM

"Democracity." Regardless of party affiliation or time period, few New Yorkers would have ever voluntarily characterized their city with such a word. Perhaps for this reason, planners of the 1939–1940 New York World's Fair held in Queens coined this term to name their model urban utopia. The Democracity pavilion promised to provide for all the needs of metropolitan citizens in the twentieth century—needs that the current political system appeared unable to meet. Democracity offered visitors an idyllic glimpse of city governance that could prevent depression and war. The scale exhibit of the "City of Tomorrow" served as the centerpiece of the fair, with millions of visitors transported via platforms high above the exhibit, witnessing the marvels of well-financed urban development . . . at least in miniature.[1]

Democracity appeared at a time of intense experimentation in the mechanics of democracy in New York City. Although the display did not mention this context, it was certainly on the minds of the planners as they developed the design for Democracity. In a radio interview in December 1936, the committee chair responsible for the fair's "World of Tomorrow" theme declared, "The seeds of great changes lie all around us today. They are found in the streamlined train, the airplane, the modern house. They are also

Democracity, the City of Tomorrow, glimmered as the centerpiece of the 1939–1940 New York World's Fair, held in Queens. Designers wanted the exhibit to captivate viewers with its futuristic vision for democratic urban planning. *New York World's Fair 1939 and 1940 Incorporated Records. Courtesy Manuscripts and Archives Division, New York Public Library, New York City; Astor, Lenox, and Tilden Foundations.*

found in such less tangible things as new forms of organization in government and business, and new techniques like proportional representation and cooperation."[2] In constructing the ideal metropolis, Democracity's designers considered governmental reform just as critical a component as the technological marvels of the day.

One month earlier, in November 1936, by a margin of nearly 2 to 1, New Yorkers had replaced their local government's board of aldermen with a city council elected using proportional representation (PR).[3] Most significantly, the PR electoral system enabled voters to rank candidates on their ballots. If a voter's first choice did not win, then that ballot would be distributed to the voter's second choice, or third choice, and so on. Under PR, if one wished to support a marginal candidate who lost, then the voter would still be able to support a second-choice candidate perceived as more viable. Rather than traditional winner-take-all elections among a few political parties, PR guaranteed victory to *all* candidates polling more than 75,000 votes. Instead of party nominations, candidates only needed to garner 2,000 petition signatures to automatically have their names added to the election ballot. Thus, any candidate representing any political organization could conceivably be elected. The system required multiple ballot counts and transfers to determine vote totals for the remaining candidates who garnered fewer than 75,000 votes. At the end of the first count, candidates receiving fewer than 2,000 votes were removed, with their second-choices distributed to the remaining candidates. This process continued, with one candidate removed following each subsequent transfer, until each borough possessed its designated number of council members. Proportional representation required continual reapportionment of council seats in the city's five boroughs because each borough was allotted one seat for every 75,000 votes cast for council candidates within its borders. The total number of seats depended upon the total number of votes cast in any given election cycle. This style of apportionment caused the size of the council to expand and contract like an accordion from term to term.[4]

In the long shadow cast by decades of single-party (Democratic) rule in local politics, PR posed a distinct threat to the city's political establishment. Reformers and minority-party members saw the procedure as a means of gaining local political power. Various progressive city organizations focused on the malfeasance of Tammany Hall (the Democratic Party's physical and symbolic structure in New York City) to contend that voters needed PR to recapture democracy at home in the midst of the Great Depression and growing totalitarian rule around the world in the 1930s.[5] To reformers, the old board of aldermen was nothing more than a municipal disgrace—a body that cared more about naming streets, the enrichment of lazy aldermen, and corrupt patronage than the city's welfare. On the other hand, the new city council elected by PR represented progress in urban governance, with the council empowered by a revised city charter to address New Yorkers' needs in a turbulent era.

Between 1937 and 1945, the voting system enabled the election of the most diverse governing bodies in New York City's history, including unprecedented numbers of third-party representatives. Under PR in 1941, Adam Clayton Powell Jr. became the first African American to win a seat on the city legislature. New Yorkers also utilized PR to elect the largest number of female legislators in the city's history. Most notably, Genevieve B. Earle, who helped draft the reform referenda that brought about these sweeping changes in local government, served as council minority leader for nearly all of PR's tenure.[6]

The logistics of PR as practiced in New York City were messy, to say the least. Borough-wide contests brought dozens of candidates into competition with one another. The Democratic-controlled Board of Elections withheld funding for counting machines, forcing scores of canvassers to tally and recheck ballots manually, with final totals requiring weeks to determine in some instances. Given the statistical prowess necessary to successfully manage a PR election under the best of circumstances, the point person for PR in the United States (and New York City) from the Depression era to the Cold War was a mathematician. George H. Hallett Jr. received his PhD in mathematics from the University of Pennsylvania in 1919. Dismayed by what he considered the unrepresentative nature of American democracy, Hallett saw the statistical complexity of a system like PR as a potential solution that promised greater equality of representation. He both crafted and advocated electoral reform from the 1930s until the 1980s.[7]

In spite of the counting delays and the relatively high cost to implement this new system, PR reshaped democracy in the nation's largest city. The system made possible the representation of numerous third-party organizations in City Hall, including the American Labor Party (ALP), the Liberal Party, and, most strikingly, the Communist Party USA. The Democratic machine, which had maintained virtually total control of the board of aldermen since the early nineteenth century, had only a tenuous working majority in the new council. Yet, the increase in minority-party representation led to rifts between the smaller parties. The ALP garnered five spots in the first PR election in 1937, two more than the Republican Party. Almost as soon as Republicans realized that their status as the secondary party in the city was threatened, they began to join Democrats in opposition to PR. Measured

Party Representation in the Board of Aldermen/City Council, 1935–1949

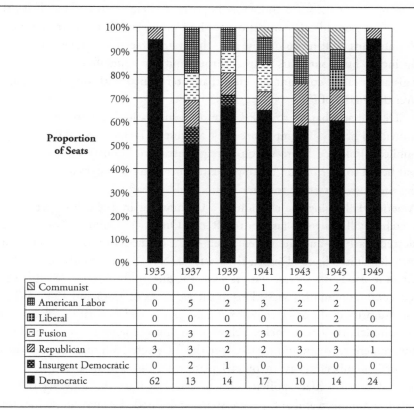

	1935	1937	1939	1941	1943	1945	1949
◨ Communist	0	0	0	1	2	2	0
⊞ American Labor	0	5	2	3	2	2	0
⊞ Liberal	0	0	0	0	0	2	0
⊟ Fusion	0	3	2	3	0	0	0
▨ Republican	3	3	2	2	3	3	1
▧ Insurgent Democratic	0	2	1	0	0	0	0
■ Democratic	62	13	14	17	10	14	24

Election rules permitted cross-party endorsements for council candidates. This table presents party affiliation according to each council member's main party affiliation. The Citizens Non-Partisan Committee endorsed several winning candidates, but none succeeded without ties to another organization. In 1941, Louis P. Goldberg won a council seat as an independent. After losing his bid for reelection in 1943, Goldberg won with the Liberal Party's support in 1945.

Source: For 1935 and 1949 figures, see Shaw, *History of the New York City Legislature,* 28 and 245. For remaining years, see *Annual Report of the Board of Elections in the City of New York for the Year 1937,* 45–46; *Annual Report of the Board of Elections in the City of New York for the Year 1939,* 29; *Annual Report of the Board of Elections in the City of New York for the Year 1941,* 32; *Annual Report of the Board of Elections in the City of New York for the Year 1943,* 29; and *Annual Report of the Board of Elections in the City of New York for the Year 1945,* 29.

proportionally, though, Republicans actually gained representation under PR—three members in a council of 26 representatives compared to three members in the 65-person board of aldermen. However, the Republican leadership viewed their party's diminished representation vis-à-vis the smaller parties as the greater concern. The incorporation of anti-Communist rhetoric into the PR discourse provided disgruntled Republicans a means of proving their patriotism and, more important, their status as the only legitimate (i.e., nonradical) competitor to the Democrats. With more and more Republicans shifting to oppose PR, the system faced two repeal attempts during its first four years of use. Throughout the council's early terms, the legislators faced constant scrutiny that intertwined with ongoing debates over the merits of PR.

Democrats characterized PR as an undemocratic threat to freedom and individual liberty. To emphasize their argument, Democrats (and some Republicans) likened PR to various foreign threats to US national security. As war began to rage in Europe, opponents portrayed the system as fascist, raising the possibility that totalitarianism could spread like a cancer to invade America. Following the election of a Communist in 1941, PR's detractors switched villains from fascists to "Reds." Opponents vilified Communists elected via PR—and the system itself—as a method for Soviet infiltration into the United States. Despite these attacks, New Yorkers continued to elect Communist Party representatives with PR during the Second World War, with two Communists victorious in the elections of 1943 and 1945. While the minority coalitions elected by PR never attained majority power in the city council, they nevertheless achieved an unprecedented diversity in local government representation. Moreover, the PR-elected minority utilized their council membership as an official platform from which to advocate enhanced social welfare policies and to stand against the growing tide of anti-Communism and anti-progressivism that flooded American politics following World War II.

Rather than isolating the contests over democratic rule in New York City, *Defining Democracy* connects local political struggles with broader historical processes. In the midst of global crises concerning the purpose and power of government during the Great Depression and Second World War, New Yorkers debated the meaning of self-rule in the United States. Using New York City as a microcosm of political culture in the United States, this book attempts a partial explanation for the hegemony of the two-party system in the United States—with local, urban politics at the center of ongoing struggles over the structure of democracy in this country.

For many, New York City government served as the antithesis to Democracy. High-profile investigations into municipal corruption littered the city's history. Generation after generation, self-anointed reformers and their press allies depicted the city's political structure as ineffective, wasteful, and corrupt. The Sisyphean battles for so-called good government never quite cleansed the city to the degree promised by reformers; however, these campaigns did prove beneficial in establishing a consistent means for New York's upper class to benefit from political participation without explicitly seeking to do so. Some of the wealthiest men in the country, including Peter Cooper and John Jacob Astor, contributed their seemingly infinite financial resources to reform campaigns that framed their self-interested, anti-populist struggles for elite political power as benevolent forays in civic improvement. Far from being a temporary phenomenon, this reform versus corruption trope provided the foundation for a series of political figures to rise to national prominence in the nineteenth and twentieth centuries. As justifications for their presidential campaigns, New York politicians from Samuel Tilden to Theodore Roosevelt to Franklin D. Roosevelt to Thomas Dewey cast themselves as victorious warriors who had fought against the city's vile forces of malfeasance, preparing them to combat any domestic or foreign threat as president.

This book presents cities as laboratories of democratic development. Rather than traditional depictions of municipalities as harbingers of democracy's doom, this study posits urban centers as constructing vital frameworks of democratic experimentation. In fact, it was often because of the challenges that city political mechanisms posed to the Democratic and Republican parties' monopoly of power that urban centers became represented as threats to democracy.

George Hallett and other activists forged international campaigns for electoral reform, resulting in fundamental changes to the structure of democratic practices in cities and nations throughout the world. Reformers in London and New York City shared resources, strategies, and encouragement during years of victory and defeat. To give one of many examples, PR elections were conducted in Dublin, Ireland, and Cleveland, Ohio, within months of each another in 1923. Hallett and his counterpart in London's Proportional Representation Society wrote the guidelines, trained the canvassers, and monitored the tallies performed in both cities.

While histories of democracy in the United States have often looked to struggles for the expansion of voting rights to situate their studies, *Defining Democracy* seeks to reorient our perspective to consider the importance of how democratic systems are structured in connection to their electoral outcomes. From the Nineteenth Amendment's ratification in 1920 to the Voting Rights Act of 1965, the United States has witnessed momentous extensions of voting rights during its history. Yet the structure of elections within this country has become remarkably static, particularly during the twentieth century. The expectation and acceptance of two political parties (Republican and Democratic) competing against each other with one victor and one loser in each election has remained a hallmark of American electoral politics for generations. Despite periods in which so-called third, or minority, parties succeeded, the dominant paradigm has remained the two-party framework. As this study suggests, one of the reasons behind this consistency has been the ongoing control by the two dominant parties of an electoral system that preserves their hegemony. However, as PR's use in New York City makes clear, this system of self-government has not been immune to fundamental change—and the quality of American democracy must be measured by diversity in representation as well as by diversity in voting rights.[8]

To contextualize the electoral rights campaigns of the 1930s and 1940s, the book begins with an overview of the nineteenth-century battles over government reform that precipitated the struggle for proportional representation. This section positions the movement for electoral reform within the context of long-standing competition between political coalitions over power in municipal affairs. The birth of municipal reform as an organized political platform coincided with elite New Yorkers' loss of local authority to Tammany Hall (the Democratic Party's Manhattan-based apparatus) in the nineteenth century. As part of this struggle for urban political power, PR gained credence with reformers as a policy for improving city governance through the transformation of municipal representation—a transformation that would entail the return of political power to an elite cohort of business owners, financiers, and lawyers.

Civic activists campaigned on the premise that reform would provide the electorate with an open political apparatus that would permit independent candidates and what reformers labeled a truer, more representative form of democracy. Yet these elite activists openly expressed their distaste for popular rule, often characterizing the masses as threatening progress in municipal government. Faced with little chance of unseating Tammany candidates under the established electoral system, reformers pursued a series of policies that could be instituted without popular approval, including unelected charter commissions and legal investigations of Tammany leadership. In this milieu, reformers devised PR as a means of ensuring elite, rather than mass, rule. Reformers structured PR as an electoral system that would increase the ability of elite candidates to win election independent of Democratic or Republican party support.

From the late 1880s through the 1920s, reformers' notion of what constituted reform shifted to incorporate the broader electorate as crucial participants in what they labeled a "Good-Government" movement. This change occurred as a diverse coalition of political activists joined good-government groups in calling for the ouster of Tammany Hall and affiliated organizations that had long monopolized power in New York City. By the time Judge Samuel Seabury, appointed by then-governor Franklin Roosevelt, concluded his investigations of municipal corruption at the height of the Great Depression, a reform alliance had coalesced that included Communists, Socialists, labor unions, anti-Tammany Democrats, Republicans, and women's rights activists, along with the elite civic associations that had campaigned for reform since the nineteenth century. Proportional representation provided the nucleus to which these political elements gravitated. Activists from across the city's political spectrum saw PR as the key to their quest for municipal power—an electoral system they believed would restructure local politics to weaken Democratic and Republican operations throughout the five boroughs and ensure their own representation in city government. This coalition of civic activists campaigned to fundamentally alter the city's balance of political power, culminating in a successful referenda campaign for charter reform and PR in 1936.

The electoral reform movement's greatest victory in the United States brought swift reaction, with activists arguing for PR's further expansion into statewide elections, and opponents rapidly maneuvering to prevent PR from ever being implemented in New York City despite its popular victory. Withstanding a series of legal challenges, and a prolonged public debate over the system's merits, the city conducted its first PR elections with the council tally of November 1937. New Yorkers utilized the system to elect the most politically diverse governing body in the city's history. Yet the Democratic Party, soon joined by the Republican Party, organized a vigorous assault against PR and the progressive council members elected by the system. Less than one year after the new council members assumed office, the state legislature pursued a statewide ban of PR. The repeal measure failed to attract support, primarily because many Democratic and Republican officials viewed the referendum as a crude attempt to reassert state supremacy over municipal government. In their eyes, retention of the system that threatened their hegemony appeared a lesser evil than a return to manipulation by the state legislature. As the debate over PR evolved, party officials and civic activists on both sides strengthened the notion that the fate of voting rights in New York was fundamentally tied to broader struggles over the nature of democracy in the United States and the expansion of totalitarianism globally.

The onset of World War II in Europe transformed political discourse in New York City. Local and international symbols fused in debates over municipal policies, elections, and voting rights. The opponents of proportional representation altered their rhetoric to more directly portray the electoral system as part of a Communist plot to weaken American security. This tactic sharpened with the appointment and subsequent resignation of a Communist Party member from the administration of Manhattan Borough President Stanley M. Isaacs. By the fall of 1940, Tammany Hall's attacks on PR fully incorporated rhetoric of national security, anti-radicalism, and anti-Communism. To repulse these increasingly grave depictions of PR, the system's supporters altered their arguments in ways that mirrored the tactics of their opposition. Long-time PR advocates developed visions of Tammany Hall that equated the political machine with international threats to domestic safety. As PR's detractors inflamed and directed anti-Communist sentiment toward the system, PR's supporters mobilized anti-fascist and anti-Nazi rhetoric to target organizers of the repeal movement.

The victory of one Communist Party representative in the 1941 council elections and two in 1943 cemented anti-Communism as the central rhetorical weapon for Democrats and Republicans in their assault on PR and progressive policy making in New York City. Against the backdrop of World War II and the continued presence of Mayor Fiorello H. La Guardia and President Franklin Roosevelt in city politics, the Communist legislators and PR survived the first half of the decade. Moreover, the two Communist council members actually won reelection *after* the war's conclusion, in November 1945, as the national anti-Communist fervor of the Cold War began to swell. Postponing a popular campaign against PR, the electoral system's most powerful opponents (who included New York City Parks Commissioner Robert Moses) designed a repeal strategy to implement following the conflict. The death of Roosevelt and the close of La Guardia's tenure in 1945 clarified the organizers' timeline, with the next off-year elections, in 1947, deemed the best opportunity to defeat the system.

With the repeal of PR framed as a referendum on Communism in the United States at the onset of the Cold War, the measure succeeded by a margin comparable to PR's victory in 1936. As predicted by the system's advocates, PR's downfall soon narrowed the spectrum of representation in local government. Changes in the city's political culture had dramatic consequences for the future of politics and government in urban America. Coupled with the end of the La Guardia and Roosevelt administrations, PR's defeat also blocked the legislative careers of progressive policy makers who struggled in vain to build a Second New Deal in the postwar era. Ironically, PR supporters succeeded in expanding proportional voting as part of post–World

Proportional Representation (PR) Referenda Results

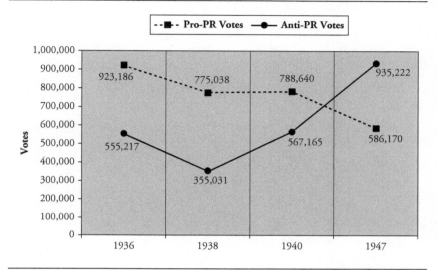

Although voters throughout the state of New York participated in the 1938 referendum vote, the figures shown here include only those votes tallied from New York City.

Sources: Annual Report of the Board of Elections in the City of New York for the Year 1936, 208–209; Annual Report of the Board of Elections in the City of New York for the Year 1938, 79; Annual Report of the Board of Elections in the City of New York for the Year 1940, 112; and Annual Report of the Board of Elections in the City of New York for the Year 1947, 60–61.

War II reconstruction projects in Germany and Japan. In the early twenty-first century, the State Department endorsed a form of proportional representation during the US occupation of Iraq as a means of ensuring greater diversity in the new Iraqi parliament.[9] In New York City, though, PR's defeat fostered a Democratic-Republican monopoly of power that continues to this day.

1

THE POLITICS OF ELECTORAL REFORM IN NEW YORK CITY HISTORY

During the second half of the nineteenth century, New York witnessed a series of battles over the city as a political entity as well as a symbol of American democracy. As the federal government fought to reassert its supremacy over the states of the former Confederacy during Reconstruction, the city experienced a protracted, often violent struggle of its own to determine who would control the reins of municipal government. Labeling themselves "Reformers," patrician, elite, Protestant New Yorkers attempted to retake supremacy in local governance from the Manhattan-based Democratic Party organization known as Tammany Hall. Although Tammany had influenced city politics since its inception in the late 1780s, the organization underwent a significant change in leadership and constituency during the middle decades of the nineteenth century. The Democratic Party leadership began to structure its municipal campaigns around the support of the city's burgeoning poor, immigrant (particularly Irish Catholic) communities. By attracting the masses, Tammany sought to establish a base of political power independent of the merchants and large-scale property holders who had previously controlled city government.

William M. "Boss" Tweed, who led Tammany from 1863 until his conviction for corruption in 1871, began his political career in the 1840s as a patron of anti-Catholic organizations. Nativist groups flooded city (and national) politics during the 1840s, campaigning for policies to prevent immigrant representation in government. One such group, the Native American Party, campaigned strenuously for electoral restrictions on recent immigrants. Anti-immigrant activists called for constitutional amendments enabling these restrictions without popular consent, including a proposal to reverse changes made to the New York State Constitution in 1821 that abolished property restrictions on certain voters, in effect extending the franchise to all white men.[1] According to historian Leslie M. Alexander, the city's free black male population actually held suffrage rights under the state constitution of 1777. While removing property restrictions for white male voters, the revised constitution of 1821 "required free Blacks to reside in the state for three years and own $250 in property in order to vote."[2] Following their intent to diminish black political empowerment, these stipulations resulted in stark racial inequality with regard to voting rights. In 1840, fewer than 90 black men were eligible to vote, yet the city's black population stood at more than 16,000.[3]

During the subsequent state constitutional convention of 1846, opponents of black male suffrage stressed the possibility that voting rights could lead to "negro masters," using fear-mongering rhetoric to present black New Yorkers as "aliens" unfit for citizenship.[4] The 1846 convention retained the property tax requirement for African American men.[5] Proponents of anti-democratic laws had amended the state constitution to compel the formation of a state constitutional convention every twenty years. In effect, this requirement established a consistent mechanism for altering the structure of city government, as well as a mandated opportunity to reverse any laws created by rival groups during the interim.[6]

Despite this successful first step by anti-Tammany elites to challenge the Democratic Party, Democrats organized sufficient opposition to scuttle the restrictions. While the city's upper class continued to direct mayoral elections through much of the nineteenth century, with the Republican and Democratic parties content to nominate business representatives to maintain the slightest semblance of respectability, every other level of municipal government shifted to representatives of the lower economic rungs aligned with Tammany Hall. For instance, the number of merchants serving in the Common Council decreased by half between 1838 and 1850. Small-business owners and workers replaced their wealthier counterparts, with most of these members of the nascent working class moving under Tammany's growing political umbrella.[7]

Tweed, who led a volunteer fire company during the antebellum years, provided a striking example of this demographic shift and the creation of a new political class. Following his nativist activism of the early 1840s, Tweed changed tactics and worked to galvanize support for Tammany from Western European, working-class immigrants. He rose through Tammany's ranks in the 1850s, as the organization strengthened its political power through practices aimed at gathering popular support and economic sustenance. Exemplifying the growing political voracity of Tammany and Tweed, the group adopted the tiger logo of Tweed's fire company as its public symbol. Block by block, neighborhood by neighborhood, district by district, Tammany and Tweed created networks of mutual support between the political organization and the masses. In return for food, clothing, employment, fuel, and sometimes cash, the city's poorest residents supported Tammany-endorsed candidates at the ballot box. Once elected, these officials directed civic projects and created patronage positions—the city's police force being perhaps the most prominent example—that further entrenched Tammany within working-class communities.[8]

The extent to which Tammany gained political support from New York's burgeoning immigrant population did not mean that the organization pursued policies contrary to the city's economic elite. Through much of the nineteenth century, Tammany bosses and the city's wealthiest bankers, merchants, and lawyers maintained a mutually beneficial balance of power within the Democratic Party. Tammany did not endorse economic radicalism or any particular policy that would have dramatically altered the city's economic structure. Both groups used the support of the other to mine the city's laboring masses for economic and political enrichment. The most glaring example of business-Tammany collusion involved the Common Council's fire sales of public assets during Tweed's aldermanic tenure in the 1850s. The City of New York leased and sold property, franchise rights, and development contracts to economic allies of the Democratic Party. The proceeds lined the pockets of Tammany's leadership, who used their bulging bank accounts to establish themselves as members of a new class of urban politician, able to finance party operations without the assent of the city's establishment.[9]

Even before the violent, chaotic years of the Civil War and Reconstruction, the tenuous alliance that bonded economic elites and Tammany within the Democratic Party fissured. In 1852, several of the city's wealthiest individuals joined forces to develop a political movement aimed at retaking municipal authority from Tammany. Led by Peter Cooper, the City Reform League labeled its objective as "reform," a term proponents wielded to define

opponents as self-interested, lower class, and corrupt. These same "Reformers" presented themselves as selfless, virtuous, and native-born leaders em-
barking on a crusade to cleanse municipal government of venal influences. In
this context, "reforms" effectively meant structural changes in local and state
government aimed at strengthening reformers' political power.

Though many self-designated reformers aligned with the recently created
Republican Party, they created anti-Tammany propaganda that incorporated
conflicting elements of pro-slavery and abolitionist rhetoric. As Republicans
developed a mythology of themselves as benevolent civic crusaders, they
often appropriated pro-slavery imagery in their struggle to weaken Tammany
Hall. Wealthy, predominantly Protestant reformers defined Tammany, which
was supported by Irish Catholics and other immigrant working-class communities, as a mongrel organization. Reformers caricatured Tammany as a
simian creature that achieved power through brute force, possessing neither
the education nor the temperament necessary to govern. While reform's
meaning evolved in coming decades, the term's rhetorical thrust remained
good versus evil.[10]

Through the rest of the 1850s, reformers pursued policies to dismantle
Tammany's sources of economic and political sustenance. With the rising
power of the Republican Party, the city's economic elites found it to be an
organization that could serve as their conduit to battle Tammany and retake
municipal power. Building on earlier success in establishing constitutional
conventions as a means of altering the political structure, the nascent reform
community saw the state legislature in Albany as an avenue for circumventing
Tammany, and New Yorkers', control over city government. Upstate Republicans, eager to control a legislative majority, allied with reformers in New York
City to revise the city charter and strip the municipality of its fiscal powers.
The state legislature created an unelected New York County Board of Supervisors to further supplant the Tammany-controlled, and popularly elected,
Common Council.[11]

Nominally separated from the city-state power struggle by a term in the
US House of Representatives, Tweed succeeded in gaining a seat on the Board
of Supervisors in 1857. He quickly consolidated his authority within the
board and developed a network of political power that came to be known as
the Tweed Ring, which connected Tammany Hall with all levels of city and
state government. As Tweed rose in Tammany's leadership, the organization's
influence expanded to incorporate the municipal judiciary and many of the
consolidated departments originally created by reformers as a means of
moving power away from Tammany.[12]

With the onset of the Civil War, the struggle between the city's economic and political elites exploded in violence. Tammany supporters drove the contest into the streets in protest of Republican policies for abolition and a federal draft. The war revealed intense divisions within the Democratic Party between Tweed's supporters in Tammany Hall and the merchants, bankers, property owners, and lawyers who had controlled local politics for decades. The Tweed faction criticized President Abraham Lincoln relentlessly, fusing charges against federal policy with anti-Republican and anti-elite rhetoric aimed both at weakening the Republican mayor and Tammany's own opposition within the Democratic Party. The Democratic Party split over support for the Union war effort, with Tammany gaining control in the tumult of 1863 and many wealthy members leaving the party leadership.

The Draft Riots of July 1863 ruptured the city over ongoing tensions concerning the nature of race and civil rights, economic power, and political authority. Rioters objected to Republican policies through murderous assaults on blacks and destruction of symbols of elite prosperity, including a Brooks Brothers clothing store. Likewise, key components of the city's Republican hierarchy defended their assets with violent force. Anti-Tammany publishers wielded Gatling guns along Newspaper Row, and Wall Street merchants defended their economic core as though it were a medieval fortress, ready to rain acid and incendiaries upon any perceived threat. The violence left at least 119 people dead and hundreds more wounded.[13]

In the riots' aftermath, Tammany and its opponents continued their war for municipal power, struggling to define the riots and proper punishment for those deemed responsible. The violence served as a lightning rod for anti-Tammany groups, and the city's economic leaders expanded their earlier reform networks to create a public campaign to wrest control of local government from Tammany.[14] Several of the city's wealthiest individuals, including John Jacob Astor and Peter Cooper, created the Citizens Association, which joined the recently constituted Union League Club and the Taxpayers' Union.[15] The groups brought allies to the cause of reform, which from their perspective meant the removal of the political apparatus that had enabled the riots. Republicans sought to decimate Tammany's base of popular support, calling for mass convictions and executions of the Irish Catholic immigrants they charged with responsibility for the uprising. Tweed, who became Tammany's leader in 1863, further enhanced his standing by negotiating a middle ground that urged prompt, just punishment while cautioning against investigations that discriminated against immigrants and the poor. By the war's conclusion, Tammany, through Tweed's leadership, had gained exclusive control of the New York City Democratic Party. Disaffected elite Democrats responded by joining Republicans in the reform coalition.[16]

Emboldened by growing Republican power in Congress following the war, New York City Republicans entered Reconstruction arguing for a slate of reforms that linked the urban chaos of the riots with miserable social conditions exacerbated by Tammany misrule. Reformers argued that social improvements would remove the causal factors—overcrowding, poor housing, and inadequate public health services—that, they claimed, led to the riots. Echoing earlier notions of reform, policies advocated during the immediate postwar period served to weaken Tammany power as much as improve living conditions in New York City. Reformers in the state legislature established a new spate of unelected, ostensibly independent commissions that were granted the authority to restructure the city's approach to fire control, health care, and housing. These policies centralized municipal authority within specific departments, in the hopes of more efficiently dealing with the city's problems. Efficiency, in this context, meant abolishing patronage offices that had positioned Tammany allies throughout the municipal bureaucracy. In one example, reformers ended city contracts with independent fire companies—long a means of directing government funds to Tammany allies—and switched to a centralized department controlled by the municipality.[17]

Displaced from power in the war's aftermath, the Tammany-controlled Democratic Party campaigned to supplant Republican majorities in city and state government through a race-baiting platform that linked local Republicans with their radical counterparts in Congress. Fusing city, state, and national politics, Tammany contended that Republicans subverted democratic, majority rule through their sweeping civil rights policies. Tammany declared that these reforms empowered blacks by disenfranchising working-class European immigrants—the Democratic Party's base of political support in New York City. In the 1868 elections, Democrats regained their majorities in the city and state legislatures.[18]

During Reconstruction, Tammany recognized reform's saliency and co-opted the term. In 1870, Tammany called for reforming the unequal power balance between New York City and the state in the hope of returning municipal authority to the city. Local Democrats supported revisions in the city charter, endorsed by former Tammany member and then-governor John Hoffman, that would be initiated by the Democratic state legislature. Rather than simply dismantling the municipal improvement programs begun by elite reformers, Democrats expanded these projects and the related patronage employment opportunities, to the benefit of the local citizenry and Tammany Hall.[19]

In July 1871, as after the Draft Riots of 1863, violence provided the core element of a Republican campaign against Tammany Democrats. Protestant Republicans supported a parade of Irish Protestants, known as Orangemen or Hibernians, along Eighth Avenue in Manhattan through a predominantly Irish Catholic neighborhood. Seemingly to no one's surprise, a violent confrontation erupted along the parade route, as local residents objected to the march. The so-called Hibernian Riots that ensued resulted in more than 60 deaths, and Republicans immediately called for their assumption of power in the name of innocent victims of Irish Catholic government under Tammany Hall. Anti-Tammany activists jumped on the incident in much the same way they reacted following the Civil War Draft Riots, with Republicans attempting to regenerate their recently lost municipal and state majorities by portraying the carnage as a stark example of Tammany misrule.[20]

Troubled by the anti-elite forces that organized the Paris Commune months earlier, Republicans fused the violence in Paris and New York City into a thesis that the upper class was under siege from a communist threat that extended across the Atlantic. According to historian Mary P. Ryan, reformers sought to develop a category "capable of transcending the ethnic division" in New York City and provide them with a means of unifying privileged residents across party lines. That category became "taxpayer." Ryan cites *Civil Rights, the Hibernian Riot, and the "Insurrection of the Capitalists": A History of Important Events in New York in the Midsummer of 1871* (New York: Baker, 1871) as the primary reform text created by wealthy Protestants to mobilize support for their reform plans. Republicans framed their campaign for municipal reform as crucial to a larger battle for economic progress against a class-oriented foe that sought to crumble capitalist wealth. To a far greater degree than previous arguments, the fusion of Tammany corruption with the Paris Commune and the Hibernian Riots swelled middle- and upper-class support for reform.[21]

Taxpayer, property owner, and citizen were equated—but those who did not meet certain property and income requirements were excluded from the civil rights and civic power afforded by citizenship. This coalition of property-owning taxpayers threatened to usurp government (meaning Tammany) authority by refusing to pay taxes until Tweed, Tammany, and the Democratic Party were removed from power. This warning also sought to shift the political loyalties of Tammany's patrons in local government, as municipal employees relied upon government finances for their livelihoods.[22]

The *New York Times* and other prominent anti-Tammany publications enhanced the threat facing wealthy New Yorkers by adding anti–Irish Catholic prejudice to their vision of an anti-capitalist conspiracy. In editorial articles and cartoons, the *Times* argued that Tammany power provided for an Irish Catholic takeover of the city's political, social, and economic structure. Recalling imagery from the 1850s, cartoonist Thomas Nast depicted reformers as uniformly virtuous, both politically and morally, with their goal of cleansing an innocent city of Tammany apes—simian caricatures also used in derisions of Irish Catholics—who threatened to raze the city. It was at this time that Nast developed caricatures of Tweed and his patrons that galvanized anti-Tammany rhetoric. Cartoons such as "Who Stole the People's Money?" published by the *Times*, depicted the Tammany Ring as a cohort of bloated figures utterly absorbed with their own wealth and unable to admit responsibility for municipal corruption. These cartoons crystallized elite arguments into an ironically populist vision of reform fighting to save the masses from urban political corruption that would endure for decades.[23]

Month after month in 1871, Tammany's strongest opponents in the press and the Republican Party, along with anti-Tammany rivals within the Democratic Party itself, built momentum for an official investigation into corruption under Tweed's leadership. Brandishing bold mission statements ostensibly focused on removing corruption throughout city government, both the New York City Council of Political Reform and the so-called Committee of Seventy, formally titled the Executive Committee of Citizens and Taxpayers for the Financial Reform of the City of New York, formed in 1871 specifically to destroy Tammany. These groups, populated by a narrow selection of wealthy reform advocates, operated under the guiding principle that the most expedient means of ending Tammany rule would be to remove Tweed. Reformers, though, made sure not to take their case to the public. Their strategy held that criminal investigations, rather than popular referenda, provided the highest likelihood of success. Tweed's ultimate removal in 1871 amounted to a municipal coup. The investigation avoided public participation, with Tweed's arrest, trial, verdict, and imprisonment brought by anti-Tammany interests that included the reform groups, allied judges, and Democrats who had competed with Tweed for control of the party.[24]

Samuel Tilden, who led the New York State Democratic Committee from 1866 until his gubernatorial victory in 1874, endorsed the Tweed investigations and subsequently directed a state commission designed to restructure city government to further weaken Tammany. As part of this civic reformation, Tilden and other Swallowtail Democrats, so called because of their expensive frock coats, strove to enact structural changes in the city's electoral process to increase "minority" representation. At the time, reformers defined minority to mean the educated, upper-class members of society who had been prevented from holding office, they argued, by Tammany. Reformers pursued the restriction, rather than the extension, of voting rights as the solution to corruption as well as the deathblow to the Tammany political apparatus. Ironically, Tilden had risen to power in New York City and then state politics as a Tammany Democrat whose rhetoric on voting rights echoed the exclusionary, racist diatribes of the party's leadership during the antebellum period. In 1868, Tilden implored other Democratic leaders to emphasize that the party's "position must be condemnation and reversal of negro supremacy."[25] In this context, Reconstruction-era reformers ushered proportional representation (PR) into New York City politics, with the objective of making permanent the recent shift in municipal supremacy to anti-Tammany, Protestant, middle- and upper-class Republicans and Democrats.

Simon Sterne, who created the Personal Representation Society in 1866 to lobby for minority-representation electoral systems in municipalities throughout the country, provided New York City's reformers with a framework for supplanting Tammany Hall. Sterne was influenced by the writings of Thomas Hare, a British jurist who devised a form of proportional representation that incorporated the single transferable vote (STV), which allowed for voters to mark candidate preferences on their ballots. As envisioned by Hare, the STV enabled voters to move beyond party allegiance in the electoral process to diversify representation in government. In 1865, Sterne met in England with Hare and John Stuart Mill, Hare's most prominent supporter, and returned to the United States to advocate the use of proportional representation, particularly in New York City. Sterne preferred the list model of proportional representation rather than the Hare transferable vote model later used in New York City Council elections. As the list system allotted legislative seats strictly according to the percentage of votes received by each party's list of candidates, this format would have ensured greater non-Tammany representation in City Hall.[26]

Sterne's *On Representative Government and Personal Representation*, published in 1871, outlined how to empower economic elites politically by creating electoral regulations that guaranteed their legislative presence. For Sterne, reform meant a limited suffrage that would effectively disenfranchise the working-class, immigrant masses, thus diminishing Tammany Hall's electoral base. Sterne's model for ensuring greater "personal representation" heightened voter eligibility requirements and created a more complex balloting process to reduce popular participation in elections. Sterne's allies in the wealthiest circles of the city argued that electoral reform would, at the same time, increase their own power in local government and weaken political machines such as Tammany Hall.[27]

Sterne served on the "Committee of Seventy" as secretary, using this position to endorse a new electoral framework for the board of aldermen that contained key elements of later proportional representation systems. Nine aldermen represented five separate districts. The cumulative system allotted nine votes to each voter, with voters able to distribute their selections to as many or as few aldermanic candidates as they desired. As with later PR proposals, reformers supported this system as it bypassed Tammany Hall to permit a variety of candidates to run and win election in multiple-representative districts. Unable to defeat Tammany candidates in single-victor campaigns, the plan provided the opportunity for electing some non-Tammany representatives even if Tammany continued to win many or, as proved more likely, most legislative seats.[28]

After Governor Hoffman, a Tammany ally, vetoed the charter on the grounds that it violated the state constitution, a city charter commission devised an alternate aldermanic election process in 1873. This system, which endured until 1887, expanded district representation to three aldermen each. Voters could vote for two candidates in their district and up to four of seven at-large representatives. This form of limited voting, as it was termed, increased minority representation by allotting more seats than voters could select, thereby diminishing voters' ability to defeat specific candidates.[29] In the context of New York City political battles, the limited vote enabled candidates to gain office without the assent of the Democratic or Republican party machines on a district-by-district basis.[30] The use of the cumulative vote for the city legislature occurred during what historian David Hammack has called the "Era of the Swallowtails," a period between 1872 and 1886 when "every man elected Mayor of New York City was a prominent merchant who owed his nomination to the most important politically active group of Democrats among the merchants, bankers, and lawyers who directed the city's economy."[31] Through electoral reform and influence over Democratic *and* Republican party nominations, New York's economic elite sought to permanently replace Tammany Hall as the dominant force in municipal politics.

Following Tweed's removal in 1871, Tammany's leadership strove to strengthen the organization's infrastructure in the face of mounting reform challenges. After Swallowtail Democrats replaced Tweed with "Honest John" Kelly, Kelly defied reformers and enacted the structural changes that created the basis for Tammany's return to dominance within the local Democratic Party by 1875. Kelly's Tammany Hall returned to power through consolidation of political operations throughout the city. Tammany implemented a hierarchical structure that connected district operations throughout the city, with the organization focusing its resources on gathering the support of the city's Irish Catholic neighborhoods.[32]

Attempts by Tammany to quell reform activism and vice versa continued through the decade, with reformers again attempting, in 1876–1877, to dismantle Tammany by altering the municipal code. Governor Samuel J. Tilden created a reform commission in 1876 with the complementary objectives of weakening Tammany and increasing Tilden's political prominence during his campaign for the presidency against Republican Rutherford B. Hayes. The Citizens Association and the New York City Council of Political Reform spawned the Civil Service Reform Association (CSRA), which sought to regulate Tammany's control over municipal appointments. Many in the press who had previously endorsed the Tweed Investigations again called for attacks on Tammany. George William Curtis, editor of *Harper's Weekly*, and E. L. Godkin, editor of the *Nation*, led the new CSRA, along with Carl Shurz.[33]

Rallying support around the mantra of taxpayer privilege, Tilden and his commission argued that the franchise must be limited to improve government in New York City. The commission proclaimed that power should be held by a narrow subset of the population—"the choice of the local guardians and trustees of the financial concerns of cities should be lodged with the taxpayers."[34] The chief supporter of proportional representation, Simon Sterne, served on the commission and endorsed Tilden's campaign as a means of instituting the electoral system in the nation's largest city.[35] Sterne marshaled the specter of communism as a threat to New York City's political, economic, and social stability—a threat augmented by expanded suffrage laws, in this case referring to increased voting access for recent male immigrants from Europe. Against a backdrop of increased labor activism amid a nationwide economic depression in the 1870s, reformers contended that popular (white, male) suffrage fostered corruption and could lead to social rebellion. As the *Nation* characterized the situation, "Communists and bosses" stood against Governor Tilden's Municipal Commission in 1877.[36]

Sterne commented that the commission, charged with reforming city government, had rightly concluded "that the only remedy for the manifold evils in the government of our cities lay in a limitation of the suffrage."[37] As the *New York Times* covered Sterne's address to the Political Science Association on June 5, 1877, Sterne argued that property must be considered a requirement of participation in the electoral process. Without such a requirement, the *Times* paraphrased Sterne, "the adoption of universal suffrage in municipal

Governments had worked incalculable injury to the property-holding class, which should by every law be the governing class, and had given rise to a dangerous system of communism."[38] For Sterne, universal suffrage equaled communism, with the open vote bringing peril to the wealthy. Sterne saw this threat "of aggression" as one of suffrage's central effects, equating political corruption with "ruffians who steal a man's purse in the open street."[39] Sterne concluded that proportional voting offered the only hope of attracting the elite to the polls as "it was folly to expect that the property-holders generally could be induced to take that interest in Municipal political affairs that they ought to take when they knew that they were casting their votes for nothing and that their influence was as powerless for good as idle wind."[40] Sterne portrayed expanded white male suffrage as violent and potentially revolutionary. This conception recast antebellum-era anxieties of black male empowerment into a figure of ambiguous racial ancestry who desired to steal wealth and political power from those deemed, because of their already elevated economic status, best suited to leadership in New York City.

The Tilden Commission's proposals failed due to a coalition of labor organizations, working-class activists, and Tammany Hall, which allied around the conclusion that their constituents' voting rights must be protected. The Workingmen's Party actively participated in the campaign, organizing demonstrations to oppose the commission.[41] Tammany labeled the franchise a "sacred right" and characterized their coalition as defenders of the right to vote for the city's laboring class, comprised of immigrants struggling to establish themselves as equal citizens in the United States.[42]

Faced with defeat, reformers turned to public campaigning as another tactic in their struggle against Tammany supremacy. The "Good Government Club" movement focused on electing reformers to local government and organized district-based campaigns to rival, if not overpower, those of Tammany Hall. During the 1880s and 1890s, reform groups cross-pollinated in their efforts to expand reform's reach throughout city affairs. The Civil Service Reform Association aided the creation of the Commonwealth Club in 1886. William Jay Schieffelin helped found the City Reform Club in 1882 and eventually served as the executive director of the Citizens Union (CU). Theodore Roosevelt supported both the CSRA and the City Reform Club.[43] The City Club of New York formed in 1892, with trustees that included some of the world's wealthiest individuals, such as John Jacob Astor, August Belmont, J. P. Morgan, and Cornelius Vanderbilt.[44] The City Club played a crucial role in the establishment of the Good Government Club movement, which sought to create district clubs throughout the city—providing the basis for a reform counterorganization to the Democratic Party. The *New York Sun* derisively labeled their members "Goo-Goos."[45]

In an effort to centralize good-government activism and strengthen its political reach, a coalition of middle- and upper-class reformers created the Citizens Union as a permanent city political party in 1897. Ultimately, the CU failed as a party and in 1908 restructured itself as an activist group that critiqued municipal government and endorsed reform candidates.[46] As good-government groups formed to counter Tammany's near monopoly of power in municipal politics, Republican leaders began to characterize reform as crucial to their party's success. In the 1890s, Republicans supported several electoral reforms endorsed by civic organizations. The anti-Tammany reform coalition saw the Republican-controlled state legislature as holding the key to overcoming Tammany's dominance at the local level.

Hoping to further limit Tammany's ability to reject policy changes, Republicans looked to constitutional revision at the state level as the most viable course for reform. Although a constitutional reform proposal passed in 1886, Republicans waited until 1894, the year after they gained a majority of delegates, to actually call the convention. Once at the convention, reformers succeeded with one of their primary objectives—the installation of the secret ballot. As with proportional representation, New York reformers imported the secret ballot initiative from overseas—in this case, Australia—specifically to reduce labor representation. The New York proposal likewise won the approval of Republicans and independents for its propensity to suppress voter turnout and thereby diminish support for urban, primarily Democratic candidates. When implemented according to the new regulations, the secret ballot weakened organizational power by making it nearly impossible for party officials to tell which candidate a specific voter selected. As Tammany Hall and other party organizations succeeded in offering quid pro quo exchanges for voting the party line, the secret ballot hindered Tammany's ability to monitor voters individually.

Reflecting reformers' continuing desire to thwart the electoral power of the masses, the secret ballot also created a de facto literacy test for the voting public. Party election canvassers could no longer fill out ballots or guide voters through the selection process at the polls. Thus, the secret ballot required that voters read, comprehend, and mark the ballot correctly for their choices to be counted.[47]

Republicans attempted to further undercut electoral support for their Democratic opposition with other policies aimed at restricting the franchise in the name of reform. The convention passed a requirement that newly naturalized citizens wait 90 days before becoming eligible to vote. Another amendment required eligible citizens to submit personal applications in order to register to vote. Recognizing the Republican Party's strength in small towns throughout New York State, the voter registration amendment exempted municipalities of fewer than 5,000 residents.[48]

Reformers also succeeded in separating municipal voting from state and national elections. This amendment sought to create distinct campaigns and electoral tallies for different levels of government. By shifting mayoral and other local elections to odd-numbered years, reformers argued that candidates would address issues of municipal importance. The policy also resulted in lower voter turnout, as the electorate did not participate in votes for local offices as enthusiastically as for state and national contests.

In 1896, the Republican-controlled state legislature amended the ballot law to ease straight ticket voting while simultaneously making cross-party voting—ticket splitting—more difficult. With candidates listed in separate columns by party affiliation, voters only needed to make a single mark to vote for a single party. At the same time, the state legislature "doubled (to six thousand) the number of signatures required for statewide independent nominations and instituted a requirement for at least fifty petitioners in each county."[49]

During this flurry of so-called good-government reforms, Republicans and non-Tammany Democrats again suggested PR as a means of increasing middle- and upper-class representation. Simon Sterne and Albert Shaw advocated having the City of New York, consolidated in 1898, governed by a city council elected by PR. Consolidation expanded New York City—then encompassing Manhattan and the Bronx—by adding Brooklyn, Queens, and Richmond to the municipality.[50] These reformers attempted to persuade others that consolidation provided the opportunity for structural reform in city government—centering power in a governing body that, through PR, could not be controlled by Tammany Hall.[51] Shaw used the London County Council as a model for creating a New York City Council. Rather than single-member districts, members would be elected on an at-large basis, removing the Tammany district organizations from control over the election process.[52] Reformers succeeded in centralizing power in the mayor's office, at that point still controlled by Swallowtail Democrats, but failed to institute PR.

During the debate over city consolidation, Sterne petitioned the 1894 state constitutional convention as the president of the Proportional Representation Society of New York. In the address, Sterne linked his campaign for PR with what he termed "misrepresentation" in the state legislature. The plan called for city elections in larger districts with multiple representatives in each geopolitical unit. He argued that the current system of small, single-member districts harmed both Republicans, in city elections, and Democrats, in upstate elections. Sterne argued that PR would "promote citizenship," "encourage statesmanship within the party," and "give freedom and independence not only to the electors, but also to the elected [by placing] men of high character and marked ability into our legislative bodies." While Sterne's rhetoric incorporated earlier elements of reform campaigns, he crafted a new argument for PR that focused on the additional government representation the system would afford the masses—a seemingly populist stance for the previously anti-populist reformer. Asserting that "workingmen are not adequately represented in our legislative bodies," Sterne declared that electoral reform "appeals with special cogency to those considerable classes of voters, like farmers, mechanics and laboring men who have interests which they feel should be represented."[53]

Yet Sterne maintained the notion that the elite, distinguished by "education and independent character," would provide the masses with the best government. As he put it, "power drifts toward intelligence, and a resolute and intelligent minority injects [sic] into our legislative bodies would, in defiance of all counter and selfish interests, exert a moral influence beyond all proportion to their numerical strength." With PR used to "purify elections [and] elevate the tone of public life," Sterne concluded that the "foremost minds, the best purposes, and the highest intellects of the country" would be brought "once more into political activity." The end result would be a system that stabilized government and prevented "radical or revolutionary changes" initiated "by reasons of slight changes of public opinion."[54] This position presented the seemingly contradictory conclusion that PR would both restructure the legislature to follow more closely the will of the people and populate the legislature with independent representatives who, by virtue of educational enlightenment, would govern without regard to public opinion.

As historian David Hammack has written, Sterne's rhetoric may have represented a broader shift in reform politics, with an emerging sentiment that reform should seek to improve the entire city's social and economic welfare. Sterne, Shaw, and other PR advocates asserted that the benefits of PR extended beyond the election of superior government officials. They contended that a reformed, consolidated New York would enable the creation of citywide programs to improve social conditions, including health and economic services for the poor. These arguments represented an important change in the rationale behind reform in general and PR specifically, which shifted to incorporate progressive reform as a crucial benefit to governmental and electoral reform.[55]

Sensing that an enlarged city would bring greater opportunities for political power, Tammany initially favored the 1894 consolidation referendum. The prospect that consolidation could benefit the reform movement, though, altered Tammany's perspective. It joined the *Brooklyn Eagle* in opposing the measure shortly before Election Day. Brooklyn political interests feared takeover by Tammany, which concluded that the forces behind consolidation strove to wield reform as a weapon to weaken Tammany.[56]

As consolidation moved closer to becoming a reality, opposition also grew among civic groups that had formerly supported the proposal. For instance, the City Club and the Union League Club opposed consolidation, as they feared a Republican plan to essentially use consolidation to take over the patronage positions and city departments controlled by the Democratic Party. The consolidated city charter included only minor structural changes— so as not to lose too much support from both Republicans and Democrats.[57] According to Hammack, Greater New York City ultimately emerged to suit the interests of the city's mercantile interests and the Republican Party.[58] While the charter incorporated certain aspects of reformers' goals for municipal reform, such as placing fiscal powers in a board of estimate and apportionment rather than the city legislature, and a centralized public school system, it ultimately resulted in a mishmash of departments and regulations that enabled Tammany Hall's resurgence for the next 30 years. Consolidation won by a vote of 176,170 to 131,706. Kings County (Brooklyn) voters, though, only narrowly passed the measure, with a margin of less than 300 votes—64,744 to 64,467. The county's strong opposition to consolidation lingered in ongoing battles over apportionment versus Manhattan that continued far into the twentieth century.[59]

In the years following consolidation, Tammany Hall collaborated with Republican Party leadership in an electoral strategy to preserve exclusive, two-party dominance in City Hall and the five boroughs. Even when anti-Tammany candidates, such as Columbia University President Seth Low in 1901, won office, they possessed little ability to institute structural reforms during their tenures. Low, a Republican who ran without the endorsement of his party's establishment, served only a single, two-year term.

For political activists who desired representation outside of the Democratic-Republican hierarchy, reform offered the only successful path to power. At the New York State Constitutional Convention of 1915, reformers articulated a new message that appealed to the city's antagonistic relationship with the state legislature in Albany. The American Proportional Representation League and the New York State Proportional Representation League provided the central arguments for installing PR as the primary electoral method for the state legislature. The most important matters considered during the constitutional convention were legislative apportionment and home rule, specifically relating to the power of New York City to govern itself independent of the state legislature. At the time, the state maintained budgetary authority over the city and sole control over whether and how the municipal structure could be altered.

In addition, although New York City held more than half the state's population, the majority of seats in the state legislature belonged to representatives of districts outside the five boroughs. As the Tammany Democratic organization monopolized power in the city, the Republican Party dominated the rest of the state. The unequal distribution of seats in the state legislature, with the more populous city holding fewer seats proportionally than less-populated areas, meant that Republicans held a wide majority in the legislature. During the 1915 convention, Republican delegates outnumbered Democrats 116 to 52.[60]

Not surprisingly, New York City Democrats argued that the most important issue to be debated at the convention concerned "Home Rule." Home rule intended to transfer fiscal control over the City of New York from the state government back to City Hall. In attempts to weaken the Tammany machine during the nineteenth century, the state legislature had shifted the balance of fiscal authority over the city to Albany. This policy shifted, rather than decreased, corruption to the halls of the state government, with legislators representing towns throughout the state battling for authority over New York City tax revenue. The home rule issue presented New York City Republicans with an acute dilemma—whether to support the state party's position at the expense of increasing the city's, and potentially their, overall governmental authority. In this instance, city Republicans and independents joined Democrats in support of home rule. Home rule's opportunity for municipal enrichment even spurred a limited reevaluation of the merits of proportional representation, as this temporary coalition incorporated a version of PR in their supplemental proposal for increased city representation in the state legislature.

Future Democratic US senator Robert F. Wagner led the reform coalition at the convention. With his focus on securing greater city power in Albany, Wagner argued that statewide proportional voting was necessary to better reflect the city's will in state affairs. Wagner and allied delegates thus supported a version of PR quite similar to that proposed by good-government reformers for city elections. Wagner situated PR within a language of civil rights, arguing that the current apportionment policy "discriminated" against New York City.[61] He marshaled a pro-PR rhetoric that framed the system as representing core national values—equal representation, majority rule, and patriotism—and framed the opposition as anathema to those ideals. Opponents chided Wagner and his proportional representation platform, arguing that the nation was founded on majority rule, not minority representation. At the heart of the argument lay a struggle for power in state and municipal government, but delegates framed that argument in terms linked to an underlying disagreement over the structure of democratic government in New York City and state.

With concern for city representation in the state legislature outweighing long-standing divisions over which political organizations held power within the city, the 1915 constitutional convention provided a crucial moment when a broad coalition of city political interests joined in support of electoral reform and PR. Democratic and Republican politicians who argued against PR for New York City before and after the convention endorsed the system when it offered the possibility for greater city representation in the state legislature.

The convention's proposal failed before the voters on November 2, 1915, primarily because convention delegates appeared to scuttle the reforms by packaging them in a single, win-or-lose referendum. Many of the central reforms presented in the constitutional referendum, including the short ballot and home rule, succeeded in later years as separate measures. Home rule passed in 1923–1924 and the short ballot in 1926–1927.[62]

During the decade after the 1915 constitutional convention, New Yorkers and Americans more broadly experienced the tensions of the First World War and its aftermath and the competing impulses produced by the conflict—leading to various calls for the expansion or contraction of political participation and representation. One dramatic example of the era's promise and perils was represented by the success of suffrage with the ratification of the Nineteenth Amendment in 1920 and the growth of the postwar Red Scare. These historical processes held powerful ramifications for local struggles over municipal democracy and PR in New York City.

The limitations of major-party support for proportional representation in the state legislature, much less the New York City Board of Aldermen, was made apparent following the election of several Socialists to city and state government amid the Red Scare following the Russian Revolution in 1917. In 1920, Republicans and Democrats allied to vote 140 to 6 to bar the seating of five Socialists elected to the state legislature. Four of the Socialists had already served terms in Albany, but anti-Communism provided justification for the dominant parties to overrule the election results.[63]

Calling for protection against supposed Russian-sponsored threats to domestic security, the Democratic-Republican establishment successfully quashed leftist and moderate political activism in postwar New York State. State senator Clayton Lusk directed far-reaching investigations of radical, pacifist, and progressive activists. Aided by hundreds of police officers, the so-called Lusk Committee used police raids to intimidate critics and narrow the spectrum of political views deemed permissible in the state. Buttressed by the federal Espionage and Sedition Acts of 1917–1918, Lusk considered the committee's purpose to be one of ensuring national security by rooting out seditious activity—not simply gathering information, but actively working to destroy what he characterized as anti-American radicalism.[64]

In New York City, the Democratic Party used its majority standing in the board of aldermen to end Socialist and reduce Republican representation. In 1917 and 1919, New Yorkers elected seven Socialists to the 67-member aldermanic board. The Socialists possessed little authority in the board. Yet the mere presence of a vocal minority upset the status quo balance of power to such an extent that Tammany Hall endorsed dramatic steps to ensure its control of local government. At the time when the state legislature barred Socialist representation as a matter of security, the Democratic Party pursued city-wide redistricting for the same ends. In the 1921 elections after redistricting, Socialists received roughly the same percentage of the vote as before but could not elect a single candidate.[65]

The Democratic redistricting plan dramatically reduced Republican representation as well. Whereas Republicans maintained a respectable membership in the board of aldermen during the first two decades of the twentieth century, even holding majorities in four of the 10 two-year terms during this period, the party saw its membership in the board dwindle after 1921. Republican representation decreased throughout the 1920s so that by 1932, the board possessed a membership of 64 Democrats and one Republican.[66]

Threatened by the escalation of Democratic power in the board of aldermen during the early twentieth century, reformers resumed their advocacy of proportional representation as a means of ensuring democracy in the nation's largest city. For many good-government activists, the creation of a charter commission in late 1921 seemed the perfect opportunity to resume their struggle for PR. On the heels of a series of victories that had occurred in cities nationwide since 1915, reformers set their sights on New York City as the potential jewel in the crown of the electoral reform movement. For them, victory in the nation's largest city could propel the PR campaign nationally and even globally, serving as a symbol of the movement's vitality and necessity.

By 1922, several American towns and cities had adopted the Hare PR method, distinguished by the single-transferable vote and multi-representative districts. These municipalities included Ashtabula, Ohio (1915); Boulder, Colorado (1917); Kalamazoo, Michigan (1918); West Hartford, Connecticut (1921); Sacramento, California (1920); and Cleveland, Ohio (1921).[67] In each municipality, good-government activists directed the creation of charter reform bodies that presented public referenda for PR's incorporation. Reformers argued that referenda offered the best opportunity for success, with the voting public providing a means of circumventing the established political parties. In Ashtabula, shortly after altering their municipal government to a city-manager plan, voters approved the system by a tally of 588 to 400.[68] Five years later, residents defeated a proposal to scuttle PR by a margin of 2,775 to 2,336.[69] After voting to install the system in 1917, Boulder voters twice decided to retain it: 2,730 to 1,340 in 1923; and 1,709 to 1,284 in 1925.[70] With these successes, the Proportional Representation League continued its quest to spread electoral reform throughout the country, offering advocacy and legislative consultation as other charter reform committees promoted municipal reform referenda that included PR.

In Ohio, Michigan, and California, public approval of PR spurred a series of legal objections that resulted in competing rulings from state to state. The primary charge against PR rested on the claim that the system violated voters' constitutional right to participate in every election for representatives of a given political district. According to this reasoning, PR enabled multiple representatives per district and thereby prevented voters, who could vote only once, from participating in the election of each of their representatives. The constitutional provisions on which opponents based such charges originated in laws designed to end property requirements and other regulations used to restrict voting rights. The legal interpretation that voters held the right to vote for every elective position that represented their given district threatened PR's use in cities throughout the country, as the system achieved diversity in representation by expanding the number of representatives per district and permitting voters to rank candidates for those offices. In non-PR elections, voters often decided between two candidates for any given office and thereby held the authority to vote for one candidate and effectively against the other. By having voters submit only one vote for candidates in districts with more than one member, and many more candidates than seats, PR limited voters' ability to prevent the election of unfavorable candidates. The system thereby expanded the array of candidates able to win elective office. The latter's impact engendered PR's support among reformers and opposition from the political parties that dominated municipal politics. By diversifying democratic representation at the local level, PR removed the monopoly of authority Democratic and Republican organizations held over the nomination of candidates, the boundaries of political districts, and the size and structure of municipal legislatures. This expansion of electoral power outside the Democratic and Republican leadership caused the parties to mount legal challenges in every city that adopted PR.

In February 1918, Kalamazoo voters approved proportional representation by a margin of 2,403 to 659. In the city's first PR election two months later, a Socialist Party member gained a seat on the town commission, unleashing a wave of charges that PR aided radicalism. Shortly after the second PR election in 1919, in which the Socialist won reelection, the Michigan Supreme Court ruled the system unconstitutional. The court concluded that since the commission contained seven members, "Each elector had the right to vote for seven candidates."[71] Thus, according to the court, PR violated the state constitution's requirement that voters be able to vote in all elections.

In addition to attacking PR on constitutional grounds, the Michigan court asserted that the system's use internationally, coupled with the public's inability to understand its operation, required the system's removal. Going out of its way to connect PR with the specter of Communist expansion, the court emphasized its use in Poland and Russia to conclude that "those countries least experienced in systems of government with sovereign power vested in the people adopt [PR] with greater avidity than older nations of long experience which have made that form of government fairly successful and stable."[72] Coupled with its characterization of the Hare system as "too intricate and tedious to be adopted for popular elections by the people," the court's emphasis on PR's use in Eastern Europe implied that a larger crisis of democratic instability necessarily followed PR's use in Michigan.[73] The supporters of proportional representation charged that the court ignored the variants of PR operating in Western Europe and Scandinavia to spuriously connect the system with the creation of the "Socialist Soviet Republic."[74] In the context of national anti-Communist and anti-Socialist campaigns that followed the end of the First World War, the Michigan court's implication that PR abetted the spread of radicalism in Europe fused the system's legality with the domestic Red Scare—a link that ended PR's use in Michigan and threatened its standing in several other states.[75]

On November 30, 1920, Sacramento voters approved by a margin of 7,962 to 1,587 a new city charter that incorporated PR for council elections. During the city's initial use of the system in May 1921, voters uncharacteristically elected to the nine-member council three independent candidates, as well as the city's first female council member and first labor union representative.[76] In the fall of 1921, a California Superior Court ruled the electoral system constitutional. Yet, the following year, a California District Court of Appeals overruled the lower court and proclaimed PR illegal. In language similar to that used by the Michigan Supreme Court, the California appellate court concluded, "The right to vote 'at all elections' includes the right to vote for a candidate for every office to be filled and on every proposition submitted."[77] The court voided the election results and ordered a new vote held under the city's previous electoral regulations.[78] During the next election held without PR, the labor representative lost, along with each of the independent candidates.[79]

In 1908 Oregonians voted to legalize PR with a nearly 60 percent majority, but the Republican-dominated state legislature subsequently stalled legislation that would have implemented the system. The People's Power League, a direct-democracy proponent that railed against the power of political parties, endorsed PR as one of a number of structural changes needed in local government. With the next election cycle in 1910, the legislature presented the electorate with a referendum essentially proposing that they overrule the 1908 measure. The voters refused by a wider margin than in 1908. However, PR's supporters came five percentage points short of passing a broader reform package that would have also mandated PR elections for the state legislature. Following well-financed, statewide activism against PR, voters rejected the system in referenda in 1912 and 1914. These campaigns, which found the state's highest-circulation newspaper and its largest political party united in their opposition to the electoral system, provided a model for future anti-PR operations in other cities, including New York.[80]

These successful challenges to proportional representation, directed primarily by the political parties most threatened by the system's redistribution of electoral power, occurred in response to initial victories for PR at the polls. The system's incorporation occurred through public municipal reform campaigns, with grassroots supporters of PR referenda outnumbering opponents by frequently wide margins. As would be attempted by a coalition of Democrats and Republicans at the 1938 New York State Constitutional Convention, the Connecticut state legislature outlawed the use of PR shortly after West Hartford voters approved the system.

The constitutional status of proportional representation proved ambiguous, though, as other state courts ruled in favor of the system. While Michigan and California courts ordered PR's removal, Ohio courts approved PR after Cleveland's adoption. The Ohio courts decided that PR did not violate voting eligibility requirements, as every voter retained the ability to vote for a representative in his or her district.[81] This ruling paved the way for Cincinnati to install the system in 1924.[82]

Supporters of proportional representation in New York closely watched these legal developments, and George Hallett urged the head of the Sacramento Chamber of Commerce to write to the New York City Charter Commission to prevent its chair from getting "cold feet" and dropping PR from the commission's list of recommendations.[83] Privately, Hallett and his allies debated the legality of the system they publicly advocated. Albert Sprague Bard, chair of the Proportional Representation League, expressed concern over PR's constitutionality and feared the results of a legal test. In correspondence with the Citizens Union, Bard concluded that the legal issue was "pretty closely balanced. The question depends perhaps on one's fundamental point of view as to the constitution, and as to one's own desire for PR to be constitutional or unconstitutional."[84] When the 1922 New York City Charter Commission finally considered PR, its legal counsel recommended against including the system in any charter proposal without a constitutional amendment that specifically permitted the system.[85] Still seeking to solve the legal question in 1927, Hallett floated the idea of amending the Rochester city charter to incorporate PR, then "have someone bring a taxpayer's suit" against the city for planning to utilize an unconstitutional method of voting. He concluded that the courts would then be compelled to rule on PR's legality.[86]

The Proportional Representation League (PRL) in New York City and the Proportional Representation Society (PRS) in London corresponded frequently, developing strategies concerning all aspects of their campaigns for electoral reform. The PRL and PRS discussed the proper mechanics of PR voting (and counting), challenges they faced in convincing the public of PR's merits, and updated each other with progress reports concerning their efforts to expand PR's use.[87] Though not yet successful in New York City by the closing years of the 1920s, electoral reformers on both sides of the Atlantic had built a network of support for PR that accomplished significant changes in how millions of people voted throughout the world. In 1923, within a month of one another, voters in Cleveland, Ohio, and Dublin, Ireland, utilized the single transferable vote to elect their local legislatures. Supporters championed the list system's use in parliamentary elections in more than a dozen nations, including Denmark, Japan, Australia, Switzerland, and Sweden. The visionary British author H. G. Wells, who wrote such classics of early science fiction as *The Time Machine* (1895), *The Invisible Man* (1897), and *The War of the Worlds* (1898), advocated structural political reforms in the United States, Great Britain, and globally that centered on the incorporation of proportional representation in democratic elections. In a 1924 article, Wells characterized the progress and work still needed to be accomplished by the trans-Atlantic movement for electoral reform:

> There is a very respectable movement for Proportional Representation in the United States of America, but it has still to be realized as practical politics and a serious need by the American public. In America every citizen is born either a little Republican or else a little Democrat; it does not matter what the Republican or Democratic platform is or what sort of man is put up for him in his division, he has to vote for his party. Or else go through a crisis almost like disowning his father and mother and vote for the other party. There is nothing else in the world for him to do in politics.[88]

Wells concluded, "The United States is young, prosperous, and at a great advantage to the rest of the world; it may be able to afford its present travesty of democracy for a long time yet. Britain cannot."[89]

In correspondence with John H. Humphreys, director of the Proportional Representation Society in London, about the use of PR in electing the German Reichstag, Fritz Kauffmann described the list system in 1925 as "effective." Framing PR as "inevitable owing to the multiplicity of opinions" in Germany, Kauffmann concluded, "Only great leading minds or a strong religious or philosophical or economical movement or growing political understanding all over the whole people may diminish the number of parties."[90] The global economic crisis known as the Great Depression soon created the context for the sort of radical change in Germany feared by Kauffmann. After decades of uneven progress toward comprehensive reform in New York City, the Depression dramatically altered the local political landscape, and a coalition of reformers and anti-Tammany politicians moved swiftly to capitalize upon the ruptures caused by the economic crisis.

2 RESTRUCTURING URBAN DEMOCRACY AMID THE GREAT DEPRESSION

After three decades of virtually total control over New York City government, Tammany Hall began the 1930s seemingly in a position of overwhelming strength. Tammany directed the nation's largest city, with a population of 7 million paying property taxes that totaled more than one-half billion dollars annually. Municipal government employed 148,000 workers at a yearly payroll of $286 million. These totals provided Tammany with an enormous, self-perpetuating supply of patronage opportunities and the money to ensure Democratic hegemony for the foreseeable future.[1]

But Tammany's mismanagement and the Great Depression provided the fuel for growing popular support for reform. Unprecedented civic payrolls meant unprecedented levels of corruption—widely known, or at the very least suspected, for years. As the scope of the economic crisis worsened by the month, the Depression provided reformers with a new, compelling rationale for overthrowing Tammany.

Samuel Seabury, who at 28 had become the youngest city court judge in the city's history in 1902, had participated as an independent Democrat in anti-Tammany, good-government campaigns for decades. From a prominent Protestant family with local roots dating to the colonial era, Seabury realized that his crusade for reform could have the appearance of essentially an anti-Catholic struggle; privately he admitted, "I am afraid that Tammany is going to counterattack by saying that we are going after [Mayor James J.] Walker, [Tammany Hall leader John F.] Curry, and the others on religious grounds."[2] To quiet such criticisms, when he began his Tammany corruption investigations, Seabury hired Catholics to his staff.

Charged by the New York Supreme Court and supported by Democratic governor Franklin D. Roosevelt, Seabury began his inquiries in September 1930 with an investigation of corruption in the Magistrates' Courts. The private and public hearings continued for one year, with more than 1,300 witnesses examined.[3] Seabury's findings of collusion between the courts and the New York Police Department's vice squad, with police officers framing and grafting payments from criminal suspects, led to the expansion of his investigations to the Manhattan District Attorney's office.[4]

In March 1931, the Republican-controlled state legislature expanded the investigations to include the entire New York City government. As Governor Tilden had done in 1876, Governor Roosevelt reversed his earlier opposition to broader investigations and endorsed them, at least partially as a way to improve his stature in preparation for his 1932 presidential campaign. Also following the precedent of the Tilden Commission, advocates of proportional representation positioned themselves to take advantage of the opportunity presented by the Depression-era investigations. The newly formed Joint Legislative Committee to Investigate the Affairs of the City of New York, chaired by state senator Samuel H. Hofstadter, appointed Seabury as its chief counsel.[5]

Reformers salivated at the prospects raised by the rapidly evolving investigations, extending higher and higher into the city's political hierarchy. The possibility emerged that the mayor and the entire Democratic leadership might be indicted on corruption charges. The Hofstadter Committee's work lasted well over a year, until December 1932, and more than 2,000 witnesses testified. The hearings revealed corruption throughout the five boroughs, in courts, police departments, borough offices, and various city departments. Borough presidents, party leaders, court officers, and judges were found to have grafted money from party campaign coffers and made deals with private business interests for personal profit. Dozens of public employees amassed personal fortunes in the span of only a few years: In the middle of the Depression, a Kings County judge earned $510,000 in six years on a $12,000 salary, and a Queens borough president gained nearly $200,000 during a similar period from misappropriation of campaign funds. The committee also investigated manipulation of city unemployment relief by Democratic district officers, who appeared to have distributed money almost exclusively to fellow Democrats, regardless of need.[6]

Coupling the ongoing hearings with his own political future in 1932, Governor Franklin Roosevelt performed a feat of political theater to rival that of 1876 Democratic presidential nominee Samuel Tilden. Just as then-governor Tilden had organized an investigation of Tammany Hall as a means of increasing his stature as a national candidate, Roosevelt facilitated an election-year inquiry that served to distance him from the state's, and arguably the nation's, most powerful party apparatus. In the spring and summer, during Roosevelt's campaign for the Democratic nomination, the focus of the corruption investigation shifted to Mayor Walker. Walker symbolized the style and upper-class excesses of the Jazz Age. He particularly enjoyed flouting reformers' standards of mayoral decorum by partying into the wee hours and starting his workdays at City Hall in the early afternoon, if at all. Testimony revealed that the mayor had deposited for himself nearly $1 million from unnamed sources, much of it in cash, since taking office in 1926. The lack of restraint that characterized Walker's public persona during the 1920s, though, struck a different chord during the Depression. He resigned on September 1, 1932, providing Roosevelt with a useful victory two months before Election Day. The Roosevelt campaign used the struggle against Walker as evidence that Roosevelt was not a product of the Tammany machine, a claim that had dogged the failed presidential campaign of Democrat Al Smith four years earlier.[7]

The successful investigations, coupled with currents of despair and agitation wrought by the Depression, provided good-government advocates with the necessary foundation to restructure municipal government in New York City and beyond. Seabury connected the reform movement in New York City with anti-machine causes in other American cities. Speaking before the City Charter Committee of Cincinnati in February 1932, Seabury revealed his cause's central rhetorical traits that would be marshaled against Tammany Hall for the next several years. "The power of Tammany Hall," Seabury declared, "is not only a menace to New York City—it is a menace to the nation as well."[8]

Eager to use the municipal investigations to further the cause of electoral reform, proportional representation advocates, including Seabury himself, maneuvered for a public referendum on PR to coincide with the release of Seabury's final report for the Hofstadter Committee in December 1932. As early as February 1932, George Hallett presented this strategy to Paul Blanshard, director of the City Affairs Committee, a Socialist-civic reform organization:

> Judge Seabury suggested the possibility of bringing up the question of forming the charter commission to a vote just after he submits the final report of the Hofstadter Committee next February, in which case he would make his final hearings and report lead up to the PR-city manager charter which the commission would be pledged in advance to prepare. [Seabury] also expressed confidence that if a charter containing proportional representation were adopted by vote of the people the constitutional question could be presented to the present Court of Appeal in such a way that the charter would be upheld.[9]

This plan made clear Seabury's understanding of the steps necessary to win popular and legal success for proportional representation, with his public hearings about municipal corruption providing the springboard for an all-out campaign for PR.

Seabury and Hallett agreed that Seabury's investigations must provide the political context for an activist charge by pro-PR groups. Seabury suggested that in the process of concluding his months-long investigation into municipal corruption, he work in tandem with activist organizations calling for PR. As Seabury prepared his final report on municipal corruption, including his recommendations for revamping city government, reformers called for a special election to create a charter commission capable of proposing structural changes in local governance. Seabury and Hallett concurred that the best opportunity for the public to back such a commission would be when Seabury released his final report to the Hofstadter Committee. Seabury crafted his final report to support what reformers believed would be the central component of the commission's own recommendations—proportional representation. For Seabury, the fate of PR in New York City meant "all the difference between a sustained good government year in and year out . . . and a spasm of reform once in a generation."[10]

In fact, reformers concluded that the commission could be created with support for proportional representation already engrained. With Seabury's report backing PR, along with the concomitant creation of a charter commission designed to back it, the two remaining hurdles for electoral reform would be a public referendum on the system and a possible court challenge. Seabury, according to Hallett's recollection, believed that the most critical way of ensuring a positive ruling would be by winning a public referendum. Hallett and Seabury concluded that popular will held the key to PR's ultimate success or failure—at a moment when even the system's staunchest supporters reckoned that "not one-tenth of one percent of voters have even a notion about it."[11]

In the midst of the Hofstadter/Seabury hearings, Hallett approached the chair of the Republican Advisory Committee for New York County (Manhattan) and argued that the Republican Party should support proportional representation as a means of increasing its own political power. Hallett used the example of PR's influence on party power in Cincinnati:

> The Republican Party in New York City occupies much the same position as the Democratic Party in Cincinnati, which has elected its proper share of minority representatives under PR and, joining forces with the representatives of the independent elements in the majority party, has had a share in the control of the city and its phenomenal achievements for the last six years.[12]

The implication was clear: supporters of proportional representation urged Republicans to join a movement behind PR explicitly as a means of weakening Tammany Democrats and, as Hallett described the carrot, increasing Republican power in New York City. When he approached Republican leaders to garner support for PR, Hallett also petitioned Governor Roosevelt directly.[13]

Not surprisingly, in his final report, Seabury located the primary enemy of reform, and thus the primary cause of malfeasance, within the Tammany Hall political machine. He asserted: "In a very large measure the affairs of the City of New York are conducted, not with a view to the benefits which can be conferred upon the residents of our City, but for the profit which the dominant political organization in the City and its satellites can make out of the running of it."[14] Seabury underlined the corruption discovered and examined during the committee's two-year investigation; moreover, he emphasized that Tammany was responsible for the wretched state of local government, civic pride, and democracy. With that conclusion in mind, Seabury proposed a series of reforms aimed at destroying the machine and instituting in its place a government made up of reform-minded public officials as the arbiters of political power in New York City.

Accompanied by pages and pages of testimony concerning graft, waste, greed, and general incompetence, Seabury quoted president-elect Roosevelt's call for immediate "drastic reform in the details and structure of the administration of [the] city."[15] Roosevelt, who supported the creation of the American Labor Party to combat Tammany opposition to his presidential candidacy, thus encouraged Seabury's strident call for reform. Roosevelt and Seabury implicitly argued that Tammany corruption had exacerbated the impact of the economic depression in New York City. Both focused on the suffering experienced by New Yorkers as a central justification for a full-scale attack upon Tammany Hall.

Due to Tammany's gross mismanagement, Seabury urged the state legislature to recognize "that no substantial improvement in the processes of our City government can reasonably be anticipated unless a radical change be made in the legislative and money-spending agencies of our government."[16] Seabury argued that the only effective method of improving city government would be to ensure minority representation in the municipal governing body. Seabury coupled this call for the end of single-party rule with proposals to constrict city government, removing the patronage positions and economic practices that funneled economic and political support to Tammany Hall. Seabury's reform package pledged to:

> diminish the appropriation of large sums of money, ostensibly for City improvement but, in truth, for the creation of excuses for hiring hordes of party workers; [reduce] the number of unnecessary boards, bureaus, departments and commissions, now existing only for the purposes of patronage, and of the politically appointed and controlled heads thereof; [and offer a] critical attitude towards the functioning of all the City departments and result in the elimination of a great deal of favoritism, graft and inefficiency therein.[17]

Seabury connected PR and charter reform to removing municipal corruption by showing a direct link, through the Joint Legislative Committee investigations, between the structure of city government and the prevalence of corruption.[18] Thus, Seabury's "first and principal recommendation" would be abolishing the board of estimate and apportionment, the board of aldermen, and other commissioners and replacing them with a single legislative chamber to be elected by proportional representation.[19] He proposed, "[The new] Council shall be elected by Boroughs, upon a non-partisan ballot, without party designation or party emblems and under a system of proportional representation, the result of which would be that every group sufficiently strong to be entitled thereto would be represented in the Council, each according to its relative strength."[20] The version of PR outlined by Seabury also assured reapportionment following each council election according to the total number of votes counted.

Seabury's other proposals included many reforms long sought by good-government advocates, such as the abolition of the borough presidents' offices, the consolidation of their functions into citywide departments, the combination of numerous municipal departments into 10 specified departments, the installation of a Municipal Civil Service Commission, and the replacement of partisan primaries with nominations by petition without party affiliation.[21] Seabury's goal was a fundamental alteration of the municipal power structure, with particular focus on creating structural impediments to party machine rule and the formation of policies that would facilitate greater diversity in civic representation.

Less than a decade after Seabury and other reformers successfully campaigned for city home rule with rhetoric of independence for city governance from state tyranny, these civic activists called upon the governor and the state legislature to enact special laws to reform the City of New York. To blunt criticism that the proposal violated home rule provisions he had already advocated, Seabury urged that any policies enacted in such an extraordinary fashion by the state be required to pass a citywide referendum by popular vote. This shift underscored the reform movement's conclusion that Albany and the city electorate offered the best means to circumvent Tammany rule.[22]

The *Nation*, which had advocated governmental reform in New York City since the nineteenth century, championed Seabury's inclusion of PR: "The most important and valuable of Mr. Seabury's proposals is to be found in his plan to introduce proportional representation in the election of members of the council. By itself this would be a tremendous step forward, for it would give minority parties and groups, which are now entirely excluded, a definite voice in city government."[23] The journal's support highlighted the system's growing prominence outside of good-government circles. In addition to the emerging campaign for using proportional representation in New York City, advocates sought to expand the system's use nationally, proposing it in Philadelphia and other cities. By the time charter reform resurfaced as a possible means of restructuring New York City government in the early 1930s, the movement for PR in New York City was part of a larger movement for electoral reform throughout urban America that had been building steadily since the turn of the century.[24]

The Hofstadter/Seabury corruption investigations, Jimmy Walker's resignation, and the public division between Tammany Hall and Franklin Roosevelt during the 1932 presidential campaign caused Tammany counterattacks aimed at co-opting the reform movement. In 1933, Tammany initiated various measures it presented as reforms, which good-government activists decried as delaying tactics. Mayor John P. O'Brien appointed a charter commission to preempt the state legislature's creation of a body that would be amenable to a more critical review of the municipal structure. O'Brien's commission strove to do little more than protect the status quo, offering a ringing endorsement of the board of aldermen and a bill of good health to city government as a whole.[25]

Encouraged by Franklin Roosevelt's prominent challenge to Tammany, an alliance of Republicans, disaffected Democrats, and civic activists allied to form the City Fusion Party (Fusion). With the reform movement squarely behind the Fusion ticket, this coalition endorsed former congressman Fiorello La Guardia, a Republican, for mayor in 1933. La Guardia campaigned as the embodiment of change in city politics—someone who would govern effectively and efficiently to counter the effects of Tammany corruption and the Great Depression's economic devastation. Although fusion as a good-government strategy to strengthen anti-Tammany interests pre-dated La Guardia, the Fusion Party's founding principle—that pro-reform, independent Democrats and Republicans could join together for the city's welfare—emerged as a force in local politics through the party's endorsement of the charismatic La Guardia. La Guardia also benefited from discord within the Democratic Party, which resulted in two prominent Democrats running against the Fusion nominee—former acting mayor Joseph McKee and current mayor O'Brien.

From September to December 1932, McKee served as acting mayor following Jimmy Walker's resignation. McKee also held the presidency of the board of aldermen during the 1920s, rising to prominence through the Bronx Democratic organization led by Edward J. Flynn. Fellow Democrat O'Brien won the special election in 1932 to replace Walker and served as acting mayor during the 1933 mayoral campaign. Tammany leaders favored O'Brien's retention, leaving McKee to run on the Recovery Party line. This division split the Democratic vote, as McKee drew significant Democratic support from O'Brien and opened the way for La Guardia to win with significantly fewer votes than his two Democratic opponents combined. La Guardia received 868,522 votes; McKee, 609,053; and O'Brien, 586,672. The 1933 mayoral results confirmed both the power of Fusion and La Guardia and the fractured state of Tammany Hall and the Democratic Party.[26]

La Guardia's victory continued the recasting of good-government reform as a popular, rather than an elite, movement. As Columbia University professor Joseph McGoldrick argued in the *Nation*, "The new Fusion is not [a] silk-stocking, black-broadcloth affair."[27] McGoldrick portrayed La Guardia's Fusion coalition as "socially motivated," supported by those who sought to improve economic conditions as well as reduce political corruption. Fusion promised dramatic change in city government, but the coalition's breadth also contained its central weakness. As McGoldrick concluded, "Fusion government is a difficult adventure. It begins in the association of many men and women of widely differing points of view, whose one common purpose is to drive out corruption and colossally incompetent government. But the persons who form a Fusion differ greatly in their interests and their emphases."[28] The campaign for good government, including charter reform and proportional representation, incorporated the central tensions of the Fusion movement. Reform drew increasing support from many of the political organizations that backed Fusion, including groups normally at odds with one another—Democrats, Republicans, Socialists, Communists, Wall Street executives, labor unions, and good-government activists. The Fusion banner offered coalition members access to power previously blocked by Democratic and Republican organizations throughout the five boroughs. While similar constituencies supported reform and La Guardia, civic activists and the mayor often butted heads over who ultimately controlled the reform agenda. Reformers supported the mayor as a powerful vehicle for propelling their policies, but they struggled at times to prevent their goals from being usurped by La Guardia's personal political objectives. In similar regards, good-government groups worked to keep their reform platform from being altered by the various Fusion-coalition organizations striving to enact their own visions of municipal government.

In the early days of 1934, reformers characterized La Guardia's victory as a popular endorsement of structural change in urban governance and joined the newly inaugurated mayor in calling for the creation of a commission dedicated to rewriting the New York City charter. La Guardia urged the state legislature to immediately pass emergency charter reform legislation by a two-thirds majority vote. The two-thirds vote granted the city broad discretion to alter its charter without further approval by the state legislature.[29]

Tammany Democrats retorted by casting La Guardia and charter reform as anti-democratic. Tammany claimed that the charter commission proposal constituted an "emergency dictatorship" bill. La Guardia's Democratic and Republican opponents declared the mayor's reform advocacy a façade designed to bestow unprecedented authority in City Hall.[30] Democratic attacks on La Guardia underscored the party's fears that the mayor planned to centralize power in his office under the guise of reform. Tammany and its allies counterattacked by co-opting reform in order to scuttle it and weaken the mayor. Threatened by having lost the mayoralty and facing growing competition for other city- and borough-wide offices, the Democratic Party shifted its anti-reform strategy to the state legislature in Albany. In response to La Guardia's charter commission proposal in 1934, the Democratic majority in the state senate prevented passage of the bill until Republicans allowed Democratic participation in the selection of commissioners.[31]

When finally compelled to constitute the 1934 charter commission, Democratic legislators structured it to fail. The commission possessed an unwieldy group of nearly 30 people, with more than half affiliated with Tammany Hall. Even more to its detriment, the group included several prominent participants in the city's recent political wars. Alfred E. Smith, former New York governor and 1928 Democratic Party presidential nominee, chaired the commission. Samuel Seabury, whose investigations of municipal corruption had recently helped unseat Jimmy Walker, joined William J. Schieffelin, chair of the Citizens Union, as a good-government bloc. Even long-time Socialist Party leader Norman Thomas participated and led a subcommittee concerning the possibility of implementing proportional representation for local elections. As distilled by the New York City League of Women Voters, "The majority of the Commission disapproved of PR in principle" but still agreed to put a proposal forward as a separate issue.[32] Given its entrenched membership, the commission stood little chance of building consensus toward a new charter.

As critics expected, the commission wasted little time in breaking down over proposals for county reform. County reorganization proposed to curtail the size of each borough's government, limiting the Democratic and Republican parties' patronage abilities throughout the city. Reform measures sought to reduce the powers of the borough presidents by removing several positions in each borough's government. Reformers saw the county offices allotted in each borough as the lynchpin of the city's political party machines. As the borough presidents attempted to strengthen their power base, the distribution of patronage jobs in borough governments provided a consistent vehicle to direct revenue and political loyalty to the parties. Reformers argued that the elimination of these offices would weaken the party organizations both financially and politically—removing cash streams and individual alliances forged through patronage positions.

As county reorganization strived to diminish the parties' power bases within the boroughs, the proposal centralized municipal government in City Hall. Long a centerpiece of the good-government movement, centralization reflected reformers' strategy that local administration must be narrowed into a closely knit network of public officials serving in a hierarchy of authority. The mayor, or a city manager, stood atop the pyramid of city government, demanding accountability and efficiency from each level of the municipal bureaucracy. In the case of New York City in 1934, Mayor La Guardia provided reformers with an ally in City Hall around whom to build comprehensive reform.

In light of the recent success of the Fusion Party, the city's political machines viewed centralization as an attack upon their very existence. With a diminished revenue stream and patronage possibilities, as well as an overall reduction in the power of the parties in the boroughs that was inversely proportional to the centralization of authority in City Hall, the county reorganization proposal debated by the charter commission brought considerable opposition from the Democratic and Republican party organizations throughout the five boroughs. The outer-borough press likewise heaped criticism upon the idea of focusing the lines of power too narrowly in Manhattan. As the *New York Times* asserted smugly, "On this issue the prairies are already afire."[33]

After initially approving a county reform plan, a majority of commission members decided to retract their decision. On August 2, 1934, in what became the commission's final hearing with all of its original members, 17 commissioners voted against the remaining 10 members to close discussion on county reform and adjourn. The pro-reform faction deemed the majority's decision evidence of its support for the status quo and antagonism toward any substantive charter reforms. Smith and Seabury promptly resigned from the commission.[34] Although the pair had clashed for years over the nature of power in the city, and the extent to which the existing system required change, Smith called Seabury an ally in the commission, as a fellow member who desired to comprehensively alter the policies that governed the municipality. As Smith stated in an attempt to explain his resignation,

A modern form of government for the greater city is not a mere gadget. . . . The issue is the capacity of the many varied elements which make up the population of New York to govern themselves and to

maintain this city, the object of our pride and love, at the very front of
all American municipalities, a great magnet and center of commerce
and civilization.[35]

Although Smith eventually opposed the more radical proposals offered by the
subsequent Charter Revision Commission, especially city council elections
by proportional representation, his explanation called upon many of the sentiments expressed by PR's proponents. For Smith, charter revision afforded
New Yorkers the ability to dramatically change their municipal government
at a moment of peril—the Great Depression. In Smith's words, New York
City could, and should, serve as a beacon of modernity for the rest of the
country and the world.

After the legislature balked at the mayor's request to disband the charter
commission, La Guardia convinced Governor Herbert H. Lehman to petition the legislature on his behalf. On August 15, 1934, the legislature agreed
to Lehman's request, unanimously dissolving the original commission.[36] On
August 18, 1934, Lehman signed the New York City Charter Revision Commission Act, which created a replacement charter commission. In advocating
and ultimately signing the act, Lehman continued the anti-Tammany work of
his predecessor, Franklin D. Roosevelt. Lehman served as lieutenant governor
during Roosevelt's tenure, and he operated as city reformers' most powerful
ally in Albany. Following days, if not weeks, of personal lobbying by the
mayor, Lehman gave La Guardia the power to select each member of the
Charter Revision Commission (CRC).[37]

The decision to delegate such authority to the mayor emerged from reaction to the previous commission's downfall, which reformers blamed on the
state legislature for selecting commissioners allied with Tammany Hall. Al
Smith, in resigning from the first commission, criticized the body's majority
as made up of "stowaways who were put on board with monkey wrenches to
throw into the machinery and scuttle the ship."[38] According to the *New York
Times*, Samuel Seabury "charged that the politicians had 'loaded' the charter
commission with sufficient machine men to prevent any improvements from
being made."[39] The new charter act attempted to circumvent Democratic manipulation through the mayor's power of appointment, as well as the requirement that the electorate determine the fate of charter reform through an ex-
pedited referendum. Reversing good-government's anti-populist strategy of
the late nineteenth century, Depression-era reformers saw public campaigning as essential to outmaneuvering Tammany.[40]

Although the legislation did not list any specific reforms to be included in a new city charter, the act required that the charter be presented as a referendum for public approval and that any "provision in such charter for the election of any elective officers by any system of proportional representation" must be submitted to voters as a separate question.[41] The presence of proportional representation at the creation of the CRC underlined the significant role good-government advocates possessed in the charter reform process. By the summer of 1934, proponents of PR, with Samuel Seabury contributing the most prominent political voice for the system, had drawn the support of the most powerful elected officials in the city and the state—Mayor La Guardia and Governor Lehman.

But the act separated a proposal for proportional representation from the broader charter revision referendum, suggesting continuing weakness in support of the system among some commission members. The separation also reflected the suspicion held both by reformers and machine politicians that PR might not survive a popular vote. The split meant that the charter could pass without proportional representation but not the reverse; PR could be installed only if it succeeded alongside the charter referendum. Perhaps more important, proportional representation could be repealed without affecting the city charter. At the onset of the CRC, even reformers admitted that a charter proposal would likely have a greater chance of electoral success than PR. Reformers saw PR as a possible weakness in the charter and concluded that offering separate questions would remove the possibility that voters would reject the charter because they disapproved primarily of proportional representation.[42] Thus, PR made its debut in the 1934 CRC hearings as an expendable component of charter reform. This secondary status undercut PR's stature and supplied opponents with multiple avenues of attacking the system in the near and distant future.[43]

While civic activists appreciated the Charter Revision Commission legislation as a potentially stronger opportunity for structural reform than previous charter commissions, press commentators questioned why the Democratic Party assented to the act's passage in the first place. The *New York Times* and other newspapers posed an important question: Why would the state legislature, many if not most of whose members opposed progressive reform in New York City, unanimously support the creation of a charter commission to be appointed by the mayor? The *Times*, whose editorial board favored charter revision and often criticized Tammany Hall, relayed an ambiguously sourced explanation:

In political circles it was reported that the Democratic organizations in each of the five counties would await the completion of a new charter and its submission to the electorate and then seek to make it a campaign issue in an effort to discredit the Fusion administration. . . . Another factor was the desire of the Democratic organization not to create a charter revision issue which could be used by the Fusion party in the coming election of a Controller.[44]

The *Times* interpreted charter reform as a double-edged sword for the Democratic Party that could either be successfully manipulated to attack Fusion or vice versa. While Democratic duplicity was nothing new in city or state politics, it seems far-fetched that party elders believed increasing Mayor La Guardia's power over such a critical matter as charter reform, which the Democratic organization had impeded at the municipal and state levels for years, could somehow be turned into a weapon against the mayor. A more likely explanation might be that Democrats favored the immediate political relief of offering fleeting support for reform to curry electoral favor in the near term. Moreover, the Democratic members of the state legislature also faced an alliance of political figures, namely Roosevelt, Lehman, and La Guardia, that held seemingly limitless popular support at the time. The CRC legislation's requirement that this same public determine the fate of reform likewise held the possibility for popular opposition to Tammany as well as providing the party organization with an alternate avenue to repel reform.[45]

For his part, Mayor La Guardia minced few words concerning his desire to create a new commission allied with his particular vision of municipal reform. Following the state legislature's passage of the bill granting him sole authority in determining the new commission's membership, La Guardia declared, "We must first decide from what viewpoint charter revision is to be approached and then get persons well in accord with that viewpoint."[46] The mayor argued that the commission must be of one mind, rather than a deliberative body seeking to debate the central issues at stake in charter reform.

The fundamental mistake of the first commission was in trying to get a charter which would satisfy everybody. . . . There has been a mistaken idea—an honestly mistaken one—that varying viewpoints should be represented on the commission. This is erroneous. . . . The fight should come before the people and not in the ranks of the commission.[47]

While La Guardia emphasized the necessity of getting a charter referendum before the electorate as soon as possible, he ultimately favored deliberately selecting the commission over expediency.

The mayor worked through the fall and winter to restructure the Charter Revision Commission with a membership to his liking, maintaining secrecy over his selection process until announcing the new group on January 12, 1935.[48] Striving to outmaneuver the bloc that had quashed reform proposals in the previous commission, La Guardia designed its replacement to create a charter that would substantively, though perhaps not radically, alter the structure of city government. The group formed in the early months of 1935 included nine members, of whom none were associated with Tammany Hall. Buttressed by support from Lehman, La Guardia, and a coalition of anti-Tammany activists throughout the city, the CRC began its deliberations with the assumption that proportional representation would prove critical to the ultimate success or failure of reform.

While the previous charter commission possessed several prominent political figures, including Samuel Seabury, Al Smith, and Norman Thomas, the new body had less well-known members. To constitute the CRC, La Guardia selected a far more unified, anti-Tammany, elite group of individuals. Members of the Charter Revision Commission included Thomas D. Thacher, a former US District Court judge and former solicitor general of the United States; S. John Block, a member of the New York Bar Association and the Socialist Party; Frederick L. Hackenburg, a justice of the Court of Special Sessions; Charles E. Hughes Jr., another former solicitor general of the United States; Joseph D. McGoldrick, professor of government at Columbia University and former New York City comptroller; Thomas I. Parkinson, professor of law at Columbia University and president of the Equitable Life Assurance Society; Joseph M. Proskauer, former justice of the Supreme Court of the State of New York; Genevieve B. Earle, former president of the Brooklyn chapter of the League of Women Voters; and Charles G. Meyer, a Queens real estate developer. Serving as lead counsel to the commission was Joseph P. Chamberlain, with Laurence A. Tanzer working as associate counsel.[49] In assessing the commission's membership, the *Times* stressed, "Not a single member of the commission is considered to have close political affiliations, although in the past several of them have been prominent in party politics."[50] In an editorial supporting the mayor's selections, the paper portrayed La Guardia as having "put politics aside [to select] men . . . recognized by all as able and experienced."[51] In addition to apparently forgetting about the CRC's female member, Genevieve Earle, the *Times* also ignored the manner in which

La Guardia first gained a monopoly over the selection process and then chose a group that almost certainly would be more amenable to his desires for reform than the previous commission. Underlining how the paper's charter reform agenda fused with La Guardia's, the editorial "congratulated" the mayor for choosing "competent and disinterested men" and concluded that "the outlook for a new and more businesslike charter is brighter than it has been at any time since the Fusion victory of 1933."[52]

In announcing the commission's membership, La Guardia promised that the group, as the *Times* described, "would have an absolutely free hand and all the money needed for its work."[53] The mayor set a goal of November 1935 for the public to vote on the new commission's charter proposal. That date proved elusive as the commission encountered a series of attacks from the Democratic and Republican party organizations of the five boroughs. Tammany-allied borough presidents, including Samuel Levy of Manhattan and James J. Lyons of the Bronx, joined Board of Aldermen president Bernard S. Deutsch in attempting to block funding for the new commission. The commission's opponents challenged the initial $25,000 grant to start the CRC's work, arguing that the mayor had more pressing matters.[54] The Democratic members of the board of estimate, the body responsible for the city's fiscal policy, temporarily stopped the CRC appropriation in direct retaliation for La Guardia's objections to Deutsch's investigations of various economic relief projects supported by the mayor. Pitted against the popular mayor and mounting criticism of his opposition to La Guardia's projects, Deutsch soon relented and agreed to provide full funding for the commission.

The commission was charged with the daunting task of revising a 400,000-word charter that included a variety of almost comically antiquated rules and regulations for the city's governance. As described by historian Thomas Kessner, the document as it read in 1935 seemed the product of a lack of foresight and careless editing that spanned generations. Hundreds of amendments and thousands of statutes littered its pages without any sense of which provisions should continue to guide life within the City of New York. Restrictions on the housing of goats and sheep appeared alongside specific instructions for the care of dead horses left on city streets. In addition to modernizing the charter, CRC members appeared from the outset intent on replacing the board of aldermen with a smaller city council elected by proportional representation, forming a City Planning Commission responsible for crafting a master plan for municipal development, increasing fiscal authority within the board of estimate, and diminishing the power of the borough offices that provided patronage lifelines to the Democratic and Republican parties.[55]

On February 18, 1935, just over one month after La Guardia's selection announcement, CRC chair Thomas Thacher gaveled the group's first public meeting to order. The commission planned to draft its charter reform proposals while holding several hearings organized to elicit comment on various reform options being considered. In an attempt to block assertions that the Charter Revision Commission would make its policy recommendations without community consultation, Judge Thacher emphasized that the hearings were "designed to afford an opportunity to organizations and individuals to present in an orderly fashion their considered views on any of the complex questions involved."[56] From the initial session, the meetings, which occurred on average about once a week and sometimes more frequently, served as forums for debating the structure of democracy in New York City. With this focus in mind, the testimony recorded at the hearings conveyed the perspectives of politicians, reformers, business owners, and activists across the political spectrum concerning the ideal framework for governing a metropolis. The meetings continued through August 1936, providing a record of how New Yorkers conceived of municipal government, including its responsibilities and objectives.

Given the necessity of passing the CRC's proposals by popular vote, the hearings offered commissioners a platform for increasing awareness of and support for charter reform. While good-government representatives disagreed over certain provisions in a revised city charter—such as the power to be held by the mayor—they agreed almost unanimously on the use of proportional representation in elections for a new city council to replace the board of aldermen.

The PR model discussed at CRC hearings matched the one advocated by George Hallett—unsurprising given that Hallett drafted the policy. The CRC's version of proportional representation for New York City Council elections reflected the single-transferable-vote method developed by British barrister Thomas Hare in the mid-nineteenth century. The procedure allowed for voters to choose candidates in order of preference. A "1" next to a candidate would signify the voter's first choice, with a "2" or "3" meaning the second or third choice and so on. If one's first choice was eliminated, then the vote would be allocated according to the voter's preference in descending order. This format was intended to prevent the threat of wasted votes, with marginal candidates receiving greater support as voters would no longer fear throwing away their votes to candidates with no realistic chance of victory. In other words, if one wished to support a marginal candidate who lost, then the voter would still be able to support a more viable, second-choice candidate.

Proportional representation as conceived by Hallett and the Charter Revision Commission featured several other characteristics that, reformers hoped, would foster greater diversity in representation. Candidacies would be open to anyone gathering more than 2,000 names on a petition and victory would be declared automatically for anyone receiving more than 75,000 votes cast in a particular borough. Proportional representation incorporated a plan for automatic reapportionment of legislative seats among the five boroughs with every council election. Each borough would be allotted a council seat for every 75,000 votes cast, with each borough able to gain an additional seat if it possessed a remainder of 50,000 votes. This arrangement would cause the size of the council to change in every term, as voter participation varied with every two-year campaign cycle. Reformers claimed that this system would make party bosses impotent in choosing who could run for office but they would also have no direct control over the exact size and composition of the council's membership. The provision for automatic reapportionment attracted support for PR from activists in the outer boroughs, particularly from Brooklyn, who had campaigned for years for a more proportional presence in city government. In this respect, many in the outer boroughs saw PR as a means of gaining power held disproportionately by Manhattan.

The proposed city council would replace the board of aldermen and gain legislative powers not afforded its predecessor. The council's most important power would be the ability to recommend and pass fiscal policies, with the caveat that the board of estimate must approve such expenditures. The board of estimate, previously titled the board of estimate and apportionment, would be comprised of the same membership: the mayor, city comptroller, president of the city council (as opposed to the aldermanic president), and the presidents of the five boroughs. Holding the purse strings of New York City government, the board of estimate would continue to act as a sort of upper house over the proposed city council.[57] Ultimately, charter reform and PR represented a trade-off for the borough governments; while the revised charter threatened to further centralize authority in City Hall, the borough presidents would potentially see their power increase in the board of estimate, and PR would substantially enhance the representation of the outer boroughs in city governance.

To Democratic and some Republican officials, the possibility of incorporating PR into the city charter raised the specter that reform could extend beyond the terms of elected officials and continue long after the energy of civic activists had diminished. The system's legal codification within charter reform would also integrate proportional representation within the city's political apparatus, hampering the dominant parties' ability to remove it. In addition to the threat posed by PR, the creation of a more diverse and possibly more powerful city council loomed over the city's political establishment. Although the mayor held vastly more influence on legislative policy and fiscal affairs, a new city council would provide its members with a formal platform for continued reform efforts. As one local reporter later commented, the idea of a PR-elected council "struck cold terror into the hearts of local Democrats."[58]

Many of the speakers who favored PR represented civic organizations that had supported the system for decades, including the League of Women Voters, the City Club of New York, the Women's City Club, and the Citizens Union. Two of the first individuals who testified hailed from these groups— Hallett of the Citizens Union and Dorothy Straus of the League of Women Voters (LOWV). Formed by the National American Woman Suffrage Association (NAWSA) following passage of the Nineteenth Amendment to the Constitution, which guaranteed women voting rights, the LOWV supported PR as a means of increasing women's representation in government. In fact, Carrie Chapman Catt, one of the architects of the suffrage movement and past president of the NAWSA and the LOWV, served on the executive board of the Proportional Representation Campaign Committee in 1936. As the New York City chapter of the LOWV declared in 1934, "We urge PR because we believe that while 'the right decision belongs to the majority, the right of representation belongs to all.'"[59] In quoting French philosopher Ernest Naville's comments on democracy from 1865, the League chapter urged an expansive conception of representation that necessitated the incorporation of proportional representation in New York City elections.

Straus argued for several reforms long central to the good-government campaign that eventually became part of the charter's revamped electoral policy, including a city council with fewer members and more powers than the board of aldermen. She offered PR as her preferred method of electing the council, with nominations "made by petition without party designation, because we conceive that running New York is a business and not a political matter."[60] Straus's recommendation for government to be run with business-like efficiency, rather than by personal interests, built upon good-government arguments in favor of PR that dated to the nineteenth century. Nominations by petition struck at the soul of the political machine's strength—the act of bestowing the party's designation upon a candidate usually went far in deciding a candidate's success. Therefore, the candidate was expected to reward the favor of party designation by working to increase party power. Straus's notion of running the city as a capitalist entity reflected the significant financial stakes involved in the design and structure of the city's political parties, which utilized government as a means of raising money and staking claim to greater and greater portions of the municipality's resources and authority. The form of PR eventually recommended by the CRC included the requirement of nominating petitions, but it made party designations optional and to be determined solely by the candidate.

The second individual to testify in favor of proportional representation at the Charter Revision Commission hearings was Hallett, the primary champion of PR in the United States during the first half of the twentieth century. Speaking as secretary of the Citizens Union, he declared that PR would "secure effective representation of minorities" as well as provide "boroughs a better opportunity to present their views."[61] Hallett did not clarify which groups comprised his notion of "minorities." His argument that PR would empower the boroughs originated in the requirement of borough-wide contests and automatic reapportionment during each election. Hallett's understanding of democracy as based upon minority representation went to the heart of the public campaign for PR in 1935–1936, incorporating rhetoric of proper democratic representation in the context of growing popular resentment against Manhattan-based Tammany Hall. The desire to diminish the power of Tammany connected the goals of reformers with residents of the outer boroughs who desired greater power in city affairs.

Additional activists who testified in favor of PR included Joseph Price (City Club), Louis Waldman (Socialist Party), Frederick L. Guggenheimer (City Affairs Committee), Ethel E. Dreier (Women's City Club), Kenneth Dayton (assistant to the president of the board of aldermen), and, despite his rivalry with Mayor La Guardia, Bernard Deutsch (president of the board of aldermen).[62] Other pro-PR groups represented at the hearings included the Communist and American Labor parties, the Teachers Union, the Merchants' Association of New York, and the Central Trades and Labor Council. Despite their political differences, these minority parties, labor unions, and civic organizations joined in endorsing proportional representation as a means of shifting the balance of power in city politics from Tammany Hall and the Democratic Party.

Reformers also raised the stakes of charter reform and proportional representation by framing these policies as essential to national security amid growing international tensions in the mid 1930s. Using language similar to that offered by machine politicians in attacks against reform, civic activists linked single-party, Tammany rule with the rise of fascist tyranny in Europe. Samuel Seabury, who had directed the investigations into local corruption earlier in the decade, enlarged the impact of reform beyond the corridors of New York City government. With democracy "on trial all over the world," he framed proportional representation as a means of proving to the nation and to the world that urban America could successfully "establish truly representative government."[63] Seabury argued that without the passage of PR, charter reform would accomplish little—both to improve local government and, implicitly, to counter the expansion of fascism globally. Echoing his earlier statements concerning the benefits of proportional representation, Seabury asserted that it would "do much to destroy the partisan Tammany domination" in city politics.[64] In effect, Seabury presented PR as both a local and an international means of furthering democracy.

Sharpening the language offered in his December 1932 report to the Hofstadter Committee that emphasized the international popularity of proportional representation, Seabury's comments three years later directly implicated PR in a global campaign against totalitarianism. He declared:

> Our duty in America, and especially in our great cities, is to establish truly representative government. Mussolini, Hitler, and others throughout the world, in order to excuse the tyrannical dictatorships which they have established, indict representative government as a failure, and in an attempt to sustain their indictment they point to the abuses which take place under our present electoral methods.... I envision the great municipalities of America establishing . . . a system of representative government which will not only give their inhabitants the benefits of representative government, but will furnish an example to other communities and to the rest of the world of the advantages resulting from government that is truly representative.[65]

Not only did such rhetoric link PR with global affairs but it also strategically fused Tammany Hall with Mussolini and Hitler as antitheses of representative democracy. The shift in Seabury's rhetoric from 1932 to 1935 revealed a broader change in the PR discourse. In language that would continue to evolve over the next 12 years, speakers for and against PR found a vital piece of common ground: They agreed that the fate of the system in New York City would have national and international repercussions.

Rather than going into lengthy descriptions of its mechanics, supporters of the system who followed Hallett simply listed it as one of the components of proper urban reform. These groups had long supported similar reforms to the charter and, for the most part, received sympathetic ears from the commission members. While reformers and, in particular, leftist activists criticized certain charter proposals for failing to incorporate sweeping structural reforms, PR became the most radical policy favored by the commission. Perhaps this development explains why the witnesses who testified longest about PR were its opponents in the two major parties, who framed the system as an attack on the very foundations of American democracy.

As the borough presidents presumed that proportional representation and charter reform would threaten their centers of power, anti-PR witnesses included every borough president except for Brooklyn's reform-minded Raymond V. Ingersoll, a Republican. This group included a coalition of normally competing Democrats and Republicans who were willing to put aside longstanding ideological differences to unite against a common enemy. In fact, Queens Borough president George U. Harvey and Staten Island Borough president Joseph A. Palma hailed from the Republican Party and had received Fusion support during previous campaigns. Witnesses such as Palma and Harvey likely did not intend to champion the tactics of the Democratic Party and Tammany Hall. Rather, they opposed charter reform and proportional representation because of their likely impact on the strength of the county governments. Aside from PR, one of the primary reform proposals debated during the charter hearings involved municipal consolidation. If county offices were consolidated into central, citywide departments operated by the mayor's office, many borough positions would be abolished, thereby weakening the grip of graft from party machine–dominated county governments. Reformers also declared that consolidation would reduce wasteful or useless offices that duplicated functions performed by other divisions.

In their attempt to quash the system that threatened to weaken their power in city government, Democratic and Republican party officials created an anti-PR rhetoric that combined themes of American democracy, patriotism, and voters' rights. Opponents held that proportional representation was confusing to voters and anathema to American democratic traditions. They scoffed at the assertion that PR would raise the quality of candidates for public office. Perhaps most damning, detractors posited that PR would result in the creation of a totalitarian form of government. The language of totalitarianism used during the CRC hearings focused on the rise of fascism in Europe and would later be retooled to emphasize the peril of Soviet Communism in the early 1940s. Regardless of the arguments provided against the system, one common trait emerged: All these claims were made by individuals whose power would likely diminish with the installation of PR elections.

Testifying on April 15, 1935, Queens Borough president Harvey declared, ironically, that PR would actually make little difference in the composition and efficacy of city government. The Republican argued that the real problem lay in inherent differences in the qualities of the membership of the local political parties and that proportional representation would do nothing to enhance the efficiency, drive, and effectiveness of the body. Harvey argued that switching to a system of proportional voting would not strengthen the Republican Party and other smaller political parties; rather, PR would further weaken the party structure in a manner that would negatively impact the quality of city government. In an exchange with CRC member S. John Block, a Socialist and PR proponent, Harvey boasted of his ability to beat the odds politically as a Republican in a Democratic borough:

HARVEY: I am the greatest example in the world against PR. For example, in Queens County, we have got 60,000 Republicans and 260,000 Democrats, and still I have been able to be elected. I believe if you have got the men and you have got the issue . . .
BLOCK: You were not elected on the principle of PR?
HARVEY: That is just the point. You don't need it.[66]

The borough president voiced dismay at how New Yorkers "keep swinging around" in voting for members of different political parties such as Democrat Franklin Roosevelt for president, Democrat Herbert Lehman for governor, and Fusion-Republican Fiorello La Guardia for mayor. According to Harvey, PR would destroy the two-party system of government, a tradition that he and other PR critics argued was a core American institution that must be preserved for the nation's democracy to endure. Harvey declared, "It is a temptation to break down the two-party system, and I believe in a two-party system."[67] For the Republican borough president, proportional representation represented the greatest possible danger to the two strongest political parties in the city, state, and nation. By restructuring the electoral process to encourage the participation of more political parties, PR threatened to dismantle the foundation of Democratic and Republican hegemony. In the context of New York City politics, such a consequence endangered Republicans far more than Democrats, as the GOP faced growing competition from Fusion and the American Labor Party. For Harvey and other Republicans, a short-term alliance with their main rival in local politics, the Tammany Democratic machine, appeared more beneficial than a council elected by PR.[68]

In addition to decrying the impact of proportional representation on the two-party system as well as the power of the borough presidents, Harvey and other borough officials asserted that the system would balkanize the city. He declared, "First of all, you are going to put all the Irish in one group and all the Germans in another, the Jews, Catholics, the Greeks, and Italians, and everybody is going to have a group and you are going to be voting according to groups. . . . I think that is a bad thing, to divide people into groups."[69] In a revealing turn of phrase, Harvey argued that the system, rather than providing voters with greater electoral options, would force them into rigid groups based upon religious, ethnic, and international affiliations. The implied threat held that proportional representation would encourage un-American loyalties and cause ethnic strife on a par with the growing conflict in Europe.

While Harvey actively supported the separation of New Yorkers into blocs based upon their allegiance to either the Democratic or Republican parties, he feared the expansion of citizen loyalties outside of the two-party political structure. Opponents of proportional representation construed the system's model of electoral freedom as likely to cause the reverse: a severe reduction in democratic rights. As portrayed by Harvey, New Yorkers could not define themselves politically without the guidance of the major parties. Otherwise, the electorate would bog down in a morass of rigid blocs ill suited to the task of electing an effective city government. In the face of a strengthening, multidimensional coalition of activists eager to tear down the political machines, Republican and Democratic officials cast them as the power-hungry, corrupt party bosses reformers sought to overthrow. In addition, the anti-reform vision offered by Harvey depicted New Yorkers as essentially incapable of democratic self-government. From this perspective, any attempt to augment the electoral powers of the citizenry would actually worsen the city's political environment. Harvey's analysis also shifted blame for future political malfeasance to a foreign source, a source arising from across the Atlantic based upon religious, ethnic, or national difference. These fears likely arose from the suspicion that charter reform and proportional representation would enable New Yorkers to define themselves politically outside the purview of the Democratic and Republican parties.

Following Harvey's admonition that the two major parties must maintain their positions of power, CRC member Block asked the borough president specifically about the disproportionate power of the Democratic Party in city government:

BLOCK: If you have got 100,000 Democrats in your borough and 90,000 Republicans voting, don't you think those 90,000 Republicans should be represented on your Board of Aldermen?

HARVEY: I am a Republican, and what is wrong in this City is that as a rule the Republican candidates are not as good as the Democratic candidates. That is the reason they get licked. I hate to make that acknowledgement, but it is true. Our men are not as good.[70]

Harvey delivered a seemingly startling criticism of the Republican Party. However, his commentary avoided a more structural explanation of the imbalance of power between the two major parties. As government reformers contended, such an analysis would likely have also implicated the Republican Party as the beneficiary of similar political malfeasance. Harvey's argument implicitly justified the status quo. He approved of disproportionately Democratic power because, according to Harvey, Democrats gained and wielded their authority with greater skill than their opponents. This perspective called for more politically savvy opponents—not structural reform.

Harvey completed his remarks by noting several logistical troubles that he contended would haunt proportional representation counts in New York City. He held that PR would produce "too long of a delay with so many names on the ballots" that would annoy impatient voters and destabilize the democratic process.[71] While Harvey criticized proportional representation for its use of paper ballots and expected confusion and delays in the tally, the force of his argument remained squarely on the disruption the system would cause to traditional party power. He argued, "Two parties are all right, three parties are all right, but you do not want a dozen."[72] Other PR critics offered more specific arguments concerning the deleterious impact of multiple political parties on city governance. This anti-PR rhetoric held that the system encouraged gridlock and could not permit decisive, effective, and timely governance. For many Democratic and Republican politicians, independent and minority party legislators created roadblocks to efficient government by their very participation in government.

Bronx Borough president James J. Lyons, a Democrat, testified before the Charter Revision Commission in a private meeting on April 17, 1935. Using language similar to that offered by his Queens counterpart, Lyons argued vociferously against any attempt at charter reform that reduced the powers of the borough presidents. Declaring that public opinion leaned against reform, Lyons asserted: "Our people do not want centralization. Any new charter which embraces such theory, regardless of how good it may be in other respects, will be repudiated by the people."[73] For Lyons, consolidation of city powers into the central municipal government would unfairly curb the powers of the county governments and, in the process, distance the people of New York from their government. Instead, he concluded that the most democratic version of charter reform would move government closer to the people through the expansion of powers to the boroughs and, in the process, increase the authority of borough presidents such as himself.

Former New York governor Alfred E. Smith, chair of the charter commission that disbanded in 1934, staunchly opposed the use of proportional representation in local elections. Testifying in May 1935, Smith argued:

> I am unalterably opposed to PR. I don't think that you can make it work. I think it is a fad. I am a strong believer in party responsibility and you can't have it under that form of election. You would get all the "crack pots" and all the wild-eyed "ginks" that the world ever produced, winning out in PR—men that couldn't get a party nomination. It will never work in New York. That is my opinion of it. I am afraid of the men you get. You won't get the representatives of the Republican Party, or any party, that is the trouble about it, you will get all the wild-eyed fellows.[74]

Smith, one of the most powerful Democrats in the nation during the 1920s and the party's national nominee for president in 1928, cited the threat of proportional representation to the Democratic and Republican parties as its primary fault. He considered PR a system that would dramatically reduce the power of the local party machines to determine which candidates, and thus which officials, would govern New York City. Smith charged that independents, or "wild-eyed fellows" as he defined them, rather than party representatives, would rule the city legislature. As characterized by Smith, the alternative to machine governance would be chaos, with countless "crack pots" running for office without the slightest comprehension of the legislative process. Moreover, Smith implied, the candidates bred by PR would threaten the city's stability.

Opposition to proportional representation increased as the CRC hearings continued into the summer of 1935, perhaps due to the increasing possibility that the commission would endorse the system as part of its charter referenda. In his initial testimony on the CRC's first day of public hearings, Alexander U. Mayer, counsel for the Taxpayers' Alliance of the

Borough of the Bronx, declared that he stood "utterly opposed" to what he described as "unrestrained and unconditioned preferential voting."[75] Despite his clear opposition to the system, Mayer nonetheless concluded that he "was not opposed to submitting PR to the people."[76] But by the time of his second appearance before the Charter Revision Commission five months later, Mayer's opinion of charter reform and PR had worsened. In later testimony, Mayer described PR as "unwise, leading to unfortunate results, and, above all, unscientific and basically unsound."[77] According to Mayer, the preferential vote unjustly awarded second- or third-choice votes the same weight as first-choice ballots. Mayer labeled PR "ridiculous" as, he contended, "it becomes easily possible for a voter to unintentionally defeat his first choice by his subsidiary votes unjustly rated as 100 per cent votes and equal to the first choice."[78] Although the PR system did not transfer votes until a candidate had been mathematically eliminated, the argument that selecting second, third, or fourth choices could somehow work to defeat the voter's first choice remained a prominent component of anti-PR rhetoric through the coming years.

After criticizing the system's structure, Mayer centered the consequences of proportional representation in the international sphere. For anyone who misconstrued the possible impact of PR as described by former governor Al Smith on May 28, 1935, Mayer utilized a powerful symbol of electoral and governmental decay for comparison—the destruction of Germany's parliament and the rise of the Nazi Party. He declared, "We have learned what such an abnormal system of voting has caused in Europe. Instance Germany. Twenty odd discordant factions in the German Reichsrath (parliament). Not able to agree in their country's supreme crisis. The final dissolution of that body and the rise of the Dictator."[79] Mayer provided listeners with a simple cause and effect presentation of the impact proportional representation would have in New York City and why the system, by its very mechanics, would prove disastrous.

While the CRC continued to hold hearings on the charter and its possible incorporation of PR, civic reformers privately relayed the likelihood that PR would be approved by the commission and eventually presented to the electorate. As early as September 1935, several months before an official charter draft was made public, George Hallett wrote that the commission had informed him "personally that they favor submission of PR to the voters of New York City as a separate issue at the time when their new charter is voted on next year."[80] Hallett's comments underscored the pro-reform nature of the second commission. In addition, his comments presented early confirmation that Mayor La Guardia had succeeded in appointing a commission sympathetic to reform.

The reform package of the Charter Revision Commission appeared likely to enhance La Guardia's stature as well as that of allied civic organizations. While the expansion of powers to a new city council could install a body to compete with the mayor, La Guardia recognized that enhancing diversity in city government would likely mean a reduction in power for his primary opponent: Tammany Hall. Thus, the board of aldermen's demise could perhaps usher in a more amicable, or at least a less uniformly Democratic, council for the mayor. At the same time, reformers were wary of increasing the power of the city's legislative branch without the assurance that the body would be elected by proportional representation. The CRC balanced the goal of creating a stronger city council with the possibility that Tammany could dominate the new body if PR failed to gain public approval.

The Charter Revision Commission made public a draft charter and a separate proposal for proportional representation on April 27, 1936.[81] This followed an attempt by S. John Block to have the questions of PR and charter reform merged so as to strengthen the system's position; however, his motion was not seconded.[82] After several weeks of speculation as to the language of the proposals, the CRC released official drafts and scheduled a series of public hearings to take place in each of the five boroughs. For all the apprehensions expressed by the CRC's detractors, the commission presented a vision of a new city council with little of the legislative and fiscal independence sought by good-government advocates. The charter reform proposal went so far as to expand the fiscal powers of the board of estimate—a majority of which was comprised of the borough presidents—while limiting those granted to the council.[83] The plan granted greater legislative authority to the city council than held by the board of aldermen, but the board of estimate maintained veto power over changes to the municipal budget. The Charter Revision Commission also backed away from more extensive changes to the structure of municipal government. One such example was the commission's decision against the city manager plan, devised by reformers as a means of weakening urban political party machines.

The city manager plan called for shifting governmental power to technocratic managers who would ostensibly remain independent from municipal party politics. Under the plan, the position of mayor would become largely ceremonial, with the manager in control of City Hall. Despite its initial appeal as a good-government reform, the Citizens Union and the other organizations that supported charter revision in New York City apparently believed that the manager plan could not be passed and, if it did, would place too much authority within the mayor's office. The manager plan would have centralized power within a significantly smaller legislative body and called for the city legislature to appoint both a mayor and a city manager. Considering Mayor La Guardia's leading role in attacking Tammany Hall and the plan's reduction of the public's electoral powers, reformers dismissed the idea of transferring the power of selecting the city's most powerful official from the public to a small group of likely Tammany-allied politicians. Thus, the Charter Revision Commission concluded that the manager plan created "dangers too grave to risk."[84]

Four of the five borough presidents—titular heads of the Democratic and Republican machines across the city—continued their fight against charter reform by attacking the CRC as an anti-democratic institution. Bronx Borough president Lyons warned that if the city adopted charter reform, "A Hitler or Mussolini type of city government could prevail."[85] He charged that the proposed policy would provide the mayor with "autocratic" powers and create an "undemocratic and dictatorial form of centralized government that would be inefficient, uneconomical, cumbersome and unwieldy."[86] Of course, Lyons's power as borough president would likely diminish with the charter's shift of responsibility from the boroughs to City Hall. Integral to his argument that the "closer government is brought to the people, the more representative it will be" was the anxiety of machine politicians that charter reform threatened to decrease the number of borough government-appointed positions throughout the city. [87]

Critics merged their primary arguments against the system—that proportional representation was both too confusing to be efficiently used and that it aided anti-Americanism. These two strands of reasoning intertwined in testimony, radio addresses, press releases, pamphlets, and posters in such a way that examples of the former became evidence of the latter, and vice versa. Many thousands of immigrants in the city had fled Europe because of the rise of fascist governments in Germany and Italy, and propaganda linking proportional representation with the growth of tyrannical dictatorships in these nations conjured a distinctly menacing connotation for these communities.[88] Anti-reform rhetoric targeted them with characterizations of municipal improvement as a conduit for expanding totalitarian threats across the Atlantic, in effect following immigrants to the United States and, more specifically, to the streets of New York City.

Following his depiction of the proposed charter as an avenue for fascism to strike New York, Lyons focused his testimony on PR's other pitfalls. He characterized the system as "proposed by minorities in our city for some time."[89] While Lyons's particular definition of minorities is unclear, his use of the term fit squarely with his assertions of the charter as "an undemocratic and dictatorial" tool to steal power from the citizenry.[90] At this point in the hearing, commission chair Judge Thomas Thacher interjected:

> [Proportional representation] is not a part of the charter. It is submitted to the electorate as an alternative. If the method of electing members of the council on the basis of PR is supported only by a minority it will be defeated and will not be a part of the charter. . . . The commission has made no recommendation to the electorate as to whether it should be adopted or rejected.[91]

Thacher's comments provided a telling insight into the commission's attitude toward PR. Although a majority of the Charter Revision Commission supported PR, the legislation unanimously approved by the state legislature and signed by Governor Lehman required that any proposal concerning proportional representation be submitted separately from the new charter. Some reformers argued that this separation was necessary to protect the broader charter's passage. They feared that the public viewed the electoral system with suspicion and estimated that the chances for passage were greater for the charter than for PR. Since PR could not be installed without passage of the new charter, the separation also implied that PR was viewed as expendable in comparison to the charter. Nonetheless, many civic groups and minority parties supported PR more stridently than the charter during the subsequent referenda campaign in 1936.

For instance, despite the fact that the proposed charter needed to be adopted before PR could be instituted, the Communist Party (CP) supported PR but opposed the charter. The Communists' seemingly contradictory stance reflected the ambivalence toward the proposed charter expressed by many leftist organizations. The CP's Civil Service Branch declared that a coalition of "bankers and real estate groups . . . crippled" the original proposal offered by the CRC and forced the group to present a final proposal with "so many loopholes and reactionary measures" that made "it unworthy of passage."[92] Offering an argument similar to that of anti-PR groups, the Communists asserted that the proposed reduction of the board of aldermen to a city council estimated to have fewer than half the number of legislators exhibited "the tendency to concentration of power."[93] The Communist Party saw further centralization of power in sections of the new charter designed to strengthen the board of estimate's "supreme authority" over city finances and create a City Planning Commission with the ability "to restrict public works." Raising the same objections as the Socialist Party and several labor unions, the CP also held that, in a clause concerning the regulation of pedestrian traffic, the proposed charter granted the police commissioner the ability to "either completely prevent or limit picketing at shops . . . [and] prohibit all street meetings."[94] The CP decried the proposed provision that would permit the removal of a council member by a two-thirds council majority, wary that it could allow the ouster of radical members opposed by "the dominant political group in the City Council."[95] Ultimately, the CP urged voters to cast their ballots against the charter but in favor of PR, which the party presented as "a progressive step" in city government.

While supporting proportional representation, the Communist Party and other leftist organizations argued that the electoral proposal could be improved. The CP advocated a more "democratic" apportionment equation that granted council seats for every 25,000 votes rather than for every 75,000 ballots cast, greatly enhancing the electoral prospects for CP and other minority-party candidates. Good-government groups advocated a larger body with a seat allotted for every 50,000 votes, but the final figure was chosen to balance reformers' desire for more diverse representation with the objective of reducing patronage positions in city government. The move to install a city council with fewer than half the members of the 65-member board of aldermen reflected reformers' goal of decreasing patronage and, thereby, the power of the political machines to control city affairs.

Confident that proportional representation would be presented to the electorate in the 1936 elections, the system's supporters extended their campaign beyond the Charter Revision Commission hearings in the spring and summer of that year. The City Club, Women's City Club, League of Women Voters, and Citizens Union produced fliers, performed demonstrations, and broadcast a series of radio programs designed to increase public awareness of charter reform and proportional representation specifically. In addition to good-government groups, many of the city's anti-Tammany political parties called for public approval of charter reform and PR. American Labor Party official Eugene Connolly contended that there "is nothing more important right now than the campaign for PR" to increase diversity in local government.[96] The ALP and other progressive minority parties argued that PR would greatly enhance their representatives' ability to defeat Democrats (and Republicans)—fundamentally shifting the city's balance of political power.

As the pro-PR coalition formed its campaign, an assortment of machine politicians and disaffected minority-party officials allied to oppose the system. Though the charter proposals did not threaten home rule, which had been advocated by the same civic activists who supported the Charter Revision Commission, the group named itself the Home Rule League against Proposed Charter (HRL).[97] The HRL included Socialist Louis Waldman, who had campaigned earlier in favor of charter reform and PR, then changed his mind after the CRC made public its proposals. Joining Waldman in the HRL were borough presidents Harvey (Queens), Lyons (Bronx), and Palma (Richmond).[98]

The HRL's letterhead brandished the slogan "Vote 'No' on the Super-Government Charter," echoing the testimony of the anti-PR borough presidents who declared that the charter proposal would create, in Lyons's words, an "autocratic, dictatorial" regime.[99] The "Super-Government" reference implied that, if instituted, the new charter would install in City Hall a centralized government with total, un-democratic authority similar to contemporary fascist regimes in Italy and Germany.[100] In pamphlets distributed during the 1936 charter campaign, the HRL declared that the proposed reforms would make "Mayor [La Guardia] a dictator in fact, by transferring to him and his appointees the most important powers of the Board of Estimate and the Comptroller."[101] The HRL cited the installation of a City Planning Commission, whose members would be selected by the mayor, as an example of the dictatorial powers assumed by City Hall under the proposed charter.

The HRL's publicity emphasized the degree to which the city's Democratic and Republican organizations viewed charter reform and proportional representation as part of a broader assault upon their power. In the context of La Guardia's rise to power through the support of independent Democrats and Republicans, Tammany Hall and its allies in the outer boroughs feared the mayor would assume even greater authority over city government with charter reform. Also, the likely reelection of President Roosevelt, both an ally of La Guardia and a staunch opponent of Tammany, only heightened fears that the balance of municipal power would shift further from the local party organizations after the fall elections.

The HRL altered the meaning of home rule, which had been primarily associated with the reform movement to gain greater autonomy for the city vis-à-vis the state government. Countering reformers' arguments that charter reform and PR would create a more representative government, the HRL asserted that the charter would "take Borough Home Rule and representative government from you."[102] The group based its charges upon the proposition that reformers ultimately sought to disfranchise common New Yorkers. The HRL proposed that to go along with the "dictatorship" created by the new charter would be "a voting monstrosity characterized as 'proportional representation,' which would reduce New York's vote 40 percent, eliminating what its sponsors sneeringly call the 'dumb bell' vote."[103] The HRL chastised civic reformers as aristocratic snobs, who desired to circumvent democratic rule by instituting reforms that would instead decimate popular participation in government. The 40-percent reduction referenced by the HRL likely arose from the group's claim that a large segment of the electorate would be unable to figure out how to vote under proportional representation.

As the Home Rule League argued that New Yorkers could not understand a proportional representation ballot, the group exhibited the sort of suspicion of the city's electorate that it attributed to good-government reformers. According to the HRL, the installation of the proposed charter along with PR would aid reformers' anti-democratic ends by creating "a City Council of small membership to be elected in Borough groups on the basis of 'proportional representation' by which representatives of blocs and racial groups can name any number of candidates for the Council—even running into hundreds."[104] The reapportionment requirements of the new charter called for a reduction in the number of municipal legislators, a measure the HRL presented as part of a narrowing of authority in city affairs. Moreover, the HRL criticized PR for fostering "racial" and "bloc" voting. Although the group did not delve into the meanings of these terms, it implied a broader criticism of the new charter as a vehicle for totalitarianism to take over the city. The assumption seemed that proportional representation encouraged ethnic, religious, and racial tensions by allowing candidates to be elected simply by appealing to their self-defined constituency. These charges incited fears of minority groups overrunning the city. Of course, the HRL's understanding of bloc voting did not appear to encompass selecting a straight Democratic ticket. Perhaps intentionally, such attacks misconstrued PR's primary threat to the political powers that be—that the electoral system provided a framework for a diverse coalition of voters to elect legislators independent of the city's foremost political parties.[105] The notion that proportional representation enabled bloc voting further implicated international tensions in municipal politics. The system's opponents argued that bloc allegiances historically lay at the root of conflict in Europe, creating the social and political discord that fostered World War I and threatened to create a similar conflict in the 1930s. Increasingly, the argument evolved to encompass the idea that comparable blocs had aided the rise of Communism in the Soviet Union.

The Home Rule League coupled the rhetoric of social and political crisis with assertions that reform would prove logistically unsound, costing the city an unreasonable amount of money in the midst of a national economic depression. Surprisingly, while the group cited a figure of $10 million as the cost of implementing the new charter, it did not incorporate estimates for the considerable anticipated expense of voting (and counting) with proportional representation.[106]

While its draft proposals had been debated for months, the Charter Revision Commission did not officially present its charter recommendations until August 14, 1936, including a separate provision for a PR-elected city council. Faced with a strengthening public campaign for reform organized by a coalition of good-government groups, labor unions, and smaller political parties, the Democratic Party pursued several court challenges designed to prevent the CRC referenda from appearing on the November ballot. The party argued before New York Supreme Courts in Brooklyn and Manhattan that the CRC amounted to an unconstitutional delegation of legislative powers. According to this position, the state legislature had illegally transferred its authority over legislation to two nonelected entities: the Charter Revision Commission and the public, which through voting would ultimately decide the proposals' fate. The claim that public referenda were unconstitutional by definition underscored the skepticism with which the city's most powerful political organization viewed the electorate. Despite the Democratic Party's argument, the Supreme Court in Manhattan concluded that the CRC possessed strong legal standing with considerable historical precedent.

The Manhattan court's counterpart in Brooklyn, though, agreed with the petitioners' claim that the CRC usurped the state constitution's legislative guidelines. On September 28, 1936, Kings County Supreme Court Justice Charles J. Dodd issued the order that the charter and PR proposals be omitted from the upcoming referenda.[107] Far from allaying reformers' fears that the Brooklyn court's sympathies resided reflexively with the Democratic Party, Dodd's holding concurred in virtually every respect with the petitioner's assertions that the Charter Revision Commission violated the state constitution. Dodd argued that the home rule initiative did not provide for the CRC's creation simply because the CRC was not specified in the original home rule legislation. Dodd concluded:

The action of the Legislature constitutes an unconstitutional delegation of legislative power or, correlatively stated, an unlawful avoidance of legislative duty. . . . In a word, it is an avoidance of the ancient method that gave New York City its present charter; it is a recognition that the City itself has not sought a new charter . . . and it is an attempt to create a new method wholly unknown and unjustifiable constitutionally. . . . The Legislature itself having no power to delegate its legislative duties to cities, it seems self-demonstrative that a constitutional change must precede any power of the Legislature to delegate power to the people themselves.[108]

In addition to squelching the power of the state legislature, with the city's blessing, to create reform-minded commissions, Dodd's holding suggested that the public should be removed entirely from the policy-making process—with the abolition of popular referenda seemingly required by Dodd's interpretation of the state constitution.

Due to the competing rulings at the Supreme Court level, the Court of Appeals agreed to hear arguments on October 1, 1936, only one month before Election Day. The petitioner before the Court of Appeals was Brooklyn resident Edward J. Mooney, represented by the prominent firm Cullen and Dykman. Mooney's brief contended that the creation of the Charter Revision Commission amounted to an unconstitutional delegation of legislative authority by the state legislature. In addition to questioning the legality of the commission, the brief asserted that the eventual delegation of power to the electorate, via the public's voting on the referenda, also usurped the powers of the state and city to govern the City of New York.[109] The petitioner concluded that the CRC and its charter proposal violated Article III, Section I, of the state constitution, which placed legislative responsibility for the state's welfare solely in the hands of state legislators in Albany.

Ironically, the board of elections, led by Howard S. Cohen, joined the CRC as respondents, though each member of the election board opposed proportional representation and actively campaigned against the system in the weeks leading to the first city council vote in 1937.[110] Respondents provided a lengthy history of state and city support for city charter commissions. Directly contradicting Justice Dodd's earlier interpretation, they argued that the state legislature had legally delegated authority to Mayor La Guardia and the Charter Revision Commission through its unanimous passage of the New York City Charter Revision Commission Act, signed by Governor Lehman on August 18, 1934. Respondents added that the home rule amendments to the state constitution passed in recent years specifically provided for the process that culminated with the CRC referenda.

The bulk of Mooney's arguments against the charter referenda focused on the constitutionality of the CRC. Yet, petitioners also challenged the legality of proportional representation. Mooney counsel Jackson A. Dykman criticized the original language of the Charter Revision Commission Act of 1934 as too vague in its description of PR. Dykman argued, "The provision in the act with respect to proportional representation is a striking example of its (the charter act's) incompleteness. *No definition whatsoever is given of 'proportional representation.'*"[111] After depicting the act's treatment of PR as a "bewildering," "substantial omission," Dykman attacked the electoral system itself. He asserted that ambiguities concerning the act's definition of PR did not prevent him from finding the system unconstitutional in its methods. Dykman perceived in American history a requirement that voters should possess the ability to defeat unfavorable candidates. He declared, "It has always been recognized that one purpose of popular voting is to enable the electorate to reject unacceptable candidates quite as much as to elect acceptable ones."[112] This point reflected one of the Democrats' primary concerns with PR—the system enabled candidates, and the electorate, to operate outside of the single-victor model that facilitated Democratic hegemony.

By creating multiple routes to electoral success, PR provided a new method for gaining legislative power by groups that did not possess the resources to counter machine-endorsed candidates in single-winner district elections. In previous years, the Democratic Party determined which candidates ran and what districts they represented. The sole remaining objective involved ensuring that a preferred candidate received more votes than the opposition. Proportional representation threatened to dismantle this electoral framework. Multiple routes to office required that the Democratic Party produce several different candidates capable of garnering the most votes in a single, enlarged district. Both sides of the PR debate recognized that Democrats could not maintain their monopoly of power in such a system.

Dykman expressed the anxieties of local Democratic—and certain Republican—leaders when he bluntly asserted that any system that did not permit voters to reject "unacceptable" candidates must be ruled unconstitutional. In an attempt to provide a legal basis for the exclusion of PR on this point, Dykman recalled the Michigan Supreme Court's ruling in 1920. As discussed in Chapter 1, the Michigan court held that the Hare version of proportional representation was unconstitutional because it did not permit every voter to participate in every election.[113] In other words, since more than one candidate would be elected in a given district, with voters able to cast only a single ballot, PR elections brought victory to candidates who would represent voters who could not cast a ballot for that particular candidate. How judges responded to this concern—that PR reduced rather than expanded voter's rights—had decided the fate of PR in Michigan, Ohio, and California, among other states.

As the CRC's lead counsel before the Court of Appeals, Paul A. Windels countered the Kings County Supreme Court's ruling on several fronts. Windels argued that Justice Dodd ignored Article XII of the City Home Rule Law, which provided for independent authority for cities to alter their charters and granted the state the ability to provide additional powers through general laws that further enhanced a city's ability to govern itself.[114] Furthermore, Windels argued that Section II of the state constitution specifically provided for the creation of a charter revision commission so long as the governor declared an emergency and the state legislature agreed by a two-thirds majority—precisely what occurred in 1934.

With regard to proportional representation, Windels quoted Article II, Section I, to substantiate his claim for its legality: "Every citizen of the age of twenty-one years . . . shall be entitled to vote . . . for all officers that now are or hereafter may be elective by the people."[115] According to Windels, the constitution's language required that every voter held the right to vote for any candidate who might represent the voter's district. From his perspective, proportional representation provided for this ability, with voters able to select any of the candidates for their particular borough. Windels also argued that reformers had entered this language into the constitution in the early nineteenth century in order to prohibit elections that excluded voters who did not meet certain property qualifications. Windels concluded that PR followed this objective and did not prevent a voter from casting a ballot for any candidate in a given district.

Confirming reformers' suspicion that judicial alliances with the Brooklyn Democratic Party led to the earlier Kings County Supreme Court ruling, the Court of Appeals ruled in favor of the CRC on October 6, 1936. The justices agreed with reformers' arguments that the state constitution allowed for city charter commissions as mechanisms of municipal reform. Likewise, the appellate court refused to reverse the CRC's proposals for a new charter and proportional representation on the grounds that they did not violate the state constitution. The failure of Democratic legal challenges to the CRC meant that the fate of charter reform—and proportional representation—now depended on the electorate.

In the previous summer's campaign literature, good-government groups had anticipated the public's ultimate authority, offering populist visions of the city voters striving to overpower machine politicians. The Democratic Party labored to find a compelling argument against charter reform. Faced with defending Tammany Hall, few public figures provided alternatives to the CRC proposals. Reform advocates, on the other hand, capitalized on the precisely defined benefits of reform to counter the alleged evils of the Tammany machine—charges that reformers had consistently honed in the public sphere for the past several years.

Although proportional representation and the new charter were separate issues on the ballot, reformers' campaign literature intermixed the two, as the primary supporters of charter revision also favored PR. Likewise, pro-reform newspapers vilified Tammany as the enemy of progress and the supporter of patronage, graft, and corruption. In addition to obese party bosses, political cartoons depicted the Tammany Tiger lurking in the distance, conveying Tammany Hall as an omnipresent threat.[116]

Pro-PR publications responded to criticisms that the system favored elites by emphasizing PR's likely benefits to "average voters." "'PR' Means Proportional Representation; It also Means People's Rule," a flyer published by the Proportional Representation Campaign Committee (PRCC), defined PR as a method for the citizenry to take power from the party elite.[117] "Charter Catechism!" featured the reappearing character John Q. Voter (JQV) yelling at a fat, cigar-smoking Tammany boss, "Don't Boss Me Any More!" as he prepared to vote for the new charter.[118] Good-government activists who had supported PR and charter reform for years envisioned the average New York City voter as male, white, middle age, and middle income. The negative depictions of bankers and politicians set JQV apart as nonelite, hard working, and dedicated to the goal of municipal progress through democratic reform. The character desired the power to use his own voice in determining the structure of city government. As part of this effort, according to the pamphlets, charter reform needed to be rewritten to encourage the participation of average New Yorkers in their city's democracy. This vision of the common New York City voter belied anti-reformers' depictions of reformers as particular minority groups (defined according to economic, religious, ethnic, or racial status) that desired to circumvent majority rule. John Q. Voter's final declaration for freedom from control by the party boss continued the ongoing battle between pro- and anti-reform groups to persuade the electorate that their side supported democratic self-government while the other backed corrupt, self-interested, authoritarian government.

Charter
Catechism!

Vote YES for
New City Charter
November 3

Make Way for Progress!

(Special cartoons by Will B. Johnstone)

BOSS RULE OR "HOME RULE"?

Does this make you want to know more about the charter?

Do You Know

**Send your name and address to
Citizens Charter Campaign Committee
100 East 42nd Street, New York City
and we will mail you more information**

Proponents of charter reform distributed the pamphlet "Charter Catechism" to connect their campaign for good government reform with New Yorkers' sense of powerlessness in 1936. On the front, the old municipal charter is drawn by horse to a museum, clearing the path for new policies represented by modern automobiles. On the back, recurring character John Q. Voter defies bloated, cigar-smoking boss—"The State"—as he asserts his independence at the polls. *Citizens Charter Campaign Committee pamphlet, "Charter Catechism!" 1936. Courtesy City Hall Library, New York City; and McDougall Trust Library, London.*

As these illustrations envisioned charter reform and proportional representation as tools to enable popular rule, they highlighted an ongoing ambivalence in the good-government movement toward the role of women in civic activism and municipal politics. This vision essentially removed women from city politics, even though female activists contributed a great deal to the good-government movement in New York City. Historically, women's groups supported charter reform and campaigned vigorously for PR in the decades following the Nineteenth Amendment's passage. Yet PR publicity rarely included both sexes. While John Q. Voter appeared in his exclusively male world, the League of Women Voters produced radio announcements that presented women in a segregated political sphere.

"Charter Revision," broadcast at the time of the CRC hearings in December 1935, featured two representatives of the New York City chapter of the League of Women Voters discussing charter reform. The broadcast featured a seemingly casual conversation between Mrs. Harry Whitney and Mrs. John Philip Cunningham, both chairs of the League's Municipal Affairs Committee, as to the merits of proportional representation.

WHITNEY: Oh, yes, proportional representation. I have heard the term but isn't it terribly complicated?

CUNNINGHAM: Not as complicated for the voter as our present requirement for voting on the voting machine. And proportional representation, or PR as it is popularly called, guarantees that the will of the community will be correspondingly reflected in the legislative body. In other words, the Democrats casting 69 percent of the vote in New York City in 1935 should have elected 69 percent of the Aldermen. Actually they elected 95 percent. . . .

WHITNEY: Well, if it would really work out that way a little complication in the use of PR might be readily overcome.

CUNNINGHAM: There is no complication in the voting under PR and it has worked out exactly as I have described in the various cities in the country and elsewhere where it has been used. Furthermore there is assurance that the will of the community will be proportionately reflected in the legislative make-up. It would then be possible in New York as it has been elsewhere to find distinguished citizens willing to run for councilman . . .

WHITNEY: It would be wonderful to improve the personnel in the legislative body.[119]

The question-and-answer session by Cunningham and Whitney connected PR with women's struggle for greater representation in local government. The repetition of the phrase "will of the community" implied that the current system operated without popular consent and that proportional representation would achieve, by its very operation, the proper balance of representative authority in government. Yet this radio spot, coupled with the testimony of women's rights activists at the CRC hearings and other public demonstrations by women's civic groups, conveyed the perception that proportional representation would increase women's authority in city affairs. In this respect, as Cunningham and Whitney repeatedly noted, the "will of the community" connoted more than proportional representation of political parties; it also involved appropriate representation of women in city government.

Pro-PR advertisements such as the "Charter Revision" broadcast voiced the expectation that women were part of the political process. According to these ads by the League of Women Voters, the Women's City Club, and the Citizens Union, through its representation of the "will of the community," PR would reflect women's status in the citizenry. Although women's rights activists made few direct solicitations of women to support female candidates, their use of populist rhetoric by definition called for greater female representation.

In July 1935, Women's City Club president Ethel Dreier petitioned CRC member and future council minority leader, Genevieve Earle, to install PR as a critical component of charter reform. Dreier argued:

Under this system the citizen need not fear losing his vote entirely. . . . We believe that adoption of Proportional Representation and the use of a strictly non-partisan ballot, without party insignia, would be the one most progressive step that could be made toward a better government for the City of New York.[120]

During the 1936 referenda campaign, Dreier and other Women's City Club members marched for charter reform and proportional representation. Despite the *New York Herald-Tribune* photo caption's gentle depiction of club members "acquainting the public with charter revision," the marchers demanded attention for charter reform and PR. Moreover, their activism explicitly positioned women as participants in city politics. This demonstration expanded the meaning of their poster's signature phrase, "A New Day in City Government," to reflect both the impact of reform and the significance of women's activism in New York City.[121]

On November 3, 1936, more than 1.5 million New Yorkers voted to determine the fate of charter reform and proportional representation. The electorate approved the new charter by 952,519 to 603,072, and PR by 923,186 to 555,217. Appearing on the ballot with President Roosevelt's reelection bid, the placement of charter reform and proportional representation in the November elections aided their success as Roosevelt won by an unprecedented margin. Several members of the Roosevelt administration joined Mayor La Guardia in campaigning for the charter, linking local reform with the president's popular New Deal agenda. Through much of the city, results

Results of 1936 Charter Referendum

	Yes	No
Manhattan	219,070	139,595
Bronx	191,414	122,663
Kings	351,962	180,072
Queens	176,618	130,020
Richmond	13,455	30,722
Citywide	952,519	603,072

"Question One—Local: Shall the charter proposal by the New York City Charter Revision Commission be adopted?"
Source: Annual Report of the Board of Elections in the City of New York for the Year 1936, 208–209.

Results of 1936 PR Referendum

	Yes	No
Manhattan	207,910	131,961
Bronx	192,316	104,887
Kings	340,007	175,673
Queens	170,355	114,153
Richmond	12,598	28,543
Citywide	923,186	555,217

"Question Two—Local: Shall the system for the election of Councilmen by proportional representation provided for in the charter proposed by the New York City Charter Revision Commission be adopted?"
Source: Annual Report of the Board of Elections in the City of New York for the Year 1936, 208–209.

tallied slightly higher for the charter than for PR. Yet Bronx voters provided more votes for PR than for the charter required to allow it. Likely hoping to benefit from a more proportional delegation in the proposed city council, 66 percent of Brooklyn voters approved PR—a greater percentage than in any other borough. Richmond County (Staten Island), which maintained the city's largest percentage of politically conservative voters, opposed both referenda. Citywide, while the charter proposal received a slightly higher total number of votes than PR, the PR referendum actually received a higher percentage of votes than the new charter. Though reformers celebrated the victory of charter reform and proportional representation in November 1936 and anticipated the city's first PR election the following year, they also faced the new year with several looming challenges—including educating an electorate that didn't fully understand PR and preparing for renewed legal challenges to the system.

3 PROPORTIONAL REPRESENTATION AND THE PRACTICE OF DEMOCRACY IN NEW YORK CITY

Proportional representation's supporters and detractors took little time in turning their attention from the 1936 referenda campaign to the 1937 city council elections. New York City's primary advocates of the system, including George Hallett and the Citizens Union, moved quickly to develop a civic education campaign designed to instruct New Yorkers in the mechanics of PR, as well as persuade them of the system's benefits and ensure its integration into the city's electoral structure. Good-government groups printed thousands of instructional leaflets, held radio programs, and eagerly corresponded with newspaper reporters and editorial staffs to increase public awareness of PR. Beginning in 1937 and continuing throughout the tenure of proportional representation, its advocates conducted role-playing demonstrations of PR elections for middle and high school classes in the public school system. Demonstration scripts were also provided to teachers to conduct PR lessons on their own. Separate programs were utilized: one for fifth-, sixth-, and seventh-grade classes and the other for eighth grade and high school. From candidate nomination to final ballot transfers, the programs gave students point-by-point instruction in the intricacies of New York City's new electoral system. With pupils not yet eligible to vote, the presentations sought to engrain support for and

HOW TO VOTE THIS NEW WAY

1. Register the week of October 4th—If you don't register, you can't vote.

2. Ask for your paper ballot at the polls on election day. It should be handed to you by one of the election clerks.

3. Mark 1 in the square in front of your first choice, 2 in front of your second choice, and so on. You can mark as many choices as you want without hurting your first choice, and the more choices you mark the more certain you will be to help elect someone.

4. Put your ballot in the ballot box, and that is all there is to it!

There will be no party emblems, but party or group names will appear after the candidates supported. You will vote for people, not for labels.

DON'T BE FOOLED!

There is nothing hard about voting the P. R. Ballot for Council

YOU VOTE THIS WAY ON PAPER BALLOTS FOR COUNCILMEN ONLY

You vote the usual way on voting machines for Mayor and other City Officials

Vote BOTH Ways on Election Day

Suggestion to the Voter

It will make matters simpler if you mark your choices on a sample ballot or a slip of paper in advance and take it to the polls with you. Then you need only copy your choices on the real ballot. The names on the ballot will be in alphabetical order although the list may begin anywhere in the alphabet, as in our picture of the ballot. (OVER)

JOHN Q. VOTER
Gets a Break

By Voting the New
Proportional Representation Way!

This leaflet prepared and published by the
PROPORTIONAL REPRESENTATION
JOINT COMMITTEE
55 West 44th Street   New York City
VAnderbilt 3-1816

After successful passage of proportional representation in 1936, John Q. Voter returns to exert his power by voting with the new system. In "John Q. Voter Gets a Break," the New York City political system is exclusively male, with punny candidate names like "James Goodguy" and "Will Workhard" filling the sample PR ballot. *Proportional Representation Joint Committee pamphlet, "John Q. Voter Gets a Break," 1937. Courtesy McDougall Trust Library, London.*

understanding of the system in parents, as students explained and discussed PR with their families. For younger children, the presentation concluded with the following admonition to be relayed to their parents:

Take your ballot home to father and mother and see if you can tell them what you did. If they ask any questions that you cannot answer, or if you have any questions of your own, bring them to class next time. Tell those at home who really vote that they must use a black lead pencil when they do so. This is the law, and many of your fathers and mothers do not have their votes counted because they are illegal if marked with ink or indelible pencil; in fact with anything except a black lead pencil.[1]

Older students, whose demonstration incorporated a more extensive, and potentially confusing, overview of the counting process, received the following concluding instructions, "Now you can tell the people at home how to vote. They do not have to <u>count</u> the ballots, but they are interested in knowing how it is done."[2] These educational programs provided PR activists another means of enhancing support for the new system by presenting it to students and their parents as an essential part of civic responsibility in a democratic society.[3]

Literature issued for the general public that supported proportional representation portrayed the system as essential for civic empowerment. In a cartoon pamphlet distributed by the Proportional Representation Joint Committee, "John Q. Voter" (JQV) returned in his role of representing the city's common voter. The middle-aged, suited gentleman "Gets a Break" with PR, as the system enables him to express his political preference for candidates unaligned with the previously dominant party bosses. In the story, JQV defeats the will of two grafting party bosses who support "Sam Heel" and "Henry Mugg" for the city council. With proportional representation, JQV realizes that he is free not to vote for the "terrible" machine candidates. Rather, he can mark separate preferences for such reform-minded candidates as "James Goodguy," "Arthur Realstuff," and "Will Workhard." As the sinister bosses exclaim, "Curses!" JQV joyously proclaims that he will "get a break" with the election of independent representatives.[4] Continuing the 1936 JQV cartoon depictions of a single-sex political world, the 1937 pamphlet incorporated a new dimension to this exclusively male political spectrum: the city's candidates for office. Assuming that "O.K. Layman" and "A. Smartfella" represented male candidates, men held every line on the pamphlet's sample PR ballot.

Though PR had passed the constitutional test posed to charter reform the previous year, the Democratic Party again mobilized its legal resources to challenge the system in court. Whereas the party's primary argument in *Mooney v. Cohen*, 272 NY 33 (1936) was that the electoral system could not be instituted because the Charter Revision Commission was created through an unconstitutional delegation of legislative authority, the anti-PR argument in *Bowe v. Cohen*, 274 NY 411 (1937) focused squarely on the constitutionality of the system itself. In arguing against PR, the Democratic Party's counsel repeated longstanding contentions that the system violated the New York State Constitution's requirement that voters be able to participate in all elections. By permitting the election of more than one council member for each borough, the argument went, PR prevented voters from casting ballots for each of their representatives in the council. This interpretation of Article II of the state constitution reflected a desire to limit the membership of the council, as the smaller the number of representatives for a given geographic area, the greater the likelihood that the area's electoral process could be controlled from nomination to the final tally. Essentially, this interpretation strived to preserve Democrats' monopoly of seats in the city's legislative branch.

As with *Mooney*, the *Bowe* case emerged from competing rulings by Supreme Court justices in Manhattan and Brooklyn. In March 1937, a Manhattan judge approved of proportional representation, while a Brooklyn justice found the system unconstitutional. On March 15, New York County Justice Lloyd Church ruled:

> Under the system of proportional representation, every voter in each borough of the City may express the order of his preference for every candidate for councilman from his borough. He would seem to have a much greater power of voting under that system than under the present system of single member districts. . . . [T]his system insures to practically every voter that his vote will actually be used in helping to elect some member of the Board (city council).[5]

Referring to the *Mooney* decision, Church argued, "We doubt very much whether the Court of Appeals . . . would have permitted a proposition on proportional representation to be submitted to the voters which was unconstitutional in its entirety."[6] From Church's perspective, the Court of Appeals had already approved the use of proportional representation, leaving the legal issue moot. Eight days later, Kings County justice Philip A. Brennan reached the opposite conclusion, finding that PR would "impair the effectiveness of the individual vote and thus deprive the elector of his constitutional right."[7] Echoing his court's 1936 ruling, Brennan held that PR violated the constitutional requirement that voters be able to vote for every elected office.[8]

John E. Bowe, joined by 10 residents covering each of the five boroughs, originated the Manhattan case. The 11 petitioners included an array of primarily Democratic Party officials, many of whom had previously campaigned against the system and would continue to do so in the future. Bowe, a Richmond real estate developer, voted against the system as a member of the 1934 Charter Commission and later as a delegate to the 1938 New York State Constitutional Convention. Petitioner John Godfrey Saxe, former president of the New York State Bar Association and member of Tammany Hall's legal committee, also served in the 1934 commission but voted for PR at the 1938 convention. Other Democratic petitioners included former Bronx Borough president Cyrus C. Miller and Brooklyn State Assembly member Edward S. Moran Jr., who served as counsel in the Kings County case heard by Justice Brennan. The firm of Cullen and Dykman again represented the opponents of proportional representation. Representing attorneys included William J. O'Shea, a 1934 charter commission member, who later voted against PR at the 1938 New York State Constitutional Convention.[9]

Underscoring the party divisions over proportional representation, Democratic Party chairs for each of the five boroughs issued a brief joining the opposition to PR.[10] On the other side, Republican Party chairs in Manhattan and Brooklyn joined a coalition of good-government groups providing amicus briefs for PR that included the Citizens Union, City Affairs Committee, New York City League of Women Voters, City Club of New York, Women's City Club, Merchants' Association, and United Neighborhood Houses. Pro-PR counsel included Albert Sprague Bard, Laurence Arnold Tanzer, and Louis Waldman, who was one of the five Socialist Party legislators ousted from the state assembly during the post–World War I Red Scare. Although Waldman had rescinded his support for PR due to qualms with the charter reform bill in 1936, he renewed his support of the system after the charter's victory. The board of elections, led by S. Howard Cohen, again served as a mandatory respondent for PR although its members campaigned publicly against the system. Making their case before the Court of Appeals, PR's opponents argued that the system threatened national principles of democratic government. Petitioners declared, "Our American system of Government is based on the representative principle of majority voting. Proportional representation is precisely the opposite."[11] In addition to challenging PR as un-American, petitioners attacked one of the most critical, acknowledged procedural weaknesses within the PR policy.

Referring to the system's procedure for transferring votes, the brief labeled proportional representation a "lottery, gamble, or game of chance, or series of chances."[12] This argument emphasized the uncertainty created by ambiguities in the transfer counts as proposed in New York City. As acknowledged by George Hallett, there was no specific formula for defining an order to the transfer ballots from the first count onward. For instance, if two ballots showed first choices selected for a candidate declared to have won, the policy remained unclear as to how those ballots' secondary choices would be counted. Petitioners questioned which ballots would be kept in the winner's column and which would be returned to the count and allotted to secondary choices. According to the charter proposal, the transferred ballots would be allotted essentially at random, such that, for example, after a candidate reached the minimum votes necessary for election, or fell below the minimum necessary to continue to the next round, that candidate's remaining ballots would be distributed to secondary choices. Any remaining ballots with that candidate selected as first choice would replace ballots already distributed to the candidate possessing secondary choices. The PR regulations contained no provision for comparing the preferences of the remaining ballots' secondary choices with the secondary choices of those ballots already counted as first-choice votes. This policy meant that voting results in a given borough would likely be different depending upon the *order* in which the ballots were counted.

According to Hallett, the architects of New York's PR system created this transfer process intentionally to make the count less complicated. Ultimately, this transfer policy enabled the possibility of random, rather than proportional, distribution of the candidate's secondary choices. According to Section 1007 of chapter 43 of the new city charter:

> If during the first sorting a ballot is found which is marked first choice for a candidate already elected, but shows no choice for an unelected candidate, it shall be given to the candidate of its first choice and in its place the last previous ballot, if any, sorted to that candidate which does show a choice for an unelected candidate, shall be taken and resorted to its next available choice as if it were then being sorted for the first time.[13]

Appellants included this section as well as comments made by Hallett to criticize PR as statistically inaccurate. In a letter to the editor of the *New York Times* from earlier in 1937, Hallett defended the transfer process:

> By complicating the rules it would have been possible to eliminate chance entirely, as is actually done in the PR elections of the Legislature of the Australian province of Tasmania. But there is such a thing as taking too much trouble to get rid of an element of chance which is both infinitesimal in size and unimportant in character. The important

thing is that PR makes nearly every vote count, while under the old system a large part of the votes are wasted.[14]

The argument in *Bowe* provided one of the rare moments when PR's critics, who frequently portrayed the system as a lottery, specified a section of the policy as producing statistical chance in the final tally. Moreover, the case witnessed a recognition by the system's chief proponent that it featured "an element of chance," however "infinitesimal" and "unimportant."

William C. Chanler, in his brief supporting proportional representation, responded to criticisms of the transfer process by arguing that improvements made by PR outweighed the chance introduced during ballot transfers. Chanler asserted, "It seems far fetched to say that a voter 'loses' his vote because his favorite candidate is already elected by the votes of others and his vote is therefore counted for his second or third choice instead of his first!"[15] As made clear in the first council elections of 1937, voters' inattention to party or coalition with their secondary choices likely caused, in many cases, votes to be transferred from non-Democratic candidates to Democrats. In language it later eschewed, the Republican Party supported PR as "an honest effort to afford representation to citizens of every shade of political opinion."[16] Moreover, the party's Manhattan and Brooklyn chairs demanded that the system persevere because the voters had approved it and "their mandate should be respected."[17] Within months, Brooklyn Republicans began to shift their perspective on the system as they struggled to elect council members.

On June 2, 1937, Chief Justice Frederick E. Crane delivered the court's majority opinion in favor of proportional representation. Three justices joined Crane's ruling, with two justices concurring separately, and one dissenting. While PR garnered a 6 to 1 court majority, the justices offered only tepid endorsements of the system. Rather than lauding PR's mechanics, Crane justified his decision upon the notion that voters should be given the benefit of the doubt in experimenting with electoral policy. Crane asked rhetorically, "This proposed system may be unworkable; it may be so cumbersome or so intricate as to be impracticable, the results desired may not be obtained; the remedy may be worse than the disease, but what have all these to do with the Constitution?"[18] While anticipating difficulties in implementing PR, Crane lauded the possibility that PR could bring a more democratic form of government to New York City. He declared, "At least this Hare System of Proportional Voting is an attempt to make representative government a reality."[19] Crane chastised petitioners' claim that PR would disenfranchise voters: "In other words, *actual* representation according to numbers is illegal, although *unequal* representation according to unequal districts is legal. I cannot follow this reasoning."[20] In his concurring opinion, Justice Lehman repeated Crane's call for "innovation" as essential to reforming city government.[21]

The court's lone dissenter, Harlan W. Rippey, reiterated the most dramatic criticisms of PR produced by Democratic officials in previous months. Labeling the system a "scheme," Rippey depicted it as un-American, anti-democratic, and unconstitutional:

> The open and avowed purpose of the scheme is to secure election by minorities, and to provide for and encourage group voting, the destruction of party government and party responsibility and of the principle of majority rule which basically underlies the American system of representative government.…
>
> Ours is a constitutional democracy—*a government of law* in which majorities rule.[22]

In language that reflected the tenets of machine opposition to PR, Rippey portrayed PR as a terror that, if unleashed, would dramatically alter the city's political structure. Of course, New York's reformers and third-party activists hoped that PR would produce precisely this result in the fall elections.

Victorious before the Court of Appeals, PR's supporters continued their campaign to strengthen the public's understanding of the system and counter ongoing Democratic attempts to prevent its use. They presented optimistic portraits of what voters should expect during and after the first PR elections. George Hallett promised that the first election would prove an example of representative democracy for which New Yorkers would long be proud. Deflecting charges that, based upon Cincinnati's delayed tally, New York City's poll workers would need at least 28 days to complete their count, Hallett asserted that there would be "no excuse for taking a longer time for a PR count in New York City than in Cincinnati, even if paper ballots are used."[23] He ridiculed predictions that the city's board of elections would be flooded with council candidates as "fantastic," concluding instead that only a select crop of candidates would run for election in the five boroughs.[24] On both counts, Hallett miscalculated.

Ninety-nine candidates ran in Brooklyn alone, producing a ballot more than four feet in length. The Brooklyn count lasted for nearly a month, with 60 counts needed to whittle the field from 99 candidates to nine council members. In the Bronx, police arrested four canvassers for fraudulently marking ballots and impounded thousands of ballots for suspected tampering.

INSTRUCTIONS

Mark Your Choices with NUMBERS Only. (Do NOT Use X Marks.)

Put the number 1 in the square opposite the name of your first choice.

Put the number 2 opposite your second choice, the number 3 opposite your third choice, and so on. You may mark as many choices as you please.

Do not put the same number opposite more than one name.

To vote for a person whose name is not printed on this ballot, write his name on a blank line under the names of the candidates and put a number in the square opposite to show which choice you wish to give him.

If you tear or deface or wrongly mark this ballot, return it and obtain another.

OFFICIAL COUNCILMANIC BALLOT
FOR THE
GENERAL ELECTION
NOVEMBER 2, 1937
CITY OF NEW YORK,
KINGS COUNTY
59   ELECTION DISTRICT
22   ASSEMBLY DISTRICT

CANDIDATES FOR THE COUNCIL	
PETER V. CACCHIONE	Communist
ALEXANDER F. CASHIN	
JOHN CASHMORE	Democratic
LYTLE G. CHAMBERS	
JOHN CHRISTMAN	
THOMAS J. CONBOY	
ALPHONSUS COTTER, JR.	
J. BERRY COUGHLIN	
JOSEPH F. COX	Taxpayers Friend
ANTHONY J. DE LISIO	
ANTHONY J. DIGIOVANNA	Democratic
THOMAS J. DONOVAN	
MARGARET DOYLE	
GENEVIEVE B. EARLE	City Fusion
HERBERT S. FELNER	
MILTON FUCHS	
JOHN S. GAYNOR	
JOHN GELO	American Labor
IRVING W. GOOTZEIT	

The ballot for the first proportional representation election in Brooklyn was more than four feet long and incorporated several changes to previous ballot formats, including new instructions and the option to forgo party affiliation. Due to the chance of lottery, candidates whose last names began with the letter "C" were listed first, giving Communist Peter V. Cacchione the premier slot out of 99 candidates in this electoral district. *New York City Council ballot, 1937. Courtesy City Hall Library, New York City.*

City Council Election Results, 1937 (by borough)

Member	Party	Votes Received
BROOKLYN Members elected: 9		
Andrew A. Armstrong	ALP	75,000
Louis Hollander	ALP	75,000
William M. McCarthy	D	75,000
Genevieve B. Earle	CF/CNP	65,474
Albert D. Schanzer	D	64,155
Anthony J. DiGiovanna	D	53,392
John Cashmore	D	53,046
Joseph T. Sharkey	D	47,063
Abner C. Surpless	R	42,424
MANHATTAN Members elected: 6		
John P. Nugent	D	75,000
B. Charney Vladeck	ALP	75,000
Joseph C. Baldwin	R	74,832
Robert K. Straus	CF	64,606
Howard H. Spellman	D	60,150
William A. Carroll	D	57,584
THE BRONX Members elected: 5		
Salvatore Ninfo	ALP	75,000
Michael J. Quill	ALP	75,000
James A. Deering	D	73,398
Charles E. Keegan	D	66,056
Joseph E. Kinsley	D	44,205
QUEENS Members elected: 5		
James A. Burke	ID	75,000
Hugh Quinn	D	59,656

Charles Belous	CF	57,225
William N. Conrad	ID	54,125
John M. Christensen	R	45,908

RICHMOND
Members elected: 1

Frederick Schick	D	31,737

Abbreviations: ALP = American Labor Party; CF = City Fusion; CNP = Citizens Non-Partisan; D = Democratic; ID = Insurgent Democrat; R = Republican.
Source: Annual Report of the Board of Elections in the City of New York for the Year 1937, 45–46.

In Manhattan, suffering from cramped quarters and mounting tensions over the tally's slow pace, canvassers threatened to strike if they weren't afforded better working conditions. Ever impatient, La Guardia responded by mandating eight-hour workdays, without an increase in the $10 daily stipend for election workers, for the duration of the count.[25]

Even after enduring several delays in the official tally, the city's largest newspapers generally approved of PR's debut. The *New York World-Telegram* expressed frustration over delays but optimistically judged the system's future:

PR has made good in improving the quality of man-power in the Council and breaking Tammany's old notorious unfair predominance in the government.... The long count, three weeks for Manhattan, still longer for Brooklyn, Queens, and the Bronx, has been discouraging. Voting machines can remedy that. The encouraging thing is that Proportional Representation, in spite of die-hard opposition, has made good.[26]

The *New York Times* agreed. In an editorial published after two weeks of counting, as patience with the tally began to thin, the *Times* proclaimed that what mattered most was that "tens of thousands of citizens who have had no voice in the city's primary legislative body will have a voice after Jan. 1."[27] The *Times* argued that even the election of Tammany candidates should not deflect support for PR: "A Tammany Council membership roughly corresponding to the valid Tammany vote will not be a disaster to PR—it will show that the PR system is working as it should."[28] In many respects, such sympathetic coverage stemmed from the dramatic shift in party representation brought by PR.

Two years after Democrats won 62 of 65 seats in the board of aldermen, the first PR elections saw Tammany and allied candidates garner only half of the seats in the council. Reformers hailed the anticipated 13 to 13 council split as an unprecedented victory for political diversity in city government. The American Labor Party possessed the greatest concentration of electoral support in the PR tally, electing five of its seven candidates to the council, with each winner reaching the 75,000-vote maximum tally. Candidates from this party showed strength in three of the five boroughs, winning two seats in Brooklyn, two in the Bronx, and one in Manhattan. The party's success owed much to the ALP's decision to run a slate of only seven candidates citywide, which lessened the likelihood of competition between ALP candidates running within each borough. The ALP had organized in 1936 specifically as an anti-Tammany organization, channeling dissatisfaction among Democrats against Tammany Hall and its Democratic allies outside of Manhattan. The party's immediate goal was to direct Democrats to vote for President Franklin Roosevelt's reelection on a non-Tammany ballot line. In the aftermath of then-governor Roosevelt's support of the Seabury investigations and the ouster of Mayor Jimmy Walker in 1932, Tammany Hall actively campaigned against President Roosevelt during his 1936 reelection bid. The American Labor Party's formation provided anti-Tammany, pro-New Deal Democrats with a path to gaining municipal power beyond Tammany's control. In the 1937 city council elections, the ALP fused municipal and national political agendas by connecting its slate of candidates to the policies of President Roosevelt and Mayor La Guardia.[29]

The Fusion and Republican parties, along with a pair of Democrats who ran independent of the party organization, gained a total of eight seats in the restructured council. Given the election of 35-year-old Republican Newbold Morris as council president, who would hold a tie-breaking vote in deadlocked proceedings, the combination of Fusion, Republican, insurgent Democratic, and ALP victors presented the components for a 13-member coalition that could possibly hold majority power in the council. In reporting Morris's victory, the *Times* detailed his elite background as a "championship figure skater," "a member of one of the city's oldest families," a direct descendant of a signer of the Declaration of Independence, owner of a Park Avenue home, and "one of the best dressed members of the Board of Aldermen."[30] Educated at the Groton School and Yale University, Morris had moved swiftly through the ranks of the Republican Party in Manhattan, succeeding Joseph Clark Baldwin as alderman for the Fifteenth Aldermanic

District, the "Silk Stocking District," on Baldwin's move to the state senate in 1934.[31] Despite the prospect of Morris leading an anti-Tammany council coalition, the PR tally suggested significant electoral weaknesses for the Republican Party. Like Fusion, the Republican Party was unable to elect more than one member in any single borough. Aside from Baldwin, who nearly received the maximum total in Manhattan, the other two Republican victors placed last among the council members-elect in Brooklyn and Queens.

Responding to the considerable delays in the tally and the possibility that Democrats could still gain control over the council, several of PR's most powerful allies strongly criticized the system. Mayor La Guardia and the *New York Daily News*, the city's highest circulation daily newspaper, asserted that PR took an unacceptable amount of time to ultimately produce unrepresentative results. La Guardia and the *Daily News* based their criticism on the idea that since La Guardia had won reelection by nearly a half-million votes, PR should have elected a majority-Fusion council. In stark language, the *Daily News* went so far as to retract its earlier endorsement of the new electoral system: "We're convinced we made a mistake on this point; and now we say PR is a failure and we regret having favored it. . . . PR as operated here smells."[32] This reasoning grossly underestimated Tammany's continued strength in local politics and ignored the fact that while La Guardia defeated his Democratic opponent by just over 450,000 votes, he garnered 58 percent of total votes cast.[33] Considering that margin, the difference between the mayoral results and the PR-council tally was as not dramatic as the *Daily News* suggested.

Pro-PR activists defended the results and called for the city to purchase voting machines to enable faster tallies in future elections.[34] Although the board of elections had adopted voting machines years before PR's adoption, the board refused to purchase new machines specifically designed to accommodate a PR tally. This decision meant that voters needed to make their selections for all other contests (city/state/federal) on a machine and then complete a separate paper PR ballot for city council elections. The board justified the use of paper PR ballots over voting machines in the interest of cost reduction, but paper balloting increased the time and expense—not to mention the frustration—brought by multiple rounds of counting and transfers. The *World-Telegram* contended that the board intentionally prevented the adoption of voting machines to encourage popular discontent with the system and speed its demise.[35] Privately, George Hallett informed PR critic, and future council member, Louis Cohen that International Business Machines (IBM) had developed a voting machine that Hallett encouraged for adoption by New York City. Hallett admitted that the machines had not been field tested and would cost more than $1,000 each. With at least 4,000 machines needed throughout the city on Election Day, Hallett's minimum cost estimate for PR voting machines totaled $4 million.[36]

To address complaints from former supporters, PR advocates noted that the Democratic Party had won a large majority of the other city contests, including "all county offices except that of district attorney for New York County, most of the judicial offices, and an overwhelming majority of the City's assemblymen and the City's delegates to the State Constitutional Convention."[37] The Henry Street Settlement's Civic Education Group argued that Democrats won so many council seats "through superior organization and a seasoned, smoothly-functioning machine."[38] The settlement's report emphasized how Democrats effectively structured their council campaigns to garner the greatest number of PR ballots, particularly with publicity that guided voters to mark secondary choices exclusively for Democratic candidates.

Democratic Party success under PR was not lost on the city's other political organizations. Republican and Communist party officials criticized the unwieldy number of anti-Tammany candidates who ran in each of the boroughs. The Brooklyn Borough president's office, headed by Republican PR-ally Raymond Ingersoll, lauded PR's successful election of several minority-party candidates. But the office criticized Republican Party leadership for its inability to elect more than a single candidate in the city's largest borough.[39] The office's post-election report focused on the party's lack of an organized campaign to both limit candidates running as Republicans and to better instruct voters on how to distribute their second and third choices.[40]

The Brooklyn tally provided evidence that voters dismissed or ignored candidates' differences when making secondary selections. Sidney Keshner, with no party designation, received 2,513 votes, of which 2,007 became eligible for redistribution to the next candidates chosen on his ballots. Canvassers distributed the remaining 2,007 ballots to 65 different candidates, with an average of 31 votes each. But 292 of those votes went to the very next name on the ballot (James F. Kiernan, no party designated), and 209 went to the next lower candidate (Paul M. Klein, no party designated). While the possibility existed that voters favored Keshner because of his party independence

Candidates' Primary Party Affiliation, 1937

Independent and other	137 candidates, 0 elected
Democratic	26 candidates, 15 elected
City Fusion	24 candidates, 3 elected
Republican	14 candidates, 3 elected
Citizens Non-Partisan Committee	8 candidates, 0 elected
American Labor	7 candidates, 5 elected
Communist	4 candidates, 0 elected
Socialist	3 candidates, 0 elected
Total candidates	223
Total council members elected	26

Two of the 15 elected Democrats ran as "insurgent" or independent Democrats, though they joined the party majority shortly after taking their council seats.

Source: "PR at Work: How Progressive Unity Could Have Won—and Can Win," *State of Affairs* 4 (July–August 1939), published by the Legislative and Research Bureau of the New York State Communist Party.

and selected other candidates without party affiliations, it was far more likely that voters simply marked the next names on their ballots in alphabetical order.[41]

In addition to Republican officials and other civic activists, the Communist Party noted the methods by which Democrats shifted their strategy to succeed with PR, while the minority parties struggled to maintain their anti-Democratic coalition after the first round. Echoing the criticisms mentioned earlier, the party interpreted the results as confirming that "progressives remained disunited against an organically united Tammany."[42] While non-Democrats garnered more first-choice ballots than Democrats, non-Democrats lost nearly half of their votes after the first transfer. According to the party's Legislative and Research Bureau, non-Democratic candidates received 1,314,722 votes in the initial count, out of a total of 2,013,101 valid ballots cast citywide. But minority-party and unaffiliated candidates saw this total plummet by nearly half, to 725,982, following the first transfer. In comparison, Democrats saw their first-choice votes drop from 666,980 to 643,642—a retention rate of 96.5 percent. Overall, Democrats gained 195,084 votes with the first transfer, as many voters selected recognizable Democrats as their second choices regardless of their first-choice selections. In Brooklyn, for example, Democrats received 220,439 first-choice votes for nine candidates and succeeded in electing five. Non-Democratic candidates in Brooklyn garnered more than double that number in the initial count—476,640 votes. But following 60 counts over three weeks, that number dwindled so that ultimately only four non-Democratic candidates were elected in Brooklyn.[43]

For the Communist Party and other anti-Tammany organizations, New York City's first PR elections underscored the power maintained by Democrats throughout the five boroughs. The Democratic machine responded to the changing electoral structure by shifting its resources to take advantage of an opposition coalition lacking in both coordination and cooperation. In each borough, Democrats estimated the number of seats to be elected and ran a limited number of candidates, thereby channeling votes into a smaller number of candidates than the other parties. While the addition of independent petitions opened ballots to an array of candidates, the Democratic Party actually benefited from this diverse assortment of candidates. Democrats organized their campaigns district by district, with neighborhood captains responsible for informing voters which candidate the party favored for first-choice votes and then how to allot later choices. This strategy reduced the risk of losing votes with each round of transfers, resulting in Democratic candidates retaining votes and dramatically increasing their totals with each transfer. For all of its opposition to PR, the Tammany network quickly and effectively modified its tactics to take advantage of the new electoral landscape.

Organizations from across the anti-Tammany spectrum recognized that the city's progressive coalition must be strengthened to protect PR and supplant Tammany Hall. The Communist Party and the Henry Street Settlement built upon their respective critiques of the tally and called for progressives to shift their campaign strategies to resemble the Democratic Party's operations. The CP called for the following measures to combat Tammany Hall:

1. Achieving unity of action behind a progressive-New Deal program.
2. Putting up a united slate, with support for each other's candidates, limiting the candidates to the number to be elected.
3. Zoning the counties so as to get maximum results.
4. Conducting an effective educational campaign on how to vote, so as to eliminate the large number of "wasted" and invalid ballots.
5. Bringing out the progressive vote for registration.[44]

As bluntly summarized by the *New Masses*, "The basic lesson [of the PR elections] is that Tammany and reaction *can* be smashed—the city *can* be won for progress, provided: *the progressive elements unite and organize effectively*."[45]

As pro-PR groups prepared for the first New York City Council session of 1938, a sense of opportunity and dread pervaded their outlook on the city's political future. Anti-Tammany groups recognized that the Democratic Party had organized itself to simultaneously increase its totals under PR *and* to work to abolish the system. As the Henry Street Settlement emphasized, Democrats had consistently campaigned against PR and, despite soon possessing an effective majority in the council, would be "satisfied with nothing short of the complete domination they possessed in the Board of Aldermen."[46] New Yorkers would wait less than one year before the first of several Tammany-sponsored referenda appeared calling for PR's abolition.

On New Year's Day, 1938, Mayor Fiorello La Guardia presided proudly over appointment ceremonies at City Hall. For the first time in the city's history, a reform coalition had succeeded in reelecting a Fusion mayor, and luminaries from the Republican and American Labor parties were on hand to bask

Genevieve B. Earle proudly takes the oath of office as Mayor Fiorello La Guardia swears her in for her fifth term as a council member on December 28, 1945. Earle won in all five PR elections (1937, 1939, 1941, 1943, and 1945) but refused to run for reelection once PR was repealed in 1947. *Courtesy La Guardia and Wagner Archives, La Guardia Community College, City University of New York, Long Island City.*

in La Guardia's glow. As Samuel Seabury watched approvingly, La Guardia administered oaths of office to the members of his administration and to members of the inaugural city council, including Genevieve Earle. For Earle, a Fusion Republican and the only woman elected to the council, the mayor eschewed formality and declared that she was "one of the city's most outstanding citizens elected to the council."[47] Earle's tally of 65,474 votes, which placed her fourth in Brooklyn, demonstrated the stature she had cultivated in three decades of work in the public sector. Earle's experience came primarily from work with a variety of urban reform organizations and municipal offices that emerged during the Progressive era of the early twentieth century. She joined the Bureau of Municipal Research in 1908 and later served with the Women's Municipal League (director), the New York City Board of Child Welfare, the United Neighborhood Guild, and the Brooklyn chapter of the League of Women Voters (chair), among other positions. As the lone woman to serve on the Charter Revision Commission, Earle advocated the electoral system that facilitated her victory in 1937, as well as in every subsequent PR election.[48]

Earle later recalled as "very wise" La Guardia's admonition to her upon joining the council, "Now remember, Genevieve, women are new in politics, and they have to learn to take it on the chin. When one woman fails, all women fail. Their success will be measured by your success. So watch your step."[49] As the only woman elected to the first city council, Earle received press attention akin to that given an exotic zoo animal. Reporters tried—and failed—to reconcile their understanding of what it meant to be a woman and the new reality embodied by Earle. In 1949–1950, she recalled an interview session with reporters that occurred shortly after her inauguration:

[Reporters] wanted to make a regular home woman of me, one of these domestic ladies who are busy around the house, and who do all the things a good woman should, I presume. . . . But when I walked up the stoop [from vacation in Virginia] with my hunting jacket, my golf clubs, and my tennis racket, the reporters were overwhelmed. . . .

[The reporters said,] "Tell us about your home life." "What do you do about running the house?"

[I replied,] "Well, I have two good maids and I delegate all I can to them."

"But we'd like some pictures of you, to write up a story of you as a woman carrying on the work of a home. Can you sew?"

I said, "No, I've never sewed. I can't sew at all."

"Can you cook?" They wanted to take me to the kitchen to toss off an omelette.

I was getting a little embarrassed by this time because I couldn't say that I did any of these things regularly—the kind of things a normal woman is supposed to do. You see, during all my life I've led a semi-professional life. . . . I've been very busy.

"Can you cook?"

I said, "Not a lick."

"Well, what do you do about ordering your meals? Let's see you prepare a menu."

I reached down to get the phone to call the grocer. Oh no, that wouldn't do at all. It was too much like office procedure, you see. "All right, I'll dust the books in the library." . . . [T]o the tune of flash-bulbs and low sweet whispers from the reporters, I just negligently dusted the tops of the books.

One of the reporters said, "My Lord! We don't know whether to put you on the news page, the political page, or the sports page."[50]

The press desired to fashion Earle as a homemaker, more skilled with cooking, cleaning, and mending than with policy making. In responding to these expectations, Earle suggested her own attitudes toward the relationship between wealth, gender roles, and social status that explicitly distinguished her responsibilities in society from those women she deemed "normal," "regular," "domestic"—including the "two good maids" in her employ.

Throughout her political career, the tensions inherent in Earle's gender politics remained at the forefront of her public persona. She negotiated a tenuous path in which she argued for women to participate more actively in civic affairs and electoral politics "because of their natural instincts to improve social conditions," but Earle explicitly repelled the notion that she was a feminist. She asserted, "I certainly am not [a feminist]. . . . I think [women] are just as capable as men, but unlike the feminists, I do not want to make an issue of it."[51] Yet Earle often did make an issue of gender inequality in politics and government. As she transitioned from the charter reform campaign of 1936 to the council contest of 1937, Earle lamented that "more women than men are interested in good government in New York City," but "the average housewife is not aware of her power. It is true that public opinion is shaped to a certain degree by leaders in women's groups, but even women who do their own housework and take care of their children could find time to play the game of good government."[52] In her frustration, she appeared to dismiss the struggles that women faced in their everyday lives; constraints that Earle may have distanced herself from via her class status and public career. However, beneath the surface of such apparent oversimplifications rested a deep longing for equal footing in the male-controlled realm of politics and government and for fellow women to recognize their role and responsibility in achieving power.

Earle argued that women should not vote for her as a woman, though she admonished women for not electing more than one woman to the council in 1937. The *Times* reported Earle's post-election statements as follows:

> Women who want members of their sex to get political preference failed to take the opportunity offered in the recent election, Mrs. William P. Earle Jr. said last night a few hours after learning that she had been elected the only woman on the City Council. . . . "I learned from this election that there was no such thing as a woman vote in New York City. . . . Women do not vote specifically for another woman. *Nor do I think they should.*"[53]

Although Earle framed her legislative work as public service rather than feminist activism, she faced critiques from the press that suggested her political stature impressed upon her the expectations and responsibilities of all women. The *New York Post* patronizingly portrayed a campaign strategy session among Earle's female supporters as an example of "feminine chicanery," designed by "petticoat-politicos . . . for the purpose of perfecting a strictly feminine campaign."[54] The *Post* described a plan by which women who backed Earle would convince their husbands to pick her as their second pick on the preferential ballot, in the hopes that such second-choice ballots could ultimately put her over the electoral threshold "without the husbands getting the idea that they were being told what to do in politics."[55] The *Post's* story stressed the degree to which the city's press viewed women's political empowerment as something to be derided. But the piece also revealed a concerted effort among women to utilize the PR process to their benefit.

With a 13 to 13 division in the composition of New York's first city council, the body's initial sessions concentrated almost exclusively on determining which coalition would control the majority. Considering the balance between pro- and anti-Tammany members, Council president Newbold Morris appeared to represent the tie-breaking vote. With a Fusion, pro-PR council leader, reformers anticipated assuming effective majority power in the council.

The aspirations of reformers darkened swiftly due to a mishap altogether un-related to municipal politics.

With the council scheduled to begin meeting on January 3, 1938, and voting for committee chairs set to start shortly thereafter, all of the PR-elected legislators gathered in City Hall except for one. Michael G. Quill, the head of the New York City Transport Workers Union and representative of the American Labor Party, found himself delayed in transit returning from his wedding in Ireland. With Quill absent, the 13 organization Democrats quickly moved for a roll-call vote on the position of council vice-chairman, the body's majority leader. As in the US Congress, whichever coalition held the majority would be able to choose committee chairs and maintain power over which policies would be debated before the full council. Despite the even split between Tammany-allied and anti-Tammany council members, council member John Cashmore, Democrat of Brooklyn, recognized Quill's absence and moved to immediately begin a roll call for the position of vice-chairman. Supported by the 12-member coalition of insurgent Democrats, Republicans, Fusionists, and ALP members, Council President Morris re-sponded with several delays in which he argued that the votes should not occur until a quorum was present. [56] Morris defined a quorum to mean every member of the council; Tammany and allied Democrats defined a quorum as the majority of members seated on the council, which would allow for coun-cil votes to begin. Morris argued that council regulations prevented such a vote, as, he later recalled, "no local law or resolution could be passed except by a majority vote of *all* the members, not merely those present."[57] The interpre-tation of this rule would decide whether a Fusion coalition or Democrats would control the council.

According to Morris, upon hearing the council president's declaration that Quill's absence prevented a vote for vice-chairman, Cashmore "jumped up and yelled, 'Hitler here is depriving the people of a vice-chairman!'"[58] Soon, Bronx Democrat Joseph Kinsley charged that "democratic government was being strangled in our legislative chamber" and "pandemonium broke out."[59] Holding an ostensible 13 to 12 majority, the Tammany-allied Demo-crats pushed through their motion to begin and, with the lack of a tie prevent-ing Morris from voting on any motion, proceeded to elect their members as committee chairs in a series of 13 to 12 votes. The Democratic Party obtained a court order requiring Cashmore's seating as majority leader, along with the appointment of the Democrats' choice for city clerk and the committee leadership positions already determined. Far from deciding the issue, Morris welcomed Quill home at the next council session on January 25 and proceeded to seat Queens insurgent Democrat James Burke as majority leader, along with a new pick for city clerk.[60] As two majority leaders and two city clerks vied for supremacy in council chambers, the new body began its tenure in utter disarray, though the spectacle made for entertaining live broadcasts on the city's public radio station (WNYC). Ultimately, the New York State Court of Appeals ruled against Morris, in a decision with significant consequences for the council's evolution, its legislative agenda, and the future of PR.[61]

In accordance with the court's ruling, while the council was split 13 to 13, the Democratic Party held every leadership position aside from president. Democrats directed each of the council's committees, enabling Tammany to effectively control which proposals could be debated and voted on by the full council. Symbolically, Democrats' majority power aided their efforts to define themselves as representing the city's interests, proposing the most useful policies, and seeking to operate the most efficient council possible. Tammany and allied Democratic council members, while not holding a true majority in the council, held majority power. The Democratic majority used this status to argue repeatedly that its will was being undermined by a destructive, delaying, and undemocratic minority coalition that sought to override the majority's, and thus the city's, interests. As suggested by Cashmore's branding of Morris as Hitler and Kinsley's ensuing call to protect democracy, Democrats wasted no time in appropriating international tensions, specifically concerning fascist attacks upon democratic rule in Europe, in council proceedings through contrived rhetoric that pitted a beleaguered majority defending democracy against a manipulative, power-hungry minority. These characterizations of the council soon evolved into critiques of PR, with the electoral system culpable for whatever delays, inertia, or legislative logjams befell the council.

The defining characteristic of the council's first term was debate—something experienced by the board of aldermen on only the rarest of occasions. Council members hurled epithets—and gavels—at one another in a series of outbursts that characterized the new city council. As Council President Morris put it, "The vulgarity and rowdiness of the Council were the raw material of democracy in action in a turbulent city."[62] Labeled a "lousy ape," "a half-wit, a crook, a bastard, a hammerhead, a jackass, a drunk, [and] a brat," Morris bore the brunt of outrage from former members of the board of aldermen and other Democrats opposed to the presence of an activist minority coalition in the municipal legislature.[63] He later described an attack he suffered from a council member following a particularly contentious session, "One night after a debate, one member barged into my office, grabbed me by the neck and pushed me half across the room, kicking my shins as he knocked over the furniture."[64] Before the close of the council's first month, the *Times* exclaimed that the members had "done everything except throw desks at one another."[65]

In the wake of these tumultuous early council sessions, the *World-Telegram* published a cartoon depicting the council as utter chaos.[66] Save for Fusion council member Earle, shown silently studying legislation, the *World-Telegram* presented the governing body as a miserable assortment of ignorant hacks, corrupt machine operatives, angry radicals, and wealthy patricians, all of whom appeared more concerned with their own power than the city's welfare.

Aside from the nuisance associated with being challenged to fisticuffs in the middle of a council session, as Morris noted occurred on several occasions, depictions of legislative "bedlam" resulted in serious consequences for relations between the majority and minority, and for proportional representation as well.[67] In its journal, *Searchlight*, the Citizens Union warned readers that the majority intentionally avoided substantive council sessions not simply for mischievousness:

> Members of the old guard . . . have done their best, directly and indirectly, to make the Council look silly, hoping in that way to discredit PR. It almost seemed as if some of the majority members, instead of trying to make records for themselves, were sitting back and waiting for opportunities to keep the entire Council from making any sort of record in the hope that by doing so the old Board of Aldermen might by some miracle be brought back to life.[68]

In the Citizens Union's terms, the Tammany-allied majority sought to weaken the council specifically to scuttle the electoral system that had created it.

From the opening week, critics of council progressives and proportional representation argued that the seating of a large minority hampered effective, efficient government.[69] Majority officials labeled substantive policy debate a symbol of inefficiency and a threat rather than evidence of representative democratic government. In effect, the majority portrayed any minority objections as assaults upon the democratic process. Moreover, Tammany Democrats, joined later by Republicans, portrayed such debate, and its resulting delays and so-called confusion, as one of the primary ills fostered by proportional representation. In fact, anti-PR activists criticized the system as

Unruly council members (except for Genevieve Earle, shown quietly working amid the chaos) brandish sticks, move the furniture, threaten one another, and accomplish nothing—especially not the people's business. Each caricature is individually labeled, ensuring all legislators' humiliation in this scathing 1938 political cartoon from the *New York World-Telegram*. New York World-Telegram, *January 24, 1938. Courtesy La Guardia and Wagner Archives, La Guardia Community College, City University of New York, Long Island City.*

being designed expressly to produce slow, ineffective governance. Anti-PR rhetoric fused this criticism with foreboding depictions of international crisis, primarily in Europe. The most crucial implication of this link was demonstrated in Democratic and Republican propaganda that PR's proponents supported it to weaken city government and aid anti-American subversion amid world war.

Deadlocked with 13 members on either side of the aisle, the Tammany-dominated committee chairs used their positions to prevent most major reform initiatives from reaching votes before the full council. Thus, despite Morris's position as council president, the reform coalition rarely gained the support of a single opposition member required to pass minority-proposed legislation. Within weeks of the first council session, the two independent Democratic members began to join organization Democrats in most roll-call votes. The shift made the officially titled majority an effective one as well. On the few occasions when minority proposals gained the backing of majority members, the majority often embraced the resulting policies as their own, to such an extent that the final legislation was labeled as majority sponsored. These tactics enabled the Democratic Party to claim victory for any legislation passed by the council, regardless of whether it had devised the initial proposals. At the same time, majority status allowed Democrats to define any attempt by the minority to block their proposals as an unrepresentative check on the wishes of a majority of New Yorkers.

Good-government groups, which depicted the board of aldermen as more concerned with street naming than substantive policy making, championed the new city council as a catalyst for important municipal legislation. But, as the New York City chapter of the League of Women Voters emphasized in its review of the council's first two-year term, the first council improved on its predecessor's record in limited ways. In the council's first year, the body adopted 74 local laws. In 1939, the council more than doubled that output with 164 laws passed. Each of these figures represented a dramatic increase over the measures approved by the board of aldermen, which rarely passed more than 50 in a single year. However, exactly half of the 238 laws passed during the council's initial two-year term—119 laws—were name changes for parks, streets, and other locales. Sixty laws dealt strictly with building codes and 26 with permits. Twelve of the laws concerned taxation, and the minority coalition championed a "slum-clearance" measure as its crowning achievement for the first legislative term.[70]

Minority Leader B. Charney Vladeck, a former Socialist Party member, proposed the clearance law as part of what he and other coalition members intended to be a dramatic expansion of public housing projects in New York City.[71] A Jewish revolutionary in Tsarist Russia, Vladeck emigrated to the United States in 1908 and, within a decade of his arrival, won election to the New York City Board of Aldermen as a Socialist in 1917. During the emerging Red Scare following World War I, Vladeck gained reelection in 1919 but was defeated for a third term following Tammany-sponsored redistricting in 1921. Away from electoral politics, Vladeck turned to journalism to advance labor rights and other civic causes, eventually managing the Jewish *Daily Forward*. Proportional representation and the American Labor Party provided Vladeck a means to return to city government, and he won the maximum 75,000 votes as an American Labor Party candidate in the 1937 Manhattan election.[72] As council minority leader, Vladeck supported a series of resolutions aimed at utilizing city government as a force for the public's welfare through enhanced consumer protection laws and industrial regulations. These proposals included "municipal baby Wagner Acts," which sought to empower labor along the lines of the 1935 National Labor Relations Act, sponsored by New York Senator Robert Wagner.[73] As the nominal majority quashed resolution after resolution, Vladeck continued to argue for a stronger, more proactive governing body until his death from a heart attack on October 30, 1938, less than 11 months after his return to the city legislature.[74]

Despite the limited shift in local policy making brought by the new council, Democrats expended a great deal of effort working to diminish the power of their newly seated opponents, as well as dismantle the electoral system that created a more evenly divided municipal government. The majority attempted to restrict public access to the council through a ban on council radio broadcasts. With the narrowly split body producing consistently raucous legislative meetings, the broadcasts on WNYC brought widespread media and public attention to their early sessions. Minority allies portrayed the Democrats' fight to prohibit the broadcasts as a symbol of the majority's dismay at having its power so publicly and consistently rebuked in chambers and over the airwaves. Critics charged that only Democrats' shame over their own performances could lead them to censor these broadcasts.

During the first term, Democrats found common ground with conservative Republicans through ostensibly anti-Communist legislation that attempted to restrict the expansion of democratic rights recently afforded New Yorkers by proportional representation elections. The city's two largest political parties sought to narrow the field of possible council candidates and remove members of the minority who challenged their political authority. Council members Abner C. Surpless (Republican of Brooklyn) and William M. McCarthy (Democrat of Brooklyn) introduced a loyalty oath for council members, which required that they pledge not to be "a member of a party or group advocating doctrines subversive of our existing government system, including but not limited to overthrow by force or violence."[75] The measure also proposed a US citizenship mandate of 10 years—a policy more stringent than for members of the US Congress, which required seven years of citizenship for House representatives and nine years for senators. The New York State Legislature had no specified length of citizenship required for its members.[76] Taken together, the bill's provisions amounted to an assault on the city's political Left, which conservative council members portrayed as potentially subversive.

Surpless's narrow win over a Communist Party council candidate in 1937 likely contributed to his (and perhaps his allies') support for constricting the council's representative spectrum. In the PR results, Surpless defeated Communist Peter V. Cacchione for Brooklyn's final council seat by only 367 votes; following 59 counts, Surpless held 41,931 votes to Cacchione's 41,564.[77] Surpless and McCarthy's loyalty oath, with its extensive citizenship requirements, threatened the ability of Cacchione and other leftist third-party representatives to serve in the council.

Republican council member John M. Christiansen of Queens provided the third and final supporting vote for the loyalty oath. Why would two Republicans join a Democrat to back this proposal? As PR brought greater representation to the outer boroughs, particularly Brooklyn and Queens, political competition increased within these areas. Queens and Brooklyn experienced a schism between those who supported PR for the increased representation the system afforded and those more concerned with the success of minority parties in defeating primarily Republican opponents in council elections. The loyalty oath proposal also underscored the reemergence of nativist rhetoric in municipal politics, a rhetoric marshaled against PR during the Charter Revision Commission hearings of 1935–1936 and increasingly utilized by the majority against the minority in council sessions. Rhetoric of Americanism and security against foreign threats permeated the New York State Constitutional Convention of 1938 and served as the core argument offered against PR's broader incorporation.

In the months after New York City's first proportional representation election, the system's advocates moved to further entrench and normalize

PR and expand its use statewide. The National Municipal League and the Citizens Union, again primarily through the work of George Hallett, urged officials throughout New York to consider implementing PR in cities across the state. In addition, PR activists argued that the system should be incorporated in statewide elections, particularly for the state legislature. In private correspondence and public statements, Hallett and others expressed great optimism regarding PR's future. For them, the early months of 1938 appeared the starting point for the spread of PR throughout the state, as well as in other cities nationwide. American supporters of proportional representation also viewed their recent success in New York City as the foundation for PR's international growth.

The most immediate task for Hallett, though, remained grounded in New York state and city politics. Governor Herbert Lehman had appointed Hallett as the chair of a committee to devise a method of electing the state legislature on the basis of proportional representation. In April 1938, Hallett presented his vision for state elections via PR in a lengthy report championing the example of the city council tally from the previous fall. While Hallett and PR's coalition of supporters prepared for the Constitutional Convention to convene in the summer, their opponents were preparing a surprise assault upon the system. This attack, revealed during the final week of the convention in August, sought to abolish PR in New York City as well as prohibit its use in the entire state.

To gauge the context in which this challenge to PR occurred at the state level, it's important to consider the relationship between Mayor La Guardia and the state legislature in Albany. La Guardia's mayoral policies fundamentally altered the long-standing balance of power between Albany and New York City. In the decades prior to La Guardia's tenure, upstate Republicans competed with New York City Democrats to control a legislative majority in the state assembly and senate. The mayor's close alliance with the New Deal administration of President Franklin Roosevelt provided the city with a source of funding that bypassed both the Albany legislators and Tammany Hall. As then-governor Roosevelt had established his own political power apparatus through assaults on Tammany, La Guardia used his political alliance with Roosevelt, and support for the anti-Tammany Fusion Party, to continue to restructure the city's party structure.[78] La Guardia's connections with the federal government, which weakened both Albany's and Tammany's power in New York City, gave further cause for the rare alliance between upstate Republicans and Tammany-allied Democrats that gelled in opposition to PR. The local and state political party machines viewed the Constitutional Convention of 1938 as an opportunity to reject the mayor's growing authority in local, state, and national politics, as well as dismantle the electoral system that aided his efforts to weaken the traditional party power structure.

Ever attuned to the possibilities afforded by constitutional conventions to revise the methods of governance, La Guardia saw the convention as an opportunity to enhance his authority through the expansion of home rule powers for the city—at the expense of state legislators and Tammany Hall. Following a visit to Albany, Reuben A. Lazarus, assistant to City Council president Newbold Morris and previously counsel for the New York City Charter Commission, cautioned: "It will be more difficult to obtain favorable action on home rule than I had anticipated. . . . There is a pronounced feeling of hostility toward the Mayor. . . . Even supposed adherents of the Mayor are outspoken in their reluctance to vote an additional grant of power to the city."[79] In addition to warning La Guardia of a move against his policies at the convention, Lazarus's scrutiny contrasted with the belief held by PR's proponents that the gathering could serve as a vehicle for extending the voting system throughout the state. Supporters of La Guardia and progressive reform in New York City saw proportional representation in state legislative elections as a critical component of expanding the city's home rule authority. Coupled with the use of a single transferable vote, statewide PR would challenge the balance of power in Albany much as it had done in New York City. First, the system would strengthen the ability of third parties to challenge the hegemony of upstate Republicans and urban Democrats. Second, PR would expand the spectrum of representatives able to run for state office on the Democratic and Republican tickets. Perhaps most important, proportional allocation of seats in the state legislature would likely shift the balance of power away from rural and suburban New York to cities, with the new balance of power resting firmly within the boundaries of New York City. This combination of possible effects forged links between New York City political groups and dissolved others.

Progressive reformers saw representation in Albany as inseparable from home rule. Council President Morris, a Republican, argued that his city's battle for government autonomy inherently integrated the struggle for greater municipal representation in the state legislature. Morris, speaking before the Constitutional Convention Committee on Cities, explained, "If the city had the representation in the Legislature to which it is justly entitled by reason of its population, we would not be here today pleading for consideration. As long as we are deprived of just representation in the Legislature just so long will we be unable to obtain sympathetic consideration of our problems."[80] Echoing other supporters of home rule and proportional representation, Morris had concluded that the success of urban government depended upon more power for the city in the state legislature, and that power could be achieved through a more representative distribution of seats in Albany.

With a bond forming between home rule and PR, the New York City Republican and Democratic Party establishment, which had long argued for more power in Albany, saw a growing threat to their hegemony in city politics that overwhelmed their desire for greater representation in Albany. Although the delegates Lazarus referred to included upstate representatives, they also included a significant portion of New York City delegates who opposed additional power for La Guardia and other anti-machine interests. At the convention, Democrats and Republicans from throughout the state joined forces to block granting further independent authority to La Guardia and the New York City government. An alliance of primarily upstate Republicans and New York City Democrats identified proportional representation as the key to both controlling the influence of New York City in state government and constraining the growing power of third parties and insurgent candidates throughout the state.

This coalition, comprised of the formerly oppositional forces of Democrats and Republicans, prevented the proposal for statewide PR by the Committee on Suffrage from being debated, much less voted upon, by the full delegation. Next, anti-progressive major party delegates joined to propose a surprise measure to kill PR throughout the state. The referendum, to be voted on by the state's electorate less than three months later, would abolish the use of proportional representation in New York City and prevent its adoption in several cities then considering the system. Rather than reveling in Tammany's growing competition in New York City, state Republicans perceived PR as a threat to their power as well. While many New York City Republicans remained supportive of PR at this point, the state party regarded it as a menace to their prospects in upstate areas where Republicans dominated local government. Revealing the extent to which PR threatened the state's Republican elite, the delegate who offered the amendment to ban PR hailed from Schenectady—one of a half-dozen New York cities preparing to decide referenda on PR in that fall's elections. The anti-PR delegates waited until the last possible moment to present their proposal.

On August 19, 1938, in the final deliberative session before the convention adjourned on August 25, delegate Louis M. Killeen, Republican of Schenectady, offered the following amendment for limited debate, "Every voter shall be entitled to vote at each and every election in this State or any of its subdivisions for as many persons as there may be offices to be filled thereat. No election for any office to be filled by the people of the State or any of its subdivisions shall be conducted by any system of proportional representation."[81] Killeen argued that the amendment's purpose was to ensure majority supremacy by writing into state law that the "principle of majority rule is fundamental in our representative form of government."[82] He then quoted a *Daily News* editorial from January 7, 1938, that again claimed that first Fusion forces gained great advances in certain sectors of the city government, then PR provided an unrepresentative and disproportionate result in not wiping out Democratic rule in the city council.[83]

Killeen's professed abhorrence of New York City Democrats did not stir reciprocal animus at the convention; every Democratic delegate from New York City voted in favor of Killeen's amendment. Despite the opposition of New York City Republicans, upstate Republicans joined with their former Tammany rivals to pass the amendment banning PR throughout the state. The measure passed easily in a 96 to 35 vote, with New York City Democrats gaining the support of the vast majority of upstate Republicans.[84] The tally suggested that upstate Republicans and downstate (New York City) Democrats favored the maintenance of their long-standing balance of power over the prospect of a more representative electoral structure statewide. Fear of change in the political status quo was manifested in their arguments that PR should not spread outside of New York City—lest the system increase the power of minority parties throughout the state.

Immediately after the vote, Joseph Clark Baldwin, who served as the lone Republican opposite 64 Democrats in the 1932–1933 session of the board of aldermen, urged reconsideration:

> The City of New York by overwhelming vote adopted proportional representation, and whether I am for it or against it, or whether you are or anybody is, if we go into the teeth of that popular referendum because some of our Democratic friends here do not like it, and there must be obvious reasons why they do not, then anything that this is attached to that we submit to the people is going to be beaten, and I submit to my friend on this side of the House that if we do that thing we will be doing a very terrible thing, in my opinion, and that has nothing to do with the merits of proportional representation.[85]

For Baldwin, public perception of Democratic assaults upon New York City's democratic self-rule portended "very terrible" consequences, with the likelihood that voters would dismiss any proposal produced by the convention and, by implication, the possibility of even greater public discord on the horizon. Though he didn't discuss the "merits" of proportional representation explicitly in his convention remarks, Baldwin voted in favor of the electoral system that facilitated his election as the most prominent, and only progressive, Republican of the three elected via PR in 1937. Baldwin caucused with the minority and was the only Republican to vote for the minority's county reorganization bills to restructure municipal government.[86]

Joseph V. McKee, who briefly served as mayor of New York City following the resignation of Jimmy Walker in 1932, immediately countered Baldwin and rebuked proportional representation in language that eschewed party division to unite the delegation behind the anti-democratic amendment as a display of patriotism:

> In all my experience I have never seen such a farce in representative government as we witnessed in the City of New York at the last election, when we attempted to elect members of the new council in our city.
>
> It has not worked, it can not work. I am appealing to you men and women, not members of the Republican party or the Democratic party, but as reasonable, rational people, to support the action we took this morning in repudiating this hybrid, which is un-American and which is destructive of all the things that we represent here in the selection of our political officers.[87]

Perhaps unintentionally, McKee presented a prescient depiction of the unifying threat proportional representation posed to machine-controlled selection of the state's politicians. The Democratic and Republican party hegemony represented by McKee and his allied delegates found itself in stark opposition to the expressed wishes of the voters who had installed PR less than two years earlier. Pro-PR delegates emphasized that this amendment sought to override popular rule, particularly the independent authority of the local citizenry to determine the structure of its municipal government.

Abbott Low Moffat, Republican state assembly member from New York City, argued that the convention delegates would suffer the consequences for going against the expressed wishes of the city's electorate. Moffat laid the blame of the current assault on PR squarely on the doorsteps of Tammany

Hall. He urged upstate delegates "not to play into the hands of Tammany Hall and the Democratic organization, who obviously do not want this in the City of New York."[88] In attempting to sway his upstate party brethren, Moffat presented an alternate proposal that would exempt New York City from the PR-ban amendment. In a manner similar to Baldwin, Moffat challenged the constitutional amendment without offering support for PR specifically.

In the convention's early weeks, Moffat privately petitioned Manhattan Republican Party chair Kenneth F. Simpson to support a statewide system of proportional representation to enhance prospects for gaining a Republican majority in the state senate: "If, as would appear likely, the pendulum in the State is swinging towards the Republicans, then as the Republican strength increases, so would the chances of gaining the Senate under such a PR system. Under the present method, the Republican chances are always precarious, in addition to the unfairness of the whole procedure."[89] Moffat's correspondence focused on the benefits he saw PR creating for the state Republican Party; his later speech before the convention retained one crucial component—an emphasis on the Democratic Party as Republicans' chief opponent in the city and state. Upstate resistance to Moffat's position revealed the degree to which members of the Republican Party favored the existing division of power with Democrats over the possibility that PR would foster competition from smaller parties across the state. Similar fears of third-party competition would gradually weaken Republican support for PR during the coming years.

Louis Killeen retorted by escalating the fears he and McKee had voiced earlier. The Schenectady Republican attacked the "sinister influences" who supported and benefited from the system: "I want to warn every upstate delegate who votes in favor of [Moffat's] amendment of the sinister influences brought to bear in the City of New York and in every other city where proportional representation is now in effect."[90] McKee and Killeen's depiction of PR as an "un-American" assault upon representative government incorporated a not-too-subtle critique of urban America, particularly New York City, as the source of an advancing national security threat. For Killeen and McKee, and the Republicans and Democrats they represented, PR's "sinister influences" were the urban leftists and immigrant activists emboldened by their newfound success in municipal politics.

Manhattan Democrat James A. Foley depicted New York City voters as a "misguided populace" that had "inflicted" the "injustice" of PR upon themselves. Foley emphasized the radical and foreign nature of the threat he saw PR spawning for New York City and state: "Now, proportional representation, what did it produce? It produced men like Michael Quill, who before the Dies Committee the other day . . . was branded a Communist. We did not have a true representation of the minority in New York under proportional representation."[91] Council member Quill directed the Transport Workers Union and represented the American Labor Party. Dubbed by some of his contemporaries "Red Mike" for his leftist activism, Quill served as a focal point for federal investigations of Communist activism in New York City. The US House Special Committee on Un-American Activities (popularly known as HUAC), chaired at the time by Representative Martin Dies of Texas, seemed intent on connecting Quill's council campaigns with his union activities and association with the Communist Party.

Ignoring the reference to Quill, Republican Helen Z. M. Rodgers of Buffalo objected to Foley and declared that the amendment was superfluous, given New York City voters' ability to repeal PR as they saw fit.[92] As characterized by Foley, though, PR and its supporters had manipulated voters to such an extent that they could no longer be relied upon to govern themselves. For Foley, the rising power of PR and its New York City supporters portended ominous consequences for the rest of the state:

> The small party division brought about the reign of Fascism and Mussolini in Italy. In Germany, the same thing happened. Small parties, divided representation, no majority control, a strong man comes in and assumes the dictatorship as under Nazism, and you are going to have the same thing upstate, you cannot escape being plagued by it, because these misguided reformers who advocated it in New York City are not going to stop, they are going to try to inflict it on upstate unless we write in the Constitution a provision against this violation of our American liberty, and violation of our American form of government.[93]

With sweeping language and no lack of dire prophesying, Foley equated New York City Council elections by proportional representation to the political machinations that brought Hitler and Mussolini to power in Europe. Good-government activists, according to Foley, represented the foundation of a fascist insurgency that would ultimately menace the entire nation. In case upstate delegates misconstrued their role in defending American liberty and government against PR, Foley placed them at the forefront of the nation's defense—their most important duty being the passage of the amendment abolishing PR.

Foley and the other anti-PR delegates thus presented New York City as having already fallen to the forces of anti-Americanism, the implication being that the city could no longer be trusted to govern itself. In essence, the proposed statewide ban amounted to an anti-democratic assault on city residents. In this milieu, PR's enabling of representative urban self-government threatened both city and state political machines, which held power through an exclusionary balance that protected Democratic and Republican access at the expense of smaller political organizations. The 1938 Constitutional Convention revealed the power of this inertia and the degree to which the two major parties saw their own interests as superior to those of the electorate. The defeat of Moffat's amendment to exclude New York City from the statewide PR ban further underscored the fear that political activism in the state's largest city could serve as a destabilizing influence for the state's entire political structure.[94]

The vast majority of New York City's politicians and journalists responded to the convention proceedings with outrage. Many current and former critics of PR joined against the abolition amendment, arguing that the convention had usurped New York City's right to self-government. As characterized by Mayor Fiorello La Guardia and the *Brooklyn Eagle*, opposition to the amendment gelled through members' objections to the removal of authority for New York City over its electoral process, not because of a unified sense of support for the merits of PR. Many Democratic and Republican party leaders, and their press allies, argued against the statewide PR ban in 1938 but reversed their stances on PR in later years.

La Guardia, who had earlier criticized PR for not electing a sufficient number of his political allies, took to the airwaves within hours of the convention's adjournment to blast the anti-PR referendum as a "proposal [that] smacks of the old up-State and down-city combinations existing in the days of Tweed. No doubt this was a part of the general arrangement and the result of log-rolling which apparently took place in the convention."[95] In language echoing the indifference to PR expressed even by critics of the amendment, the mayor continued:

The question is not whether proportional representation is good or bad. At the last election, had there been no proportional representation vote, I could have carried an overwhelming majority of the City Council. A casual check of the vote in the districts would so indicate. No one will say that some of the members of the City Council elected through the proportional system have been particularly kind to or considerate of me. . . . [But] the people of this city have a right to select their Councilmen in any manner and in any fashion they may desire.[96]

A TAMMANY TRICK

Two years ago New York City voted on a new way to elect its city council. This method was called proportional representation (P.R.).

The idea was to give people who weren't voting the machine ticket a chance to elect their share of candidates.

The voters decided to give P.R. a try. They voted for it 923,186 to 555,217.

Now it has been tried once.

Some people like it.

Some don't.

But one thing is sure.

Certain politicians don't like it.

They tried to kill it in the courts—and failed.

They tried to kill it at the polls—and failed.

They tried to keep it from working in the election—and failed.

Now they have a new scheme.

They slipped in a statewide amendment to make it unconstitutional.

They will fail again—because the people know this is a LOCAL ISSUE which each city should decide for itself.

The Republican, Democratic and Labor state platforms all say so!

Defeat This Attack on Home Rule!

Vote NO on Amendment No. 7

DON'T BE FOOLED!

Whether you favor or oppose proportional representation

Remember

New York City decided on P.R. for itself. It should decide whether to keep it or not the same way.

Yonkers and Schenectady plan to vote on P.R. this fall. Let them make their own decisions!

This amendment is a direct attack on home rule.

It was a deal sneaked through the convention by Tammany politicians and certain up-state Republicans

—on the very last day

—without telling the public

—without discussion in committee

—without warning to the leaders

—too late for delegates to find out how the people felt

—too late for reconsideration.

It is a real ripper amendment.

Give it the WORKS.

Vote NO on Amendment No. 7

HOME RULE
Gets the Works

STOP THIS OUTRAGE BY DEFEATING AMENDMENT NO. 7

The Anti-Home Rule, Anti-P.R. RIPPER AMENDMENT

Copies of this leaflet may be secured from

State Committee for Home Rule on Proportional Representation

610 FIFTH AVENUE Room 365 NEW YORK CITY
COlumbus 5-4990

In this 1938 pamphlet, John Q. Voter again finds himself menaced by conniving party bosses. The state convention maneuver to repeal proportional representation, though, poses a graver challenge than in previous years, as a knife-wielding Tammany politician threatens to kill local democracy (and John Q. Voter) with a "Ripper Amendment." *State Committee for Home Rule on Proportional Representation pamphlet, "Home Rule Gets the Works," 1938. Courtesy McDougall Trust Library, London.*

La Guardia's assessment of proportional representation highlighted the system's impact on the city's balance of political power, with himself placed unabashedly at the center, and the degree to which the electorate should be represented in city government.

Acknowledging its consistent opposition to PR, the *Brooklyn Eagle* nonetheless objected to the actions at the constitutional convention. The paper's editors found the council elected under PR "disgraceful" and "virtually impotent," yet they declared that the system was "entitled to a fair trial."[97] In language that the paper would eschew in coming years, the *Eagle* declared, "It is erroneous to refer to 'PR' as the work of radicals. It should be remembered that it was warmly supported by such conservative Republicans as Charles Evans Hughes Jr. and former Judge Thomas D. Thacher, and such organizations as the Citizens Union."[98] Far from a fluke in commentary, the *Eagle* repeated its conclusion that PR deserved additional use in its series of voter recommendations printed shortly before the elections. In subsequent editorials, as in previous columns, the *Eagle* contended that the primary issue at stake concerning the convention repeal effort was not PR, necessarily, but home rule for New York City.[99] Describing the PR referendum as the "most outrageous action of the Constitutional Convention," the *Eagle* concluded that the "proper procedure [was] to give Proportional Representation a reasonable further trial here and then let the city's voters have an opportunity to decide for themselves whether the system should be continued in operation."[100] According to the *Eagle* and La Guardia, voters should serve as the arbiters of PR's fate in New York City elections. The *Eagle's* faith in the electorate extended only so far; its support for public authority soon diminished as voters, particularly in Brooklyn, opted to support both PR and increasingly radical candidates for the city council.

Three weeks following the constitutional convention, congressional hearings expanded the implications of PR's use beyond New York. On September 15–17, 1938, a subcommittee of HUAC held hearings to investigate "un-American and subversive activities" in New York City. The subcommittee focused its New York City inquiries on activism by the Communist Party and the German-American Bund, which advocated Nazism. Through several hours of testimony, subcommittee members probed the activities of supposed Communists purported to influence New York City politics. Representatives questioned several witnesses as to the party affiliation of Michael Quill, who had served on the city council since his election as an American Labor Party candidate in 1937. The subcommittee queried several self-professed former Communist Party members as to whether Quill had ever participated in party activities. The congressional delegation seemed particularly interested in the connections between the Transport Workers Union, the Communist Party, and Quill's council campaign.[101]

Interviewees referenced Peter Cacchione, council candidate and Communist Party chair for Brooklyn, in their testimony.[102] A first-generation American, Cacchione worked as an industrial laborer in Pennsylvania before moving to New York City during the Great Depression. Cacchione's labor activism was deeply rooted in the work experiences of his youth, which drew him into Communist Party politics in the early 1930s.[103] Although the hearings did not specifically discuss proportional representation as aiding Quill's victory, or contributing to Cacchione's near-miss in 1937, the subcommittee's questions and testimony underlined the degree to which labor's electoral success (via PR) challenged the party hierarchy on a national level. Representative J. Parnell Thomas of New Jersey railed against alliances between labor unions, political parties (particularly the Communist Party), and candidates for political office in New York City. He declared, "Known Communists . . . have been running for and are holding political office here in New York City. I do not think it is right to use any labor union to drum up support for such candidates, who are known Communists."[104] Thomas's objections extended beyond Communist involvement in city politics. He opposed the integration of the labor movement within New York's political apparatus. The emerging political alliance of labor unions, the American Labor Party, and the Communist Party struck the subcommittee as a subversive threat. This suspicion, enhanced by PR elections, challenged their notions of who should hold power in urban America. Committee members' fears crystallized through the ability of an activist labor coalition to participate directly in electoral politics. With PR, labor organizations and allied political parties found entry into the halls of government, not simply as an advocacy force but as a direct participant in city governance. Similar to the rhetoric of anti-PR delegates at the constitutional convention, the congressional hearings explicitly presented New York City, via its supposedly radical political culture and, implicitly, PR, as the source of a growing threat to American security. Outrage over leftist electoral victories enabled by PR was expressed at the New York State Constitutional Convention, by the US Congress through its investigation of "un-American activities" in New York City politics, and in the prohibition campaign waged against the system in the fall of 1938.

Two of the most prominent non-Tammany proponents of PR's abolition in 1938 were the *New York Sun* and Notre Dame professor Ferdinand A. Hermens, a German émigré. From 1938 through 1947, Hermens provided the intellectual foundation for multiple repeal campaigns. His thesis, which he emphasized emerged from personal observations in Europe, held that proportional representation aided the rise of Adolf Hitler and the Nazi Party in

Germany and that the system could potentially destroy democracy in the United States if allowed to gain a foothold. The *Sun's* editors relied primarily upon Hermens's arguments in their editorial attacks against the system. The *Sun* even repeated his characterization in one editorial published shortly before Election Day of "PR as a Trojan Horse." The *Sun* admonished readers to review Hermens's work in greater detail, declaring that it "would be a blessing if every voter in the state could read before election day 'The Trojan Horse of Democracy,' a forty-page pamphlet reprint of an article by F. A. Hermens in the November issue of *Social Research*."[105] The editorial then quoted Hermens's justification for overturning the 1936 referendum results:

> The various minority groups have created an atmosphere in which every one who objects to proportional representation is likely to be considered morally bad. In such circumstances one feels willing to condone the action of the Constitutional Convention of New York in proposing a ban on proportional representation. Future generations of voters in New York City would have reason to be grateful to the constitutional provision which, by overriding one decision made by the electorate in New York, has made sure that their city recovered with the majority system[—]the only instrument for the making of effective decisions in the future.[106]

Championing a notion of majority rule that would rescind the electorate's decision, Hermens and the *Sun* endorsed the argument offered by the anti-PR delegates at the constitutional convention—New York City voters should not maintain the authority to govern themselves. To present the paper's city readership with sufficient rationale for not determining their democratic structure, the *Sun* then focused on the supposed connection between PR and the rise of European fascism. The piece quoted Hermens's conclusions regarding his argument that PR "aided the development of the Communist party and Nazis" in Germany, and enabled fascism in Italy, Austria, and Greece.[107]

The Communist Party campaigned against the referendum and, in defending PR, articulated an alternate view of New York City's position within the global struggles of the day. Brooklyn Communist Peter Cacchione turned Hermens's analysis on its head, implicating the rise of fascism abroad to assert that PR must be preserved to safeguard American security and democracy:

> There are those in our country who say we're [three] thousand miles away from Europe and thankful for it. But my friends, the destruction

of democracy in Austria and Czechoslovakia has stimulated fascist reactionary forces in America in their fight against democracy in our own land.

This is the issue in our present election campaign—the issue of defeating reaction, fascism, and war—and the retention and extension of the democratic rights of our people.[108]

Cacchione's blunt characterization of Tammany Hall and its allies as fascist forces that desired democracy's destruction framed proportional representation as an essential democratic right of the people. Their differences aside, Cacchione and Hermens cast the local debate over PR as a key component of an international struggle over the future of democracy—with PR defined as either a key democratic trait or as its antithesis.

Despite arguments that PR threatened local, state, and national security, the most powerful organizations in New York state politics decided that near-term popularity was more pressing than banning PR. Two weeks after the HUAC hearings, the *New York Times* reported that both Democratic and Republican state party conventions had overruled the constitutional convention delegates and decided to officially oppose the PR ban. According to the *Times*, both parties saw support of the ban as potentially harmful to their standing with voters. Republicans backed away from the convention proposal as part of their attempt to increase support for Thomas Dewey's gubernatorial candidacy. Two blocs within the Democratic Party debated the measure, with New Dealers convincing a majority that their status would be enhanced by countering the so-called Old Guard Democrats affiliated with Tammany Hall. In essence, both state organizations recognized the popular support for PR and also considered the electorate ready, willing, and able to inflict punishment upon the groups that attempted to disregard their expressed wishes.[109]

The lack of organizational support for the abolition of proportional representation hindered the formation of a cohesive statewide, much less citywide, campaign for the referendum. Ultimately, the city and state electorate voted against the proposal by large majorities. City voters retained PR by a margin of more than 2 to 1, greater than the margin two years earlier, with 69 percent of the electorate voting in favor in 1938 compared with 62 percent for the 1936 referendum. Challenging the arguments offered by Hermens and the *Sun*, state and city voters apparently concluded that PR's retention in New York City and its possible expansion to other cities throughout the state would not threaten their liberties and would instead enhance their electoral power.

1938 State Constitution Referendum to Abolish PR

	Yes	No
Manhattan	93,010	172,197
Bronx	66,356	160,865
Kings	117,713	268,534
Queens	66,594	155,889
Richmond	11,358	17,553
New York City Total	355,031	775,038
Outside of New York City	272,092	779,366

"Amendment No. 7: Shall the proposed amendment, submitted by the Constitutional Convention prohibiting voting by any system of proportional representation, be approved?"

Source: *Annual Report of the Board of Elections in the City of New York for the Year 1938*, 78–79; and George Hallett to Charles H. Woodward, December 20, 1938, folder 52-5, "New York State Constitutional Convention 1938 Proposed Ban on PR," box 52, PRL Papers, CURB.

The 2 to 1 margin of victory for retention of proportional representation did not diminish tensions over the city's electoral structure. Instead, the system's supporters produced increasingly strident calls for Tammany Hall's dissolution while PR's detractors built upon the rhetoric of previous campaigns to frame PR as the lynchpin of a global anti-American conspiracy. Implicitly extending the central thesis of Ferdinand Hermens, the *Staten Island Advance* implicated PR's retention in New York City with ominous characterizations of advancing international radicalism:

The French general strike . . . should give proponents of "PR" in this country something to think about. The French situation is the "reduction ad absurdum" of unlimited minority representation. . . . A similar condition prevailed in the Republic of Germany prior to Hitler's seizure of power. Spain, likewise, was torn by similar extremes, with the Communists utilizing the chaotic condition to promote internationalism and affiliation with the Soviet government. . . . Chaos breeds fascism.[110]

The paper's references to fascism, Communism, labor activism, and minority representation constituted an argument that proportional representation would destabilize the United States—beginning with its tenure in New York City. In the wake of New Yorkers' broad approval of PR in 1936 and 1938, the *Advance* continued to advocate limited representation as the solution to PR's upheavals in New York City. That the *Advance* and other PR opponents couched this supposition in anti-fascist rhetoric demonstrates the threat PR posed to the major parties as they sought to retain control of municipal authority. Urging voters to reduce their political options and support the Republican and Democratic machines, the *Advance* asserted that the two-party system acted "as a brake against abuse of power" and created an environment where "democracy is possible, [and] personal liberty of speech and freedom of the press are preserved."[111] The contrary wishes of voters expressed in the recent elections only heightened opposition to the Democratic- and Republican-dominated municipal structure championed by the *Advance*.

The *New York Herald-Tribune* lauded voters' actions in the 1938 elections and offered direct appreciation of both proportional representation and the city council. An editorial declared, "Armed with the powerful weapons of the new charter and PR, the voters of the city effectually abolished those prostrate statesmen who once slept tranquilly through their terms in the old Board of Aldermen."[112] Exaggerated and mutually antagonistic as their perspectives may have been, the *Herald-Tribune* and the *Advance* reflected similar opinions in the broader coalitions for and against PR in concluding that the system's objective was the destruction of the city's political hierarchy.

Before the end of 1938, reform-minded council members engaged in a legislative struggle whose outcome suggested limitations in the degree to which charter reform and proportional representation had actually reshaped the city's power structure. This policy fight centered on county reorganization, one of the primary, though as yet unachieved, measures proposed by the Charter Revision Commission in 1936. County reorganization called for a significant reduction in the positions afforded each borough's (or county's) government. The positions to be abolished at the county level and centralized into citywide offices included sheriff, register, commissioner of records, public administrator, and commissioner of jurors.[113] Leaner borough governments meant fewer appointed jobs and fewer jobs meant reduced patronage opportunities; such reductions threatened to dismantle the Democratic and Republican parties' base of popular and economic support in the five boroughs. Genevieve Earle argued that the proposals would reduce salaries by $2.4 million; Democrats challenged this figure but admitted that at least $350,000 would be saved.[114] Eager to move forward with one of the reform coalition's most important measures, Earle proposed this restructuring plan during the tumultuous second council session of January 25, 1938, in which Newbold

Morris removed John Cashmore as vice-chairman and replaced him, temporarily as it turned out, with James Burke.[115] Earle's five bills remained bottled
in committee by the Democratic leadership through much of the council's
first year. Possessing a working majority in the council, Democrats prevented
the issue of municipal reform from being debated until the council's final session of 1938.[116]

When Earle and the council minority proposed the legislation on
December 20, the resulting debate turned into an overnight foray that tested
the council's stability and the extent to which PR had actually altered the
contours of power within local government. The round-the-clock session
lasted from 12:20 P.M. to 8:20 A.M. the following morning, with the council
stenographer collapsing at 11 P.M.[117] Earle's husband called the police at
5 A.M. because she hadn't come home. Council President Morris shattered
his gavel at around 8 A.M., moments after he exchanged threats of bodily
harm with Bronx Democrat Charles E. Keegan. Upon Keegan's refusal to
stop speaking after being ruled out of order, Morris declared, "If I come
down there after you, you'll be suing me for assault and battery." Keegan replied in kind, "You may be 6 feet 3 and you may be 9 feet 10, and you may
weigh two tons, but if you come down I'll cut you down to my size. Let's go
into the committee room and I'll take you right now."[118] With barely a moment's respite, Brooklyn Republican Abner Surpless then raised the stakes
even further by motioning to censure Morris for his conduct. Ultimately, 17
council members voted against the proposals versus only nine in favor. The
majority included all 15 Democrats on the council as well as Republicans
Surpless and John M. Christensen of Queens. The defeat of county reorganization left the reform coalition in tatters, as the final tally underscored the
inability of the minority bloc to maintain loyalty with the two insurgent
Democrats and two of the council's three Republicans. The margin also
made clear that council Democrats and Republicans would unite against the
minority on policies that threatened to weaken the two major parties' power
within municipal government.[119]

The failure of the municipal reform bill sparked competing interpreta-
tions, and accusations of fault, among city newspapers. The *Daily News*,
which opposed the constitutional referendum, returned to its earlier criticism of proportional representation for not electing more allies of Mayor La
Guardia. Perhaps because the system enabled leftist party representation,
the paper concluded that the results necessitated the electoral system's
"abandonment as a failure."[120] The *Daily Worker*, published by the Communist Party, challenged this assertion and argued, as others had previously,

that the larger concern remained the viability of Tammany Hall. For the *Daily Worker*, a PR-elected progressive alliance remained the only obstacle against the "Tammany-Tory-Republican gang in the City Council" that defeated county reform:

> Actually, PR is the most democratic electoral system the city has ever had, and the people have far more representation in the City Council now than they ever had in the Tammany-dominated Board of Aldermen. Even though county reform was defeated, it was the labor-fusion-progressive coalition which brought it up after the Board of Aldermen kept the matter buried since 1935.[121]

The paper claimed that Tammany's ability to maintain unity at the polls was the critical factor that enabled the Democratic Party to control a working majority in the council:

> The *News* pretends that there is something wrong with PR because Mayor La Guardia and his progressive reform program won a huge election majority in 1937, while the Tammany obstructionists got control of the City Council. The answer is, clearly, that while the people were most strongly united behind the Mayoralty ticket, their unity in the Councilmanic contests were not extensive and solid enough for them to elect a majority of labor and progressive candidates. That's the real trouble. And it can be remedied next time by early preparations: to defeat the reactionary obstructionists and to elect progressive Councilmen in the 1939 elections.[122]

Whereas the *Daily News* saw proportional representation as an obstruction to progressive government, the *Daily Worker* framed it as essential to altering the balance of power in New York City and bringing a truly progressive government to fruition.

Other high-circulation dailies agreed with the *Daily Worker* and viewed the defeat of the municipal reform bill as a renewed call to arms against Tammany and the Democratic Party. The *World-Telegram* defended the system through direct assaults upon the opposition's contention that PR and county reform were harbingers of fascism:

> No bunkum about "totalitarianism," "mayoral dictatorship," referenda or faulty bill drafting should for one instant conceal the real motive of

Democratic City Councilmen who plotted to kill and did kill the bills for county reorganization.... A Tammany that has totally failed in its efforts to kill PR is foolhardy indeed, we think, to invite still worse punishment from PR when Councilmen are elected next fall.[123]

Such rhetoric set the stakes for the city's political struggles in 1939. On the one hand, as expressed by the *Advance*, anti-PR groups refused to regard the constitutional referendum's failure as diminishing their quest to ban PR. Instead, the proposal's failure caused increasingly grim assertions that PR would bring the downfall of democracy in New York City. On the other hand, PR's advocates framed the upcoming council elections as the electorate's opportunity to finally end the influence of political machines in urban government.

In this respect, the state- and citywide failure of repeal in 1938 reinvigorated many longtime supporters of PR. These activists renewed their calls for expansion of the system to other areas of the state, nation, and world. The campaign to retain PR in New York City was not the nation's only PR-related election in 1938. Yonkers, New York, voted to incorporate the system in its council elections, and measures to install it failed narrowly in Schenectady, New York, and the Massachusetts towns of Quincy, Cambridge, and Northampton.[124] Cincinnati already utilized PR for city council elections and the Pennsylvania state legislature unsuccessfully debated the system's incorporation in Philadelphia in 1938–1939.[125]

Herbert C. Pell, chair of the New York Democratic Committee during the 1920s and a diplomat in President Franklin Roosevelt's administration, reflected the progressive views of many New Dealers who saw PR not only as a welcome alternative to Tammany Hall but as a blueprint for global change.[126] Writing to progressive Manhattan Borough president Stanley M. Isaacs in March 1939, Pell admitted to "Utopian" thoughts that PR's success, on the local and national level, might cause support for the system to "spread like wild fire" internationally. More than any other factor, Pell concluded that the detractors' connection of PR with international radicalism, particularly fascism and Communism, threatened the system's expansion. Pell viewed such rhetoric as potentially sowing the seeds of division within the PR coalition. He commented that supporters "must, in the face of the enemy, fear disunion more than anything else." To maintain the PR alliance, Pell argued, "It is more important at the present day to beat down the last effort of the reactionaries than it is to advance."[127] Despite his desire for the system's extension, Pell concluded that supporters needed to repulse attacks that PR aided totalitarianism rather than campaign to expand PR's reach. In the summer of 1939, international events reverberated throughout New York City's political culture in ways that destabilized PR in precisely the manner Pell feared. Longtime PR critics utilized the turmoil of the oncoming world war to buttress their claims that the system aided the formation of anti-democratic regimes abroad and at home.

4

UNDER THE CLOAK OF PATRIOTISM

SPECTERS OF TOTALITARIANISM IN CITY POLITICS

From 1938 to 1940, international events became increasingly central to the debate over electoral reform in New York City. The signing of the Nazi-Soviet Non-Aggression Pact in August 1939 and the subsequent German invasion of Poland signaled the beginning of the Second World War in Europe. While the principal organizations advocating proportional representation in the United States and Great Britain had relied upon one another for decades, that relationship changed fundamentally during the war. With Great Britain's declaration of war, London's Proportional Representation Society (PRS) called upon the movement's leadership in New York City to protect the system during the conflict. In September 1939, PRS director John H. Humphreys wrote George Hallett that "we must look to our friends in the United States for a double share of the constructive work and thinking now needed."[1] By the following summer, Humphreys described a precarious situation faced by the PRS, noting that its recent annual report might be the group's last publication "for some considerable time." Humphreys again emphasized to Hallett that "the task of providing trustworthy foundations for democratic institutions will fall almost wholly upon the friends of proportional representation in America," and he expressed hope that his counterparts "will take up the challenge."[2] The PRS continued its work through the war, even though its offices suffered damage during the Blitz, the organization had to move its headquarters, and one of its executives died in military service.[3] Distanced from the air raids and physical devastation of the war, PR's supporters in the United States nonetheless faced their own challenges associated with the conflict.

The term "Little Red Scare" connotes the wave of red-baiting and anti-progressive attacks that occurred in urban America at the war's onset in Europe. Although the United States did not officially enter the conflict for two more years, the war's beginning caused significant upheavals in New York City politics. Anti-Communist sentiment flared in municipal affairs before the signing of the neutrality pact, with results that recalled the attacks upon progressive activists during the Red Scare after World War I. Following his appointment of Simon Gerson, a Communist Party member, to a staff position in late 1937, Manhattan Borough president Stanley Isaacs became the focus of an intense red-baiting campaign. In the weeks after the appointment, minor complaints swelled into full-fledged charges that the city government was "pink" and filled with "Communists and fellow travelers." Along with his campaigns against the Democratic and Republican machines, Isaacs's staunch support for progressive policies, including his consistent advocacy of proportional representation, made him the target of the city's most powerful political organizations and press companies.

Shortly after the appointment in December 1937, William Randolph Hearst's *Journal-American* ran the front-page, banner headline, "Communist Appointed to City Post."[4] In February 1938, the *Brooklyn Eagle* ran a cartoon that placed Isaacs at a desk holding a paper titled "City Business," with a colonial figure standing before him, labeled "Democracy." Keeping watch to the side, though, appeared a mustached figure with all of the stereotypical trappings of a Soviet military officer, possessing the name "Communism." The cartoon's title, "Can He Serve Two Masters," characterized Isaacs as beholden to two interests—New York City and Soviet-directed Communism.[5] In March 1938, the *New York World-Telegram* ran cartoons on consecutive days that depicted Isaacs as a Communist dupe whose poor decisions threatened New Yorkers' tenuous security and the gains made by reformers under Mayor La Guardia. The first illustration cast Isaacs waving a "Hurray for Stalin" flag while throngs of people labeled "unemployed" looked on in dismay. The second, titled "Isaacs Puts the Red Smear on a Liberal Administration," showed him throwing paint onto a sign reading "NY City's Government under Fusion. An Honest and Decent Administration by Mayor La Guardia."

Written on the paint were the words, "Appointment of Gerson, a Communist, as Confidential Investigator."[6] These pivotal cartoons demonstrated the shift toward red-baiting in municipal politics by the late 1930s, a tactic that became commonplace during the Little Red Scare.

Political cartoonist Rollin Kirby, who drew "Hurray for Stalin" and "Isaacs Puts Red Smear on a Liberal Administration," expressed regret at having penned the illustrations shortly after their publication. On March 8, 1938, Kirby wrote to Nathan Greene,

> "I have received a number of letters such as yours asking why I made the two cartoons in opposition to the Gerson appointment. I shall answer yours as I have the others—the cartoons to which you object were ordered by the editor. That was the paper's policy but one with which I disagreed. Nothing could be more distasteful to me than to find myself fighting alongside [sic] the American Legion, George U. Harvey, the Chamber of Commerce and the rest of the red-baiters."[7]

A year later, Kirby wrote directly to Simon Gerson, admitting, "I am greatly relieved to be separated from the *World-Telegram* where, to tell the truth, I have been very uncomfortable for a long time. My attitude toward you in the matter of the two cartoons I did of you was an entirely impersonal one—I only felt an injustice was being done."[8] These reflections provided a unique glimpse into the evolution of red-baiting as a tactic in New York City political culture. Kirby admitted that he abhorred the arguments he articulated for the *World-Telegram*, yet he expressed impotence at being able to challenge the political tone mandated by his editors.

Good-government reformers considered the Isaacs-Gerson red-baiting a disingenuous strategy by local political bosses to regain their monopoly of power following the rise of Mayor La Guardia and the success of charter reform. William J. Schieffelin, chairman of the Citizens Union, defended Isaacs against such tactics. He declared, "The most vociferous critics, however, are . . . the political enemies of the present administration and the professional redbaiters."[9] Schieffelin argued that the motives behind such charges lay in Democrats' desire to create an "artificial hysteria" to regain power in city government, rather than a yearning for representative democracy. Schieffelin noted the similarity between the charges against Isaacs and earlier Tammany rhetoric portraying reform as part of a subversive conspiracy: "In the last election the public showed that it could not be made to forget about tin boxes and misgovernment by means of a red scare. . . . No believer in democracy . . . would attempt to deny Communists the right to vote or to hold office."[10]As the Gerson debacle escalated, the Republican Party considered disavowing its affiliation with Isaacs. For years, Isaacs had criticized the party's lackadaisical, and sometimes contrary, attitude toward progressive urban policy.

Amid assertions that Communists had infiltrated city government through the appointment of Gerson and the election of Transit Workers Union president Michael Quill to the city council, the Democratic and Republican parties, and their allies in the press, capitalized on international events to intensify their attacks on PR's supporters in the summer and fall of 1939. Proportional representation had seemingly passed a statewide test the previous year, but local margins against the constitutional referendum overestimated support for it. Many opponents of PR had opposed the referendum or abstained from campaigning against PR, given the massive home rule objections to the proposal. These larger organizations found ready allies in grassroots anti-radical groups that saw connections between war in Europe and the growing representation of progressives in the city council. The New York City Police Department's Criminal Alien Information Bureau conducted undercover surveillance of suspected seditious activities on both the Left and the Right. The 180 detectives assigned to the "Alien Squad" attended Communist Party demonstrations, as well as meetings of various anti-Communist groups that occurred frequently between 1939 and 1940.[11] According to historian Thomas Kessner, even the FBI and US Army intelligence were unaware of the squad's activities.[12]

The Alien Squad's reports revealed a burgeoning anti-progressive movement that organized meetings attended by dozens, and sometimes hundreds, of people. These gatherings occurred primarily in homes and halls in the boroughs of Queens and Brooklyn, where large numbers of working- and middle-class white New Yorkers lived. Participating groups included the Christian Front, Neighborhood Committee against Communism, Queens County Committee against Un-American Activities, Flying Squads of Americanism, American Nationalist Party, American Society for Americanism, Anti-Communist League, Bronx Committee to Combat Communism, Coughlinites, and Christian Minute Men. These organizations charged that various local populations, including non-Christians (primarily Jews), African Americans, women, Nazis, and Communists, threatened to ally with foreign enemies to subvert domestic security.

A coalescing conservative Right that strengthened in opposition to FDR's New Deal policy agenda perceived a threat in the increased power taken in local politics by African Americans, labor, women, and leftist political parties during the late 1930s; it claimed that these groups, combined with international threats associated with conflict in Europe, were forming a coalition that threatened to destroy American democracy, as well as the existing social and political hierarchy. The new government leadership enabled by proportional representation, including five American Labor Party members elected in 1937 and the first female minority leader of the city council as of 1940, contributed to the fear expressed by these grassroots xenophobic, anti-Semitic, racist, and anti-feminist groups. According to the spokespeople for these groups, PR's diversity posed as much of a threat to New Yorkers' security, and perhaps their own power, as Germany or the Soviet Union.

Anti-Communist groups held dozens of public meetings, attended by thousands of New Yorkers in Manhattan and the outer boroughs. Most of the participants expressed general hatred of the Soviet Union and Communism, but they also focused their outrage on specific local officials and political activities, including Isaacs's appointment of Gerson. Groups such as the Neighborhood Committee against Communism expressed a growing resentment toward Communists as well as progressive municipal politics in general. Speaking before a meeting of about 250, J. Miller voiced outrage at the power held by the "Isaacs [sic] and the Gersons" in city government. Claiming more than the threat of a single Communist member of the Manhattan borough president's office, Miller saw a Communist presence throughout city affairs, with City Hall described as a "Red spotted building" and the voting power of women labeled a "disease placed upon the man." Such diatribes exposed a particularly resonant vision of the Communist threat, which incorporated overt Communist activity with a broader critique of representative democracy.[13]

Despite his unsuccessful support of the constitutional referendum to ban proportional representation in 1938, Notre Dame University professor Ferdinand Hermens returned to the New York City PR debate during the 1939 city council campaign. Hermens used the war in Europe as a rhetorical device to justify his arguments against PR. While his rhetoric was consistent throughout the 1930s, the conflict provided Hermens a new political environment in which, he argued, New Yorkers needed to reevaluate the role of proportional representation in city government.

Shortly before the 1939 council elections, Hermens petitioned Mayor La Guardia to move against the system. Hermens wrote of "grave objections [that] have been raised against proportional representation, both on a national and on a municipal plane."[14] Hermens objected to linkages between PR and the municipal government that extended beyond the electoral process. He contended that "the school system of New York has been widely used for PR propaganda. . . . At the same time the radio station of the City of New York has given many hours to proponents of proportional representation whereas little time has been given to the opponents."[15] Hermens saw "the best interests of democracy" threatened by the system and, with war begun in Europe, continued to portray PR as a "Trojan horse" that would weaken America's defense.

Recognizing Tammany Hall as one of the most prevalent symbols used by PR's supporters, Hermens argued that an effective anti-PR campaign must be waged outside the reach of Tammany. Hermens observed that any opposition movement linked with Tammany would be perceived by voters as merely a ploy to maintain the machine's power. So, Hermens made what amounted to a good-government argument against PR. He asserted that Fusionists opposed the system and, moreover, that the system was a waste of vital government resources. Hermens echoed La Guardia and the *New York Daily News* in concluding that "the PR council was the one point at which the Fusion landslide had been stopped" in the 1937 elections.[16] Writing in the journal of the National Municipal League, which had closely aligned with the movement for proportional representation in the United States since its founding in the late nineteenth century, George Hallett chided Hermens for neglecting to mention how Fusion "lost all the county offices but one, four-fifths of the city's assemblymen . . . , and seven-eighths of the city's delegates to the state constitutional convention."[17]

According to Hermens, proportional representation had already cost the city more than $1.5 million, a figure one reviewer attributed to either a typographical error or ignorance.[18] Interestingly, Hermens explained this amount in correspondence with La Guardia by blaming the council and its predecessor, the board of aldermen, for not dismantling the bloated municipal offices that cost the city hundreds of thousands of dollars per year—offices that would have been closed had the PR-elected minority council members succeeded in the city legislature's opening sessions.[19] In effect, Hermens tried to convince La Guardia and others that PR both threatened municipal good government and national security. The mayor, who had himself earlier criticized the system as inefficient and misrepresentative, defended PR following the 1939 elections. He noted that the second PR election cost the city 62 percent less than the first, with a saving of $433,000—a cost of $267,604.68 in 1939 versus $700,893.24 in 1937.[20]

Hermens's arguments about PR's inefficiencies did not seem to resonate with public officials nor the public at large nearly as much as the deepening declarations that the system provided a means for Communists to gain power in local

This cavernous Manhattan armory is crammed with canvassers hard at work in the enormous undertaking of multiple ballot counts in the second proportional representation election. In the lower left, dozens of sealed boxes wait to have their ballots sorted, counted, transferred, and re-counted several times, a process that took many days. *165th Armory, Manhattan, November 8, 1939. Interior of Armory as Voting Headquarters. Courtesy Bettmann/CORBIS.*

government. For its part, the Communist Party agreed with assessments arising from PR's opponents that the system could facilitate Communist representation in public office. Following the first council elections under PR in 1937, the Communist Party of New York State asserted that the New York City Council, elected via PR, provided the foundation for a progressive "Democratic Front" throughout the state. From the state Communist Party's perspective, municipal gains via PR would lead to state electoral victories and, ultimately, successes "on a national scale."[21] The state committee emphasized that five members of the American Labor Party had won council seats in 1937 and that Brooklyn Communist leader Peter Cacchione had nearly won as well. The committee made clear that unity between progressive forces, enabled by PR, posed the greatest threat to Tammany Hall. At the same time, the committee proposed that anti-progressive forces had already begun to marshal anti-Communist rhetoric as a means of defeating the emerging progressive coalition in the city legislature.

Even before the Little Red Scare, during the appointment controversy over Communist Party official Simon Gerson and objections to Cacchione's near victory in 1937, the committee concluded that anti-Communism posed the greatest threat to reform and progress in local, state, and national politics. As the committee characterized the situation, "The main purpose of all Red-baiting is to defeat all progress by dividing the people so that reaction and its propaganda may triumph."[22] The Communist Party characterized anti-Communism as rhetoric designed to smear the entire progressive movement.

Communist Party leaders incorporated their own anti-fascist rhetoric into calls for unity behind PR and other progressive policies. In several speeches, pro-PR Communists linked the terms "reactionary" and "fascist" to describe their opposition. As Manhattan Communist Party leader Israel Amter labeled his opponents "fascists," the state committee emphasized, "The need of defeating reaction in New York City brought the progressives together."[23] Communists positioned anti-fascism as the driving force behind the coalition that carried charter reform and proportional representation. The party leadership wasn't the only group to develop such arguments in opposition to Tammany Hall— good-government speakers frequently portrayed Tammany Hall as a totalitarian group at odds with freedom, democracy, and progress in New York City.

Black leftists connected PR with their struggle for power against Tammany Hall in municipal politics. The Harlem Chapter of the Communist Party argued that PR presented the only viable method for progressive legislation in the city council. With PR, "the progressives could have put up a staunch and effective fight against proposed reactionary legislation."[24] Without PR, the group argued, pro-black, pro-labor representatives did not stand a chance of being nominated by the Democratic machine. For Harlem Communists, PR provided a tool to weaken Tammany's grip on the candidate nominating process, which they argued prevented progressive candidates from ever appearing on the ballot.

As the Communist Party invested significant resources behind Peter Cacchione's council campaign in Brooklyn, the board of elections decided to remove Cacchione and three other Communist Party council candidates from the council ballot less than one month before the 1939 elections. The board ruled on a legal technicality—a technicality that the board apparently ignored with regard to a non-Communist candidate, according to the Republican Commissioner Jacob A. Livingston, the lone member of the board to vote against the resolution. The resolution invalidated the Communists' nominating petitions because the board's majority concluded the documents did not contain "additional details on the witness's present and previous voting district," requirements instituted by the state legislature earlier in the year.[25] The ruling also removed four other council candidates—all either independents or minority party representatives. Despite his status as a write-in candidate, Cacchione received 24,677 votes, placing him twelfth, with seven candidates elected to the council from Brooklyn.[26] The fact that 8,096 of Cacchione's votes were transferred to Genevieve Earle—a shift that took even Earle by surprise—suggested that voters recognized how both candidates challenged the Democratic and Republican parties in Brooklyn.[27]

For all of its dire characterizations of proportional representation, the Democratic Party saw its strength in the council increase with the 1939 elections. The American Labor Party dropped from five council members to two; Fusion decreased from three to two; Republicans declined from three to two; Insurgent Democrats fell from two to one. Organization Democrats, on the other hand, increased their numerical strength from 13 members to 14. In addition, the Democratic Party saw its proportional advantage in the council rise significantly, increasing from 13 members in a 26-member council to 14 members in a 21-member council. As voter participation declined sharply from 1937 to 1939, reapportionment enabled the Democratic Party to increase its representation in the council from 50 percent to a two-thirds majority by adding only a single council member. This expansion of legislative power reflected the concerted efforts of the Democratic Party to limit its candidates throughout the city. The *Daily News* characterized Democrats' shrewd mastery of PR with a political cartoon entitled "The Cat that Ate the Canary," which showed the Tammany Tiger happily digesting a bird labeled "PR."[28]

The 1939 council elections fueled a wave of antagonism toward PR from two of its most powerful supporters: the Republican Party and the borough of Brooklyn. Brooklyn Republicans did not muster enough votes to elect a single council member. To increase their party's council representation, Republicans seemed perfectly willing to trash the system that had provided them with greater citywide membership than they previously held. Groups such as the Young Men's Republican Club of Westchester County expanded the scope of PR's threat and directly linked the system with a national dictatorial movement emerging under the auspices of the New Deal. The Republican club argued that "the greatest threat to our liberties comes not from without but from the New Deal trend toward dictatorship."[29] The group concluded that PR furthered the goals of totalitarians—specifically targeting Franklin Roosevelt—as the system proved "demoralizing to the principles of majority rule and un-American in theory and practice."[30]

City Council Election Results, 1939
(by borough)

Member	Party	Votes Received
BROOKLYN		
Members elected: 7		
Joseph T. Sharkey	D	67,533
Genevieve B. Earle	CF/CNP	66,655
John Cashmore	D	64,481
Anthony J. DiGiovanna	D	61,022
Walter R. Hart	D	60,524
Harry W. Laidler	ALP	59,507
William M. McCarthy	D	52,573
MANHATTAN		
Members elected: 5		
Robert K. Straus	CF/CNP	68,965
William A. Carroll	D	68,049
Joseph C. Baldwin	R	61,267
John P. Nugent	D	57,105
Alfred E. Smith Jr.	ID	51,424
THE BRONX		
Members elected: 4		
Salvatore Ninfo	ALP	80,181
Charles E. Keegan	D	71,892
Louis Cohen	D	66,477
Joseph E. Kinsley	D	58,863
QUEENS		
Members elected: 4		
James A. Burke	D	75,000
Hugh Quinn	D	67,283
John M. Christensen	R	50,110
William N. Conrad	D	48,419

RICHMOND
Members elected: 1

Frederick Schick	D	31,173

Abbreviations: ALP = American Labor Party; CF = City
Fusion; CNP = Citizens Non-Partisan; D = Democratic;
ID = Insurgent Democrat; R = Republican.
It is unclear why the board of elections tallied Salvatore Ninfo's
votes beyond the 75,000 maximum.
*Source: Annual Report of the Board of Elections in the City of
New York for the Year 1939, 29.*

Brooklyn's newspapers blamed PR for war in Europe and assailed the
system as undemocratic and pro-Communist—despite borough voters'
election of five Democrats, one Fusionist, and one American Laborite. The
Brooklyn Eagle charged, "We have seen the fatal results of the growth of a
multitude of minority parties in various European governments. It is charged
that their ineffectiveness in Germany and Italy, where PR was in use, had a
large part in the breakdown of the parliamentary system that led to the Hitler
and Mussolini dictatorships."[31] Certain pro-repeal writers even targeted the
vilification of Tammany Hall and asserted that good-government rhetoric
represented merely a "scarecrow" that reformers used to threaten voters into
supporting PR. Such arguments revealed a degree of irony when compared to
the flourishes of red-baiting found in the same publications.[32]

With troubles mounting for PR, prominent supporters tried to distance
themselves from the Communist Party. While campaigning for the council as
an American Labor Party candidate, Stanley Isaacs blasted David Dubinsky,
president of the International Ladies Garment Workers Union, for fostering
the "wholly unfounded" charge that he (Isaacs) had supported the Communists. Isaacs declared, "Your allegation that I have been a front of the Communist Party is utter nonsense."[33] In a letter to the editor of the *New Republic*
written in 1941, he explained his desire to avoid aiding the Communist cause.
Isaacs wrote, "Those who are bitterly anticommunist have to avoid helping
this group just as those of us who believe intensely in civil liberties have to
avoid helping the communist cause even though we insist on defending the
rights of communists."[34] By depicting Communists as a menace to freedom,
Isaacs and other PR advocates worsened the political environment in which
they struggled to defend the system. The anti-Communist stance taken by

both sides reinforced the suspicion that Communism threatened local freedom. In this rhetorical atmosphere, pro-PR activism by leftists in the Communist and American Labor parties served to strengthen the increasingly negative association between PR and Communism.

While many of Isaacs's liberal defenders objected to allegations that he supported Communism, they agreed with conservatives who declared that Communists should be prevented from serving in public office. Isaacs found himself criticizing Communism while also defending his appointment of an avowed Communist: "The events of the past few months have deepened my dislike for Communism but have likewise deepened my attachment to the Bill of Rights. I cannot see how a man, competent in his work, can be deprived of his job solely because of his real or alleged radical views."[35] Allegations concerning Gerson's appointment continued until the Republican Party refused to renominate Isaacs for the borough presidency in September 1941. Isaacs then resigned his post and ran as an independent for the city council that fall. In his letter of resignation, Gerson repeated the accusation that the Democratic Party utilized fascist tactics to force radicals and, ultimately, liberals from office: "They . . . seek to scrap the Bill of Rights and impose a storm troop rule here under the cloak of patriotism. . . . This was the classic pattern in Nazi Germany and every other fascist country—Communists first and then, swiftly in turn, every other liberal force."[36] For PR specifically and New York City politics in general, the implications of rising anti-Communism proved dramatic. The system became a flashpoint for a citywide debate over Americanism, democracy, and security. Advocates for and against PR refocused their attention to equate the potential "threat" of Communism with the immediate fear of Hitler and fascism. Throughout the city, political parties and civic organizations debated how to proceed in an environment where real or suspected Communist affiliation could be wielded as a potent weapon.

While the Republican Party began to dismantle its progressive wing, the Little Red Scare produced tensions within the American Labor Party that ultimately broke it apart. Party leaders competed for control of the organization with divisions defined around support for the Communist Party. Charles Belous, former chair of the City Fusion Party in Queens, requested aid from Mayor La Guardia as Belous saw the ALP disintegrating over the Communist issue: "Must we stand by while both factions tear the disputed child to death?"[37] As explicitly presented by Belous, mounting tensions within the city's progressive coalition of Communists, liberals, and moderates threatened to split the alliance and weaken opposition to the city's political machines. Moreover, Belous concluded that the ALP's internal battles endangered the efforts of anti-Tammany activists in the city, with Fusion members (the vast majority of whom were formerly members of the Democratic and Republican parties) increasingly alienated from their leftist allies.

Recognizing these fractures within the coalition that successfully installed charter reform and PR only a few years earlier, the Democratic Party saw 1940 as the time to strike to permanently abolish PR. In the summer and fall of 1940, Bronx Democratic Party leader Ed Flynn guided a citywide campaign to repeal PR. The system's supporters accused Democratic organizations throughout the five boroughs of gathering 275,000 of the 278,000 signatures obtained to secure a referendum.[38] In "PR Unmasked," Democratic council member Louis Cohen framed PR as a subversive threat. Defining fascism and communism as "seditious extensions of democracy," Cohen asserted, "Just as these isms are deceptive camouflage, misleading poorly informed and trusting citizens, so, too, in America we have an ism which insidiously eats at the heart of our democracy—proportional representation."[39] Despite fears that Franklin Roosevelt's 1940 presidential reelection campaign would increase anti-Tammany turnout as it did in 1936, Cohen privately expressed optimism, "Notwithstanding the national election, I feel that we will be able to obtain a sufficient number of affirmative votes for the repeal of PR."[40]

Ferdinand Hermens joined Cohen in supporting repeal and asserted their campaign hinged on which side possessed greater public activism and press support. He argued, "The superiority of the PR agitation consists in the fact that they (PR's supporters) have ample material in print that the other side almost entirely lacks. If this defect is only partially remedied the good sense of the American people can be relied upon to do the rest."[41] Hermens's perspective helped explain his public statements against PR and his persistent attempts to link its use in New York City with European electoral systems that, he argued, contributed to the rise of fascism and the Second World War.

Parks Commissioner Robert Moses, the most powerful unelected government official in New York City, joined Cohen and Hermens in strategizing the repeal effort.[42] An imposing figure, Moses used his appointment as parks commissioner to consolidate power over municipal planning throughout the five boroughs. Famously dubbed the "Power Broker" by historian Robert Caro in his Pulitzer-prize winning biography, Moses served as parks commissioner from 1934 to 1960.[43] The *New York Times* estimated that Moses simultaneously held as many as 12 different positions in municipal government, orchestrating the construction of parks, bridges, tunnels, and highways that reshaped the city's landscape.[44] The combination of his extensive appointments and Moses's own drive for increased authority left him ideally positioned to shape the campaign against PR. Ironically, Moses had supported both the good-government movement and proportional representation earlier in his career. During the truncated campaign for charter reform in 1922, Moses joined 52 reformers, including Carrie Chapman Catt, Richard S. Childs, Jane Addams, Charles Beard, Jeannette P. Rankin, Belle Moskowitz, and Samuel Seabury, in advocating PR's adoption in New York City.[45] According to Caro, Moses became estranged from the reform community because of the influence he gained as an aide to Democratic governor Al Smith in the 1920s.[46] By the time of the PR debates of the 1930s and 1940s, Moses had so turned against his former allies that his rhetoric sometimes focused on the intellectual, and even moral, depravity of government reformers.[47]

In 1933, when PR was touted as a key component of government reform in the aftermath of the Seabury investigations, its supporters knew not to look to Moses for aid. As Republican Brooklyn Borough president Raymond Ingersoll privately expressed to George Hallett, "It may be difficult for anyone to convert . . . Robert Moses to the support of PR."[48] The raucous conception of democracy fostered by PR infuriated Moses, who appreciated the ability to plan the city's development without the influence or input of other policy makers or the public. If anything irritated Moses more than PR, it was the City Planning Commission installed by the charter reform package that also passed in 1936. Reformers charged the commission with crafting a master plan for the city, a power Moses had already unilaterally delegated to himself and one that he remained quite content to manage without any competition. Moses's fervent desire to maintain his authority engendered his opposition to reformers, PR, and potential attempts to return direction of certain city functions to Albany. When city Democrats allied with upstate Republicans to propose the abolition of proportional representation in the 1938 state constitutional convention, delegate Moses abstained from voting. At that time, Moses feared a resurgence of Albany-centered power in city affairs more than the powers of a PR-elected city council.

In correspondence with Cohen and Hermens, Moses warned that the repeal effort was "lost in a great national election."[49] However, Moses approved of Cohen's plan to repeal the electoral "monstrosity" in correspondence earlier that year.[50] His only hope of swaying the electorate against PR would be to convince the "conservative papers" to reverse their editorial stances and oppose the system. Moses determined, "If the *Daily News* were to come out against it, which I think they are likely to do at the last moment, it might turn the scale. There just isn't enough time and public interest to have the subject thoroughly debated. I am hopeful, however, that PR will be beaten."[51] Moses saw the press holding the key to PR's fate, and he personally lobbied newspaper editors to run negative articles against the system.[52]

In the correspondence between Hermens and Moses during the 1940 campaign, the pair portrayed PR as an ominous, and possibly immediate, threat to American security. As in his public statements and published works, Hermens overtly linked PR's tenure in New York City with political machinations that led to the overthrow of the Weimar parliamentary system and the rise of Nazi rule in Germany. Hermens, a German refugee, emphasized his own participation in that political struggle, which served to underscore his argument that PR in New York was developing in a way similar to the system's evolution in Germany:

> It seemed well nigh impossible to arouse the leaders of Republican Germany to the dangers that confronted them. At last, two younger deputies of the Center Party were ready to assist me in a popular drive against PR. . . . However, Hitler beat us to the game. In the United States, of course, the danger of such abrupt developments does not exist. Nevertheless, precautions cannot be taken too soon.[53]

Hermens's implication was clear—the PR debate in New York City mirrored the failed struggle against the rise of Nazism in Germany. According to Hermens, failure to repeal PR would bring consequences similar to those faced in Germany: the end of democracy and the rise of a fascist state. Moses agreed, "What you (Hermens) say about PR in Germany checks with everything I have heard, and I cannot conceive of any reason why sensible people should invite a similar experience even if it were on a much less drastic and tragic scale, in this country."[54] Though this argument proved a consistent component of repeal rhetoric, it rested upon a false reading of German electoral history. The German PR format described by Hermens differed substantially from the Hare system used in New York City elections by incorporating the List model, in which each party submitted a list of candidates to voters. Parliamentary seats were then allocated in proportion to the percentage of votes each party received, rather than according to individual candidate totals.

While Hermens and Moses agreed in their criticism of PR, they differed with regard to their conceptions of democracy. Hermens sought to expand his campaign against PR into a national organization pledged to the prospect of majority rule. He proposed the "American Association for Majority Rule," with the motto, "Democracy is the protection of minorities by the rule of the majority."[55] Hermens's approach underscored his distrust of minority representation, which he concluded ultimately threatened the viability of a functioning democracy regardless of whether such representation occurred in Germany or the United States. As a Republican, though, Moses expressed concern about the impact such a plan would have on his party's power in the United States. Moses countered, "We do want a vigorous minority, for example, in Congress, but we want the minority elected on the ordinary geographical basis and not by a system which encourages group voting."[56] It's unclear what differentiated voting for Democrats or Republicans from "group voting" in Moses's mind, but his comments suggested an acute unease with the prospect of people voting in any system that did not follow the two-party, district-based model.

Reformers and their allies in the press rejoined the battle by arguing that proportional representation must be preserved to ensure diversity in local representation. Many of the city's highest-circulation daily newspapers continued to support the system and focused their pro-PR rhetoric in ongoing attacks on Tammany Hall and its allied borough organizations. The *New York Herald-Tribune* attacked the repeal referendum as a Tammany-organized attempt to subvert the electoral process—and, more directly, the power of the electorate. One reporter described the repeal measure as a "pernicious bit of knifework against . . . local liberties which the Tammany-Democratic clubhouse statesmen have slipped into the ballot with their referendum to annihilate the proportional voting system for the City Council."[57] The *New York Times* headlined City Council president Newbold Morris's charge that the repeal organizers were "cynical, selfish, bitter, reactionary political bosses, who prospered in the years when nobody cared enough to throw them out."[58] Then, the *Times* concluded, "Put in plain language, the truth is that Tammany believes that under PR the citizens of New York City have too much to say about their city government. It proposes to disfranchise as many of them as it can."[59] The *Times* continued its support of PR as an extension of American democracy that must be supported in opposition to the city's most powerful political machine. The paper characterized the drive against the system as orchestrated by "organization members of the Democratic party," and concluded that readers must vote against the repeal effort to prevent the retrenchment of Tammany Hall.[60] According to the *Times*, Tammany conceived repeal as a plot to circumvent the democratic process, remove electoral power from the hands of the citizenry, and regain total control of city government.

The *New York World-Telegram* asserted that Tammany's attack on PR was part of "bigger, nationwide schemes of bosses and machines" to use President Roosevelt's campaign for a third term as a "sinister" cover for their plans to strengthen their control over urban America.[61] Such arguments held that machine bosses throughout the country had rallied around Roosevelt's third-term candidacy as a means of strengthening their own hegemony in municipal government. These statements reflected the dominant press sentiment that the political machines posed their own threat to national security.

In grave terms, PR supporters linked the system to ongoing international conflicts. In a radio address entitled "PR Should Not Be Repealed," George Hallett declared:

> The world is tense today with a life and death struggle between two ideals of human society. . . . The same struggle is going on here in our own country, and we are in danger, as I see it, not so much from the agents of foreign dictatorships, against whom all proper precautions will certainly be taken with the overwhelming approval of our people; but some of our own people whose loyalty to America is unquestioned but whose political philosophy is strangely akin to the Nazi ideal.
>
> I refer particularly to the political machines of some of our great cities. These machines, of which no one party has a monopoly, are little more concerned with popular government than are the dictatorships of Europe.
>
> Where people are allowed no more share in their own government and no more consideration than they are allowed where one of these machines gains unchecked control, they can hardly be expected to be enthusiasts for democracy itself. It is of such stuff that fifth columns are built.
>
> We are threatened at this election with such a totalitarian regime in the New York City Council. . . . The repeal amendment now proposed in effect to disfranchise these newly represented voters, to leave them a theoretical vote but no chance to elect anyone year in and year out as in the old Board of Aldermen. This is taxation without representation just as surely as if an equal number of voters comprising the entire electorate in some particular part of the city were deprived of a vote.
>
> Most of the objections to PR boil down to criticism or distrust of the people.
>
> PR is based on the sound American principles of majority rule with minority representation, and equal voting power for all voters. . . . The only way to cure this evil (political machines) is proportional representation. . . .
>
> Here in this greatest city in the greatest democracy in the world we have a special duty in this critical hour to protect democracy's gains and

to strengthen it by making still better use of its opportunities. We shall fail in this duty to ourselves and to the world if we do not vote down overwhelmingly this political attack on proportional representation.[62]

Hallett's commentary repositioned the PR debate to frame the political machine, rather than Communism, as the primary threat to domestic security in the midst of world war. Hallett reversed the argument that PR aided the rise of Hitler and instead made the case that PR, in the spirit of the American Revolutionary War effort, protected Americans from Nazism. Hallett escalated the PR referendum to a "life and death struggle," and he declared that the party machines represented a more immediate, more powerful threat to urban America than any foreign enemy. With the imagery of the ongoing global conflict clearly presented, Hallett placed PR squarely in the forefront of an urban arsenal for democracy.

Hallett concentrated his rhetoric on threats posed by political machines, the driving force he saw behind the move to repeal PR. Yet, he also stressed the public's critical role in the fate of local security and, therefore, "democracy itself." In delivering this radio appeal, Hallett raised the specter of popular revolt. He characterized a public stripped of its democratic authority as a likely source of subversion. According to Hallett, the removal of voting rights would foment mass rebellion—but not rebellion for liberty and democracy. Hallett declared that the loss of PR and the machine's return to hegemony would cause rebellion by a public allied with foreign-led totalitarianism. Hallett's argument left listeners with few options—PR provided New Yorkers with their only defense from totalitarian control directed either from above (political party officials) or from below (the masses). It's difficult to determine who would escape such a vice, but Hallett implied that democracy, embodied by PR, guaranteed safety.[63]

As feared by Moses and Cohen, PR benefited from the large voter turnout brought by Roosevelt's national reelection campaign. The citywide repeal attempt in 1940 failed, but by a significantly smaller margin than the 1936 referendum or the city tally for the 1938 state constitutional proposal. Whereas the 1938 victory might not demonstrate support wholly for PR, as many opponents of PR opposed the statewide repeal measure because of its origins in Albany, the 1936 results offer an intriguing point of reference with which to compare the 1940 figures. From 1936 to 1940, opposition to PR remained relatively steady, with anti-PR votes of 555,217 and 567,165, respectively. However, pro-PR votes declined greatly over this span, from

1940 Referendum to Abolish PR

	Yes	No
Manhattan	123,743	175,740
Bronx	119,490	160,478
Kings	197,372	262,233
Queens	108,479	175,764
Richmond	18,081	14,425
Citywide	567,165	788,640

"Proposition No. 1: Shall the proposed amendment to the New
York City Charter, providing for the abolition of proportional
representation in New York City and providing for the election
of Councilmen by senate districts, be approved?"
Source: *Annual Report of the Board of Elections in the City of
New York for the Year 1940*, 112.

923,186 to 788,640. PR's margin of victory dropped from 25 percentage
points in 1936 to 16 points in 1940. Perhaps more telling, the victory margin
fell most dramatically in the city's most populous borough, Brooklyn. Following the *Daily Eagle*'s turn against the system, the Republican Party's poor
showing in two consecutive elections, and the controversy over Communist
Peter Cacchione's removal from the ballot in 1939, Brooklynites still favored
PR in the 1940 vote. However, the margin dropped from 32 percentage
points in 1936 to 14 points in 1940. Citywide, the successful retention of PR
obscured the worsening political environment in which the system's advocates operated. Anti-fascist and anti-Communist attacks on PR fused with
depictions of a global totalitarian threat to polarize debate over PR, with both
sides claiming to fight for the future of democracy. Within this rhetorical
atmosphere of extremes, advocates for and against PR created a situation in
which maneuverability and compromise proved impossible.

In the midst of the 1940 repeal campaign, George Hallett dismissed anti-
Communist criticism of PR by declaring, "No avowed Communist . . . has
ever been elected in any one of the more than 50 PR elections which have
been conducted in American cities." With the election of Communist
Cacchione to the council in 1941, PR's supporters could no longer condemn
their would-be allies without implicitly challenging the system itself.[64] Under
the banner, front-page headline "Stalin Urges U.S., Britain to Open 2D
Fighting Front," the *Brooklyn Eagle* edition of November 6, 1941, alerted its

readers to a Communist development much closer to home. Directly below the main international story, the paper announced, "Boro Red Up Front in Early PR Count." The same article that reported the likely election of Cacchione also noted that despite major citywide Democratic losses, particularly the victory of Fusion Mayor Fiorello La Guardia to a third term, "the Democratic aspirants for the city's legislature were more than holding their own."[65] But, the main story of the coming days would be the election of the first Communist Party member to the New York City Council from, as the *Eagle* lamented, the borough of Brooklyn.

When the final results appeared one week later, the *Eagle* and the Democratic Party swiftly moved to characterize the election as a further indictment

City Council Election Results, 1941
(by borough)

Member	Party	Votes Received
BROOKLYN Members elected: 9		
Genevieve B. Earle	CF/CNP	75,000
Joseph T. Sharkey	D	75,000
Edward Vogel	D	71,355
Walter R. Hart	D	70,022
Anthony J. DiGiovanna	D	60,926
Rita Casey	D	59,412
William M. McCarthy	D	57,143
Louis P. Goldberg	I	50,726
Peter V. Cacchione	C	48,536
MANHATTAN Members elected: 6		
William A. Carroll	D	75,000
John P. Nugent	D	71,302
Adam Clayton Powell Jr.	ALP/CF	63,736
Stanley M. Isaacs	CF/CNP	56,058
S. Samuel DiFalco	D	55,883
Meyer Goldberg	R	47,314

THE BRONX
Members elected: 5

Charles E. Keegan	D	75,000
Louis Cohen	D	73,638
Joseph E. Kinsley	D	72,958
Salvatore Ninfo	ALP	68,347
Gertrude W. Klein	ALP	63,678

QUEENS
Members elected: 5

Hugh Quinn	D	69,644
William N. Conrad	D	69,163
James A. Phillips	D	62,875
John M. Christensen	R	60,948
George E. Donovan	D	45,061

RICHMOND
Members elected: 1

Frederick Schick	D	36,878

Abbreviations: ALP = American Labor Party; C = Communist; CF = City Fusion; CNP = Citizens Non-Partisan; D = Democratic; I = Independent; R = Republican.

Source: Annual Report of the Board of Elections in the City of New York for the Year 1941, 32.

of PR. The paper interviewed four of Brooklyn's council members-elect, all Democrats, and published their charges against the electoral system:

ANTHONY J. DiGIOVANNA: "Proportional representation should be abolished. There is no proportional representation in it. When the Communist Party, with a possible registration of 40,000 to 45,000 voters in Brooklyn, can elect a member of the Council, and the Grand Old Party, with an estimated registration of 200,000, is unable for the second successive election to elect one of its members, there is something wrong."

RITA CASEY: "You have only to look at the ballots to see the slithering slimy head of intolerance. I hope to educate the voters to the viciousness and costliness of this system."

WILLIAM M. McCARTHY: "It has done much to create religious and racial hatred."

EDWARD VOGEL: "It discourages the party system in a democracy and it invites a racial, religious, color and class vote."[66]

Taken together, these comments combined many of the central criticisms that anti-PR activists had levied against the system since its inception. Yet these Democrats compounded the usual fears of racial, religious, and class solidarity with a new mantra of proportional representation as an avenue of Communist conspiracy. As described by Rita Casey, PR and the growing Red Menace stood inseparable. She admonished Brooklynites, apparently insufficiently

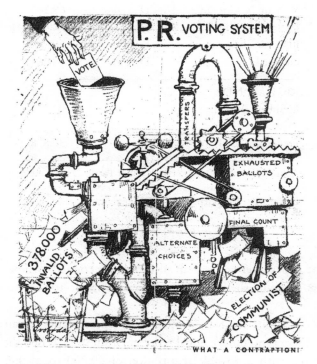

The PR system is depicted as a Rube Goldberg-style contraption, a mess of tubes, gears, and alarms that ultimately results in only two outcomes: invalid ballots and the election of a Communist (Peter Cacchione). Cacchione's election mobilized the *Brooklyn Eagle* and other critics, transforming their disapproval of the system into an immediate, outraged campaign for repeal. *"What a Contraption!"* Brooklyn Eagle, *November 14, 1941. Courtesy City Hall Library, New York City.*

educated to correctly utilize the single transferable vote, to review the ballots, leaving unclear how another look at the ballots would reveal "the slithering slimy head of intolerance."

For several days, the *Eagle* continued its onslaught against PR and Cacchione, with front-page headlines concerning a "Red" being elected to the council, interviews and editorials lambasting PR as "un-American," and cartoons such as "What a Contraption!" This drawing depicted PR as a dehumanizing machine that manipulated voters' choices through a series of superfluous, confusing processes that ultimately distorted the voter's initial preference into two categories: invalid ballots and a pro-Communist tally. As represented in the cartoon, each vote began by being deposited into a large funnel resembling a trash bin, which, after going through a maze of secret, destructive stages, is finally spewed out as two piles of refuse. One primary heap of garbage gives victory to a Communist, while an overflowing trash basket of wasted votes remains as the system's by-product. Although the borough of Brooklyn elected the lone Communist Party member to the citywide council of 26, the drawing suggested this single victory as the defining result of the election.[67]

As opposed to PR advocates' contention that the mechanism reformed corrupt elections and promoted efficiency and more effective voting, the *Eagle* made the opposite conclusion—that PR obfuscated the voter's original intent through a series of arbitrary, unsupervised stages labeled "alternate choices," "transfers," and "exhausted ballots." Rather than dozens of human counters and election officials undertaking the vote tally, an inhuman, overworked machine spews ballots without a care to the voter's original intent. The drawing conceived of the city's electorate in a telling way, representing voters as uniformly male, middle to upper class (suit and shirt cuffs with well-kept nails), and white. This depiction could alternately be seen as presenting PR as a system that overrode the wishes of elite male voters with the wishes of New Yorkers of different classes, races, and gender. The masses churned election results into invalid ballots through ignorance and into Communist support through radicalism.

The Communist-backed *Daily Worker* responded that such attacks veiled the majority's hope to remove all minority representation in local government:

> Some shout: "Destroy PR because under it a Communist was elected." They speak in bad faith. They would be opposed and are opposed to minority representation under any election method. . . . No, it's not PR alone they're after. They want to destroy the possibility of third party

representation under any election system. In short, they want to weaken and mutilate the democratic process.[68]

For Brooklyn Democrats, Republicans, and newspaper editors, the election of Cacchione overshadowed the increased representation afforded the borough under PR. In fact, the borough's extra representation in the council enabled Cacchione's victory as much as the single transferable vote. Cacchione's tally placed him ninth in the borough's standings, Brooklyn's final member elected to the council. Despite Cacchione's narrow victory, the Communist's success spurred precisely the kind of assault anticipated by the *Daily Worker*. With the Communist victory in 1941, the "Red issue" fully replaced fascism and Tammany Hall as the PR debate's central villain.

The immediate result of this change came with a revision to the council's agenda for its first session after Cacchione's election. On November 25, 1941, at the behest of council member Louis Cohen, the council debated another proposal to end PR in New York City elections. Cohen, who had led the unsuccessful campaign against the system in 1940, presented the repeal question again for the November 1942 elections. The question to be posed to voters would be, "Shall the proposed amendment to the New York City Charter, providing for the abolition of proportional representation in the City of New York and providing for the election of councilmen by senate districts, be approved?" Section 2 of Cohen's bill called for a manner of reapportionment that sought to maintain the proportional apportionment afforded by the original PR legislation. This would be accomplished by election of at-large members to the council in the following numbers: three for the Bronx, four for Queens, three for Brooklyn, and one for Richmond.[69] The *Daily News,* the city's highest circulation daily paper, echoed the sentiments of Cohen and PR's other antagonists who desired repeal following Cacchione's victory— "The proper target is PR itself."[70]

On December 4, 1941, the council chambers in City Hall filled with advocates gathered to debate the merits of Cohen's proposal and, ultimately, the proper structure of democracy in New York City. The ensuing theatrics recalled the council's initial sessions of 1938. The *New York Times* distilled the meeting's essence into the headline, "Gavel Is Hurled at Hearing on PR; Cohen Lets It Fly at Critic, Rushes at Him—Missile Hits Mrs. Casey's Foot."[71] Robert Moses spoke at length in favor of the bill, characterizing PR as a "freakish," "cumbersome" "gadget." Moses declared PR to be a primary cause of the Second World War: "It was precisely this device and others of the same parentage and origin that caused most of the troubles that have brought about the present war."[72] He depicted its advocates as an obsessed lot unable to recognize the terrible consequences the system inflicted at home and throughout the world. He concluded, "Now I kind of grew up with a good many reformers, and I am ready to testify that when they get hold of a question of this kind they are the most fanatical people in the world. Anybody who does not agree with them is damned. Anybody who does not subscribe to what they are for is an ignoramus and a menace to the city."[73]

In its editorial against PR that followed this hearing, the *New York Sun* framed Moses as an expert on municipal affairs, who, from previous experience working with reformers, was in the best position to determine whether PR should survive. The paper asserted, "Commissioner Moses will never be accused of being an old fogy but, as he said, he was brought up among reformers and he knows that when they get hold of a gadget like PR they become fanatical: [Quoting Moses], 'Anyone who does not agree with their opinion is damned.'"[74] Repeal advocates' eagerness to call for another referendum on PR reflected a marked shift in their perceptions of public sentiment for the election law, and the perceived power of anti-Communism in municipal campaigns. Three days after the chaotic council hearing that suggested PR's imminent demise, the Japanese military attacked Pearl Harbor and the United States formally entered the Second World War. With the council's attention at least temporarily reoriented toward the conflict, it ultimately tabled Cohen's proposal. The war delayed another citywide repeal campaign for years, and, in the interim, New Yorkers witnessed the political uproar created by the Communist Party's representation in the city legislature.

5 A RED (IN THE) CITY HALL

On March 28, 1941, FBI director J. Edgar Hoover signed a memorandum recommending that Peter V. Cacchione, the head of Brooklyn's Communist Party organization and city council candidate in 1937 and 1939, "be considered for custodial detention in the event of a national emergency."[1] Hoover's classification of Cacchione continued a trend in federal surveillance of suspected threats to domestic security that increased dramatically in the months following the start of World War II in Europe in 1939. As early as 1936, according to historian Richard Fried, President Roosevelt had authorized Hoover to monitor domestic Communist and fascist activism as potentially dangerous.[2] With the onset of the Second World War, Hoover, with Roosevelt's assent, broadened the scope of this surveillance to include the creation of a Custodial Detention Index. This list included Cacchione and other Communists, as well as members of the German-American Bund, a fund-raising organization that supported the Third Reich.[3]

Officials at city, state, and national levels mobilized their resources to contain suspected threats to domestic security. In 1940, the US Congress passed the Smith Act, which outlawed membership in groups that advocated revolution.[4] In New York in 1940–1941, State senator Frederic R. Coudert and Assemblyman

Herbert Rapp formed a committee to investigate subversive teaching in New York City colleges. The popularly known Rapp-Coudert Committee spurred the municipal board of education to fire 20 teachers, with 11 more resigning under suspicion of Communist association.[5] Moreover, Rapp-Coudert buttressed a state apparatus that facilitated police surveillance of suspected radical activism associated with New York City politics. At the municipal level, the Bureau of Criminal Alien Investigation of the New York City Police Department (NYPD), dubbed the "Alien Squad," monitored potentially subversive organizations throughout the five boroughs. Historian Thomas Kessner argues that the FBI did not know about the full extent of surveillance operations undertaken by the NYPD under Mayor La Guardia's direction.[6] While the level of coordination between surveillance operations at the city, state, and federal levels remains unclear, authorities clearly created a series of surveillance operations that focused directly on the Communist Party in New York City, its perceived allies, and, after the November 1941 elections, the nation's only democratically elected Communist legislator, Peter Cacchione.

As proportional representation provided the electoral means by which Cacchione, and then fellow Communist Benjamin J. (Ben) Davis Jr., won election to the city council of the nation's largest city, surveillance officers increasingly focused their attention on PR. In a field report dated October 23, 1941, an FBI agent reported consulting with the offices of the NYPD's Alien Squad as to Cacchione's residence. The FBI's characterization of Cacchione took a dramatic turn following his election to the New York City Council in November 1941. On November 12, the New York City office telegraphed the bureau's national headquarters with news of Cacchione's victory. On the following day, a memorandum addressed to Hoover described the election as of "outstanding interest to the Bureau" and cited a *Daily Worker* article that attributed the victory "in no small part to the second and third choice votes cast for him by other than Communist supporters."[7]

On December 5, 1941, in a directive sent to the special agent in charge of investigating Cacchione in New York City, Hoover classified Cacchione as a member of the most dangerous class of individuals being monitored by the bureau, "Group A. Individuals believed to be the most dangerous and who in all probability should be interned in event of War."[8] From this point in 1941 until Cacchione's death in 1947, the FBI's surveillance amounted to a running tally of Cacchione's activities as a New York City Council member, candidate for reelection, and advocate for PR. Field reports included press clippings and interviews with undercover informants concerning Cacchione's public addresses and legislative work in the council, testimony before the

Rapp-Coudert Committee, and his refusal to testify before HUAC. Perhaps unintentionally, the file also contains an extensive examination of the mechanics of democracy as practiced in New York City Council elections under proportional representation. Following Cacchione's reelection in 1943, Special Agent E. E. Conroy informed Hoover that Cacchione benefited from PR and that he received the largest first-ballot count of any council candidate in the city. Moreover, in detailing Cacchione's campaign strategy, Conroy revealed the get-out-the-vote tactics necessary to elect Cacchione by such a wide margin. Concerning Cacchione's activities, Conroy stated that:

> the organization of his campaign began as far back as January, and that the Communists started to prepare their literature in March. [Cacchione] stated that 300 canvassers started to work for him in June, that the number was boosted to 800 in September and to 1,000 in October. In the latter part of October [Cacchione] asserted that 1,200 canvassers were "knocking on doors and punching doorbells, 600 of them working six nights a week and on Sunday."
>
> In addition, his literature was extensive and he bought space in the newspapers and time on the radio.[9]

While Cacchione's opponents charged that he won his council seat through manipulation and "un-American" politics, they did not charge Cacchione with any illegal activity. The reports of municipal, state, and federally sponsored surveillance of Cacchione, and later fellow Communist council member Ben Davis, did not reveal any examples of illegal campaigning or corruption.[10]

As Communists contributed significant resources to defending proportional representation, surveillance officers included extensive coverage of pro-PR activism in their confidential reports. While the reports did not necessarily single out PR as a subject worth further investigation, the coverage shed light on the extent to which Communist activists championed PR and reveal the attention that police investigators and their government superiors paid to the PR campaigns.

In contrast to the white, male-centric imagery that dominated the city's political landscape, council candidate Cacchione and the Communist Party employed dramatic illustrations in targeted appeals to the city's less powerful citizens. In one pamphlet, an army of racially diverse women helped one another wield massive banners proclaiming their unity against Hitler and fascism. Another brochure depicted a swastika-clad Hitler reenslaving a black family. The reverse of that brochure showed a fierce Tammany tiger suckling its twin cubs, labeled "Race Hatred and Appeasement." Another pamphlet, written in Polish, superimposed a depiction of war-torn Warsaw over the New York City skyline. The implication—that the horrors of war in Europe could easily spread to American shores—compelled Polish New Yorkers to support the Communist Party in order to secure their safety. Taken together, these pamphlets empowered New Yorkers as a force against totalitarianism; all they had to do was vote for Cacchione in a PR election.[11]

As Cacchione and the CP became adamantly pro-war following the German invasion of the Soviet Union in the summer of 1941, the repercussions of this shift continued the schisms within the American Labor Party in New York City. Underscoring the fusion between local and international politics, leftist party leaders required council candidates to publicly declare their support of US intervention in the war in order to receive the party's endorsement in the fall elections. When Brooklyn council member Harry Laidler refused, he was denied the party's endorsement for reelection in 1941. Announcing the party's decision in September 1941, an ALP spokesperson declared, "You can say all you want that foreign policy has nothing to do with a city election. But you are either against Hitler or you are for him."[12]

Though Cacchione's ninth-place finish in Brooklyn garnered the lion's share of press and government attention following the 1941 elections, the PR tally also brought the victory of the Reverend Adam Clayton Powell Jr. in Manhattan. As the first African American elected to the city council, Powell's victory marked a milestone in New York City history. *Time* magazine declared in its lead that Powell's triumph meant "Harlem's 200,000-odd Negroes had their first representative in the New York City Council," perhaps unintentionally suggesting that white officials did not—and could not—represent black New Yorkers in government.[13] The national newsmagazine emphasized how Powell's campaign strategized a get-out-the-vote effort with the logistics of proportional representation in mind: "Helpfully he mailed 200,000 sample ballots to voters showing how to mark the complicated proportional representation ballot. In Harlem, which gave him some 50,000 No. 1 votes, there were fewer spoiled ballots than anywhere in the city."[14] Biographer Charles Hamilton describes how Powell supporters rallied around PR as a means to elect the first African American council member. Many Harlem residents responded to this "elaborate electoral scheme" with a "genuine grass-roots campaign, opening storefront headquarters in various neighborhoods, blanketing the community with leaflets, and holding small street-corner rallies day and evening."[15] For the first time, Hamilton argues, the city's black community participated in a campaign with a legitimate opportunity to elect one of its own. Powell soon used his council position as a springboard to national politics, running successfully for Congress the following year.

In the 1943 council elections, Powell endorsed Communist Ben Davis as his de facto replacement. An African American native of Georgia, Davis graduated from Harvard Law School in 1928.[16] He came to prominence as a civil rights lawyer through his defense of Angelo Herndon, a black labor activist accused of inciting insurrection in Atlanta, Georgia, in 1932. After Herndon was sentenced to 20 years of hard labor for his leadership of a peaceful demonstration, Davis and the Communist Party championed Herndon's appeal all the way to the Supreme Court, which ruled in Herndon's favor in 1937.[17] In March 1940, Davis testified before the Senate Judiciary Committee, offering fiery testimony that challenged the senators' stance on civil rights and resulted in W. E. B. Du Bois's endorsement of Davis's political style in the pages of the *Amsterdam News*.[18] By the time of Davis's council candidacy, he, Powell, and Du Bois led the short-lived leftist Harlem paper, the *People's Voice*.[19] Although he received 44,344 votes, far below the 75,000-vote quota for automatic victory under PR, Davis's tally placed him in Manhattan's fourth council seat and only a few thousand votes shy of the totals received by the two Democratic Party candidates elected in 1943.

Historian Michael Denning locates the elections of Powell and Cacchione in 1941, and Davis in 1943, as part of broader Popular Front activism that leftists organized following the Nazi-Soviet Pact of 1939 and the onset of World War II in Europe.[20] Veterans' groups, conservatives, and increasing numbers of moderates focused their opposition on proportional representation as the source of the Left's recent electoral successes. In reaction to the Communists' victories, most of the few remaining pro-PR newspapers switched to negative editorial stances. Following the 1943 tally, the *New York World-Telegram* titled an editorial "Smaller and Redder" to describe the new council, which would include two Communists and fewer members overall due to reapportionment.[21] Council seats decreased dramatically following the 1943 vote, with the body reduced by slightly more than one-third to 17 members from 26. Numerically, this shift in apportionment meant that the Communist Party actually tripled its portion of the legislature, increasing from about 4 percent of council seats to nearly 12 percent.

Anti-Communist reaction to the election of Davis and the reelection of Cacchione overshadowed, perhaps intentionally, the significant decline in Democratic Party representation following the 1943 election. Though it was expected that every party experienced a reduction in council representation

City Council Election Results, 1943 (by borough)

Member	Party	Votes Received
BROOKLYN		
Members elected: 6		
Joseph T. Sharkey	D	74,716
Peter V. Cacchione	C	69,149
Genevieve B. Earle	R/CNP	67,241
Walter R. Hart	D	67,234
Anthony J. DiGiovanna	D	47,853
Edward Vogel	D	47,041
MANHATTAN		
Members elected: 4		
Stanley M. Isaacs	R	75,000
John P. Nugent	D	48,835
William A. Carroll	D	48,035
Benjamin J. Davis Jr.	C	44,334
THE BRONX		
Members elected: 3		
Charles E. Keegan	D	68,913
Michael J. Quill	ALP[a]	67,195
Gertrude W. Klein	ALP	55,314
QUEENS		
Members elected: 3		
James A. Phillips	D	74,455
Hugh Quinn	D	60,824
Alfred J. Phillips	R	57,593
RICHMOND		
Members elected: 1		
Frederick Schick	D	19,453

[a] Officially, the board of elections did not record a party affiliation for Quill.

Abbreviations: ALP = American Labor Party; C = Communist; CNP = Citizens Non-Partisan; D = Democratic; R = Republican.

Source: Annual Report of the Board of Elections in the City of New York for the Year 1943, 29.

with the narrowing of the council's size due to reapportionment, the Communist Party's rise in power made clear that this wasn't the case. In every borough except Staten Island with its lone council member, the Democratic Party saw its numbers reduced. In the Bronx, the American Labor Party held two of the borough's three seats, right under the nose of Democratic National Committee chair Ed Flynn, who also controlled the borough's Democratic Party operations. In Brooklyn, Democrats still held a majority of seats, though Cacchione and Genevieve Earle (Republican/Citizens Non-Partisan) placed second and third, respectively. Earle's performance reiterated her strength with the electorate, but Cacchione's rise from ninth place in 1941 to second in 1943 suggested that the Communist had built a substantial public following during his first term.

Perhaps most significant, in Tammany Hall's home borough of Manhattan, Democrats could only manage to split the borough's allotted council seats. The party's two victors gained only a few thousand more votes than Communist Ben Davis, who finished fourth. Moreover, Stanley Isaacs, endorsed by the Republican Party, reached the 75,000-vote threshold, the only candidate in the city to do so in 1943. The high vote totals of Isaacs, Cacchione, Earle, and Mike Quill (American Labor Party) in the Bronx also underscored the coalescing of popular support for leftists that would be difficult to overcome electorally under proportional representation. As anti-PR activists had argued for years, the electoral system made it virtually impossible to campaign *against* any particular candidate. Therefore, the Democratic Party and its press allies primarily attacked PR for the outcome of the 1943 elections, the implication being that the system had caused undemocratic results.

Yet as attacks on PR increased, many of the system's chief proponents expressed concern over Communist success under the system. George Hallett, writing as secretary of the Citizens Union, declared, "The CU executive committee is so far from being sympathetic to Communism that in the election last fall it refused to recommend . . . any candidates of the Left Wing of the ALP, in which there is thought to be strong Communist influence."[22] The Commerce and Industry Association also expressed a "deep concern 'at the threat to the American constitutional system from Communist agitation'" and urged voters to separate the issue of proportional representation from their supposedly just fears of Communism.[23] Anti-Communism forged the coalition that campaigned against PR, but it also weakened support for the system among some of its formerly most ardent and influential advocates. Laurence Tanzer, who served as associate counsel for the Charter Revision Commission that proposed PR in 1936, emphasized the power of anti-Communism in his later recollections about PR's repeal. He noted, "I think the feeling, in which I share, against the Communists was so strong as to obscure all questions of actual justice and democracy in popular representation."[24]

For their part, Davis and Cacchione championed themselves as the defenders of the ideals of American society in the face of anti-democratic threats during the Second World War. The 1943 Communist Party leaflet "Don't Let Your Country Down" listed the following reasons that voters should support Communist candidates:

> IF YOU FAIL TO VOTE in the City Elections, reactionaries or politicians-as-usual may take over the City Council.
> Do you want to win the war? And the peace to follow?
> Do you want to win unconditional surrender of the Axis?
> Do you want to strengthen the unity of the United Nations?
> Do you want to smash the defeatist fifth column at home?
> Do you want a strong home front behind the military front?
> Then ... KEEP DEMOCRACY WORKING on the HOME FRONT
> ... VOTE FOR WIN-THE-WAR CANDIDATES FOR CITY COUNCIL ON NOVEMBER 2, 1943.[25]

Echoing the *Pittsburgh Courier's* wartime Double-V campaign for victory abroad (over the Axis) and at home (over racial prejudice), the CP presented its policies as crucial to the fate of democracy at home and abroad.[26]

Privately, Davis and the CP's leadership presented an alternate rationale for Communist representation that, again, seemed similar to the goal of local political power that drove Democratic and Republican operations. According to an FBI informant, Davis focused on the practical gains afforded by his election to the city council in a presentation to CP leadership:

1. It would tend to give the Party prestige
2. It would be a talking point in securing new members
3. New avenues would be opened to the Party and its activities
4. Patronage[27]

Given the inflamed rhetoric directed toward Davis and the CP following his victory, the aforementioned benefits, if reported accurately by the informant, reflected long-standing goals of minority political parties. From this perspective, Davis viewed his service in the legislature as a means to legitimize the party, strengthen its popular support, and gain the monetary and authority benefits of filling patronage positions in local government. As had good-government reformers since the nineteenth century, Davis and the CP recognized that the Democratic Party maintained its hegemony in New York City politics primarily through its control of municipal largesse.

Davis's election also came on the heels of a violent summer in Manhattan. In August 1943, long-standing tensions between Harlem residents and the New York City Police Department exploded into riots that ended with more than 600 arrests, nearly 200 injuries, and six deaths.[28] Davis's insistence on anti-discriminatory reforms coupled with this violent atmosphere to foster a series of racially charged criticisms of Davis and the electoral system by which he gained power. Both Cacchione and Davis highlighted civil rights policies in their campaign platforms and called for reform in the police department, but Davis's victory fostered a backlash unequaled by the attacks that followed Cacchione's victory in 1941. The *World-Telegram* published a two-part series by reporter Frederick Woltman arguing that the Communists won because of propaganda "capitalizing on the troubles and feelings of race and nationality." Woltman described the Communists' campaign strategy as including "door-to-door, bell-ringing canvass in the Irish neighborhoods that would have put Tammany Hall to shame." The day before, Woltman wrote that the Communists waged a campaign "throughout the city which deliberately exploited racial, religious and nationalistic feeling to the virtual exclusion of municipal issues." By framing civil rights as anathema to municipal politics, Woltman issued a charge against Davis, leftists, and proportional representation that increased momentum for the system's repeal—that, by seeking electoral support on the basis of specific policies designed to benefit particular socioeconomic, racial, and ethnic groups, rather than party allegiance, progressives unfairly manipulated the democratic process.[29] This argument, repeated by both Democrats and Republicans, narrowly defined the purpose and power of municipal government. This conservative perspective constrained democratic politics, often automatically negating policies that arose from groups outside the two dominant political parties.

A consistent coalition of independents, Republicans, anti-Tammany Democrats, and Communists never formed, and the minority experienced an almost complete breakdown. Prior to Cacchione's victory, the council minority met before each council session, reviewing the meeting's agenda and legislative proposals. When Cacchione joined the council in 1942, these practices ended and the minority coalition split apart. As Genevieve Earle recalled, "The Minority jumped on horseback and went off in different directions.... [W]e didn't even try to have a coherent program of any kind ... there was no coherence in the Minority."[30] Davis later wrote, "One of the biggest things I learned at the preliminary minority session was that it was utterly impossible to whip that group into an organized, politically unified minority even on a minimum progressive council program."[31] With little internal cohesion, the council minority proved unable to maintain a working coalition that could challenge the Democratic majority.

On a personal level, Earle described her relationship with Davis in terms that combined perspectives about region, gender, and race, "[Davis] was not only a Communist but the only Negro [in the council] and a Southerner." Earle recalled that she once told Davis to call her "Gen," which prompted Davis to reply, "Mrs. Earle, I thank you, but I'm too much of a Southerner to ever call a lady by her first name. If you'll forgive me, I'll continue to call you Mrs. Earle." Earle remembered her reaction, "Here's this corrupt Communist with the courtesy of a cavalier."[32] Earle's characterizations of her Communist counterparts combined criticism of Communist ideology with guarded admiration for Davis and Cacchione's contributions to the legislature. She recalled, "Except where matters of their ideology as Communists came in conflict with the other general thinking of the political groups in the Council, they were good, hard-working and valuable members, but when it came to the point of the Communist slant, then there was never any doubt where those boys stood."[33] It's unclear how Earle understood Communist ideology or what she meant by "Communist slant," but her recollections seem to conclude that, from her perspective, Davis and Cacchione were beneficial members of the council minority until they argued for their political interests. For Earle, Davis and Cacchione "were always Communists, and, of course, when they disagreed violently with anybody, they never failed to call that particular person or group 'Fascists' in unmistakable terms. They called them 'Fascists' just as some Democrats and Republicans call everybody they disagree with 'Communists.'"[34] While this comment suggests a significant distance between Earle and her Communist counterparts, it also highlights the tense political culture that characterized the PR-elected council of the World War II–era. Earle emphasized that anti-Communism, and anti-fascism, were rhetorical tactics, wielded indelicately, broadly, and often without clear connection to the political platforms of the targets under attack.

Stanley Isaacs, who succeeded Earle as minority leader in 1946, echoed her consternation with the inability of the council minority to forge a productive coalition. In personal correspondence from the period, Isaacs went further in castigating the council as a whole, concluding, "The New York City Council is a bore. I am a minority member of a powerless body, with only one or two people to work with for whom I have real respect."[35] He added separately, "The Council has very little power, and as a member of the Minority, I have very little chance of sharing that, so there is very little that can be accomplished. It is a good forum, however, and I have used it for that purpose on several occasions."[36] As his conclusion made clear, one of the few powers that Isaacs perceived in the council was the "forum" it provided. Many of his fellow minority members shared this understanding, and they used the council as a platform from which to advocate an array of policies, few of which stood a chance of being passed by the Democratic majority. One other point of agreement among the minority council members rested in their support for proportional representation, which provided their best, and perhaps only, means of winning election. As Isaacs summarized, the council had "very little power and wastes a tremendous amount of time, [but] if you do have a Council then the proportional representation system is the best way to elect it."[37]

Though divisions among the minority members prevented the formation of a steady coalition in the council, a certain fluidity developed in interparty relations that belied the divisive rhetoric that often dominated city political culture. For instance, the Communist Party found itself supporting certain citywide candidates endorsed by both the ALP and the Democratic Party, such as William O'Dwyer for mayor and (future mayor) Vincent Impelliteri for council president. The Davis campaign supported ALP council members such as Eugene Connolly but also Republican Stanley Isaacs.[38] In 1945, Tammany Hall went so far as to endorse Davis for reelection, albeit temporarily. The Manhattan Democratic Party organization designated him as a Democratic candidate for the council in an attempt to increase its power in the council and, in particular, to strengthen its influence in Harlem. Within a week of the announcement, Tammany rescinded the endorsement. Davis viewed Tammany and the Democratic Party in general as opportunists, who railed against the Communist Party as a threat to domestic security when such rhetoric seemed beneficial and offered it a hand when such a move appeared to provide political capital.[39]

In council sessions, this schism, based upon competing conceptions of democratic government and hardened by competition for legislative power, grew more apparent in the isolation of progressive minority council members from the Democratic majority. Few of the more than 200 Communist-sponsored bills became law.[40] Yet pure ideology did not explain the refusal of Democrats to endorse minority legislation. On rare occasions, such as when the council passed an anti-discrimination requirement for future public housing projects initially proposed by Stanley

Isaacs and Davis, the Democratic leadership took control of the legislation and assumed the final law as their own to celebrate.[41] The law barred public funds from being used to build housing projects that discriminated on the basis of race. Adam Clayton Powell Jr. had initially called for the measure with Isaacs to force the Metropolitan Life Insurance Company to rescind racial discrimination in its Stuyvesant Town Housing Project. Met Life received substantial tax exemptions from the city in order to build and maintain the property.[42]

For the most part, the only way the minority ever succeeded in the council was when it focused significant resources on a particular issue pressed by its constituent groups. Davis's few legislative successes involved council resolutions concerning race and national policies—areas decried by critics as beyond the purview of a municipal legislator. These resolutions included proclamations against lynching and celebrations of George Washington Carver Day and Negro History Week.[43] Though the anti-lynching measure passed, Davis recalled that Democratic council member William Hart challenged the measure in stark terms, quoting Hart as charging, "The Communist members of this body are constantly taking the floor to press for adoption of measures foreign to our system of government. They frequently take the side of a foreign power. No one in this Council condones lynching. But, at least, *those who do it are Americans*—no matter how misguided they may be."[44] According to Davis, Cacchione immediately retorted, "So are the innocent negro victims of the lynchers Americans?"[45] These exchanges underscore the vitriol that was common to council sessions during the Second World War and, from the Communists' perspectives, the racist undercurrents that influenced New York City politics during the period. Davis's campaign literature made no distinction between local and national (or global) policy recommendations; rather, it positioned Davis's objectives in the following categories: "Jobs," "Equality," "Transit," "The People's Living Standards," "Education," "City Employees," and "G.I. and Veterans' Rights."[46] The measures listed included resolutions to integrate major league baseball, federal legislation to eliminate the poll tax, "investigations of anti-Semitic disturbances," and a variety of programs designed to aid in the city's reconversion to a postwar economy.[47] Davis emphasized these points as evidence that he addressed the concerns of New Yorkers struggling to move beyond the fears of the Great Depression and World War II.

While the minority possessed little capacity to pass legislation on its own, its conception of the council as a platform for local, national, and, in certain circumstances, global activism fundamentally transformed the New York City Council. Enabled by proportional representation, this expanded conception of municipal governance began a new period in the history of the council in which the minority could participate in the legislative process—if not controlling passage at least providing a check on policies they opposed and an official platform from which to champion particular causes or measures supported by their constituents.

The Democratic majority objected to most measures proposed by the minority, and it expended considerable effort to protect its control of the council and the local political structure. During La Guardia's tenure, the council devoted much of its resources to investigating the mayor and hampering his ability to create and administer various social welfare programs associated with the federal New Deal. Rather than opposing La Guardia purely for ideological reasons, though, the Democratic majority's later policies suggest that objections to La Guardia's political authority also influenced their agenda. During the tenure of Mayor William O'Dwyer, a Democrat, which immediately followed La Guardia's, the Democratic council not unsurprisingly reduced its investigations of the mayor. But, the council also pursued a few liberal policies that it had opposed when proposed by La Guardia or the PR-elected minority. Majority Leader Joseph T. Sharkey, a Democratic mainstay who won election five times under the PR system he relentlessly criticized, went so far as to usher through a comprehensive housing policy to preserve rent controls in 1947.[48]

Perhaps the most surprising legislative accomplishment of the war era proved to be the extension of council terms, passed in 1945.[49] This feat seems paradoxical given both the presence of two Communists in the council at the time and the majority's declarations that the presence of avowed Communists in City Hall was anathema to democracy. It appears that Tammany legislators and their allies favored expanding their terms even if that decision also meant lengthening the tenure of Communists and their allies.

In the 1945 council campaign, Davis and Cacchione presented a municipal platform that included a comprehensive package of social and economic policies designed to forestall recession and retrenchment following the end of World War II. In its focus on city government as crucial to preserving civic welfare, the policies also recalled the government expansion associated with the prewar New Deal. Communist posters called for massive investments in "post-war construction," "housing," "anti-discrimination," "education and child care," "price control," and "transportation and utilities." In order to finance these projects, the Communist Party declared the need to "Amend the City Charter to give the City Council equal power with the Board of Estimate in matters of City finances!"[50]

The Communist council members also incorporated the city's diversity and culture in their campaign material. The party produced a series of flyers that explained in multiple languages how to successfully mark the PR ballot for Cacchione, with text in English, Spanish, Hebrew, Italian, and Polish. Without always labeling Cacchione a Communist in these illustrations, the CP attempted to attract immigrants and working-class Brooklynites.[51] The Davis reelection campaign used the same format for its "Vote this Way" pamphlet, with the notable difference in the tones used to color the figures in the voting process. In addition to a white female election worker and white male voter, Davis's "Vote this Way" illustrations included a person of darker skin following the white male in the voting process.[52]

Ben Davis's campaign tactics continued the Popular Front fusion of culture and progressive politics of the 1930s. The Davis campaign sponsored public entertainment events as a means of increasing political support and

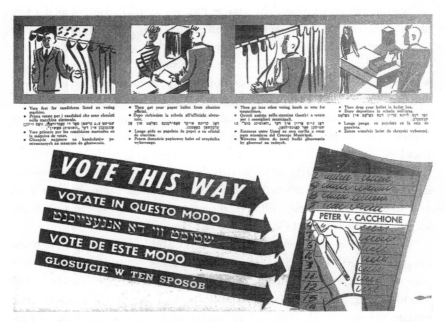

Competing against dozens of candidates in borough-wide elections, council candidates appealed in multiple languages to ensure that all New Yorkers would understand how to vote under proportional representation. This pamphlet, for Communist Peter Cacchione, uses more space to explain the system than to promote the candidate's policies, and includes text in English, Italian, Hebrew, Spanish, and Polish. Citizens Committee to Re-Elect Councilman Peter V. Cacchione, "Vote this Way," 1945, Peter V. Cacchione Papers (TAM 073), folder 20, box 7. From the microfilm, film R-7823, reel 3. *Courtesy Tamiment Library and Robert F. Wagner Labor Archives, New York University.*

raising money, including an "All Star Victory Show" featuring performances by Duke Ellington, Louis Jordan, Billie Holiday, Art Tatum, and Josh White, among many other prominent musicians.[53] Historian Michael Denning terms this collection of activist musicians organized for Davis a "jazz Popular Front."[54] The campaign emphasized the membership of such luminaries as Holiday, Count Basie, Lena Horne, Langston Hughes, Canada Lee, and Paul Robeson in the campaign's coordinating committee.[55] Internal documents underscored the campaign's strategy to approach New Yorkers through a variety of public activities, including parades, concerts, rallies, signs, door-to-door canvassing, print ads, "street ads," and even $60 for peanuts to be given away at rallies.[56]

The enthusiasm of the Davis reelection effort evolved in the midst of a rapidly changing political climate in 1945. The death of President Roosevelt in April convulsed the Democratic Party, which struggled to discern its policy objectives as it organized around a new leader for the first time in 12 years. In New York City, Roosevelt's death, along with La Guardia's decision not to seek reelection in 1945, fostered the perception that the reins of City Hall were theirs for the taking. With these changes in mind, it's important to consider the creation of the Liberal Party (LP) in 1944. During the war, the American Labor Party reeled from internal divisions between Communists and anti-Communists. Communists asserted that anti-Communists were conservatives in sheep's clothing. Anti-Communists argued that Communists within the party sought to surreptitiously hijack the party for their own radical interests. As one critic argued:

> Concealing their Communist affiliation, and mouthing slogans which are popular at the moment, they succeed in getting perfectly estimable and well meaning people to join them. Hiding behind the names of such people, they form the so-called "left wing" of the ALP, through which they seek to gain control of YOUR party, as they gained control of other organizations you are familiar with.[57]

Defeated in elections for leadership positions within the American Labor Party, the anti-Communist wing formed the Liberal Party in 1944. The LP's infrastructure included Adolf A. Berle (chairman), David Dubinsky (first vice-chairman), John L. Childs, George S. Counts, Alex Rose, and Reinhold Niebuhr (vice-chairmen), and Ben Davidson (executive director).[58]

Similar to the ALP, the LP cast itself as a haven for liberal Democrats who opposed Tammany Hall. In its first platform, the party patriotically emphasized that "Our first task is to win the war." Envisioning postwar America, the LP called for a return to New Deal policies as a means to strengthen democracy at home: "American democracy rests upon a foundation of general economic welfare that can be maintained only through full employment, full production, and a high standard of living."[59] Striving to establish a rationale for its existence, the LP competed with the ALP/CP—the Liberal Party considered these organizations inseparable—for control over the New Deal's, and later Franklin Roosevelt's, legacy.

In its formational documents, the LP focused on the inadequacies of the Democratic, Republican, and ALP/Communist parties, describing these organizations as Southern racists (Democrats), economic reactionaries (Republicans), or totalitarians (Communists).[60] During the campaign to repeal proportional representation in 1947, the party prepared speakers' guides to prep party representatives on certain key messages that should be emphasized to convince potential members that they should join the Liberal Party. One guide for speakers to trade unionists defined the political parties in the following terms:

a. Republicans: Traditionally conservative and tool of moneyed interests. b. Democrats: Stress southern reaction, machine politics of Tammany Hall, Hague, Pendergast, etc. c. ALP: Controlled by Communist Party and party liners, with no roots in American progressive movement. d. Liberal Party: Only truly democratic, progressive party in New York State.[61]

The Liberal Party's policy goals incorporated local and national agendas, including defending labor against the Taft-Hartley Act, strengthening the Federal Employment Practices Commission, working for housing subsidies and "against rent increases [and the] rising cost of living," increasing the minimum wage, and retaining the five-cent subway fare.[62]

The Liberal Party appealed to "liberals of all economic groups" and emphasized its broader ambitions, seeking "nation-wide expansion when conditions and forces are ready."[63] The LP positioned itself as continuing in a long line of historical movements in which new political parties emerged from tumultuous periods, with "Lincoln and the Republican Party" listed as one prominent example.[64] Viewed from a distance, and given the party's relative lack of subsequent success, the Liberal Party's aspirations may seem overly optimistic. Yet, understood within the context of the tumultuous political climate of 1944–1945, the LP's emergence continued a wave of antagonism against Tammany Hall and the Democratic Party, which began with the formation of the American Labor Party the previous decade. The Liberal Party provided another avenue by which disaffected liberals could participate in electoral politics and government without following either the Democratic or Republican parties. Considering the growing anti-Communist sentiment of the Cold War, the LP also sought to benefit from its standing as an explicitly anti-Communist minority party.

During the 1945 council elections, the Liberal Party focused its rhetoric against both the Democratic and Communist parties. As Communism supplanted fascism as the most powerful villain in local politics, the LP resurrected the Tammany Tiger as a threat powerful enough to overcome, or at least compete with, the symbolic power of the Red Menace. With its campaign poster "Tiger in the Streets," the Liberal Party literally recalled Thomas Nast's iconic depiction of Tammany from the Reconstruction era. As employed by the LP in 1945, the Tammany Tiger once again menaced the streets of New York City at the behest of corrupt political bosses. The LP appealed to a sense of civic pride and urged New Yorkers to defeat Tammany to protect their jobs, children, and livelihoods. Although this imagery empowered anti-Tammany organizations in earlier decades, the political landscape had shifted to such an extent that these visuals paled in comparative force to the LP's—and the anti-PR coalition's—red-baiting.

In opposing the Communist Party, the Liberal Party focused on Ben Davis's seat in Manhattan. The LP, along with the Republican Party, endorsed Benjamin F. McLaurin, an African American organizer who had served as vice-president of the Brotherhood of Sleeping Car Porters.[65] In his opening campaign press conference, McLaurin specifically argued that Davis, and implicitly any Communist, could not represent Manhattan's black community, "The 400,000 Negroes of our borough are entitled to representation in the City Council." He continued, "These conditions will only be overcome when the Negroes have a spokesman in the City Council who is free and is not bound by a commitment to any totalitarian movement, either within or outside our country."[66] Like his Democratic opponents, McLaurin argued that Davis merely served as a puppet for the Communist Party, rather than in the interest of Manhattanites.

McLaurin called upon New Yorkers to rally behind a candidate who served their interests rather than those of a foreign power and sought to create "equal educational opportunity for all," "jobs in the post-war period," "a city free from discrimination, . . . decent housing, and adequate health, welfare, recreation, and social service facilities for the underprivileged citizens of New York."[67] McLaurin and the Liberal Party criticized Tammany as unresponsive to the needs of New Yorkers and the Communist Party as utterly under the control of the Soviet Union. McLaurin chastised Davis as a radical, distant from the lives of black New Yorkers who, according to McLaurin, "want no part of Communism, no segregation in any form, but do want complete integration in all patterns of American life."[68] Within days, the Davis campaign publicly requested that McLaurin end his campaign "in the interest of unity and to guarantee the election of a Negro to the City Council this year."[69] From the perspective of the Davis campaign, McLaurin's candidacy threatened to end black, as well as Davis's, representation in the council.

Although McLaurin failed in his candidacy, the Liberal Party joined the tenuous minority coalition against Tammany Hall with victories in the 1945 council elections. The new party succeeded in electing two council members, giving it equal numbers with the Communist Party and the American Labor Party, falling just one member short of the Republican total. Publicly, the Liberal Party highlighted its two council victories as evidence that the party had created a platform from which it could challenge the Democratic and Republican parties in municipal and state politics. Privately, state party chair John L. Childs described the results of the 1945 municipal elections as "very disappointing."[70] According to Childs, the party exited the election season "with a diminished prestige and with a substantial financial deficit," having "received a much smaller vote than had been anticipated in view of the results in 1944."[71] In his statement before the party's state executive committee, Childs concluded that after "twenty months of hard and devoted work" to create the party," the Liberal Party stood "at the most, not much stronger than when [it began]."[72] Childs framed his remarks around a series of recommendations he deemed essential to strengthening the party into an entity that could survive the maelstrom that enveloped the "labor-liberal" cause in the aftermath of World War II. He emphasized that there could be "no compromise" on the exclusion of Communists from the Liberal Party, but he also argued that the party must expand its base to become something other than a tool to be manipulated by the Republican and Democratic parties. Though the party continued to function for several decades, the problems outlined by Childs in December 1945 characterized the central dilemmas it faced throughout its tenure in New York City and state politics.[73]

While the Liberal Party criticized Davis and his fellow council member Peter Cacchione for bringing Communist representation to the city legislature, the party strongly favored the retention of proportional representation, the electoral system by which these Communists had won election to the council. The Liberal Party's leadership viewed the survival of PR as absolutely essential to their quest to become a viable political organization in New York City and state. In an August 1945 position paper, the LP lauded the system as

a tool that "has strengthened the voice of the average citizen in his government and has made for more effective popular and democratic control."[74]
While praising proportional representation for "raising the caliber of city legislators," the Liberal Party warned that further work was needed for the
system to remain and for its full benefits to be experienced:

> The party is also of the belief that the friends of proportional represen-
> tation must conduct a far more vigorous educational campaign than in
> the past regarding the workings and values of the [PR] system, and
> must at the earliest possible moment consider constructive plans for
> improving the mechanics of the system's operation and for extending it
> to the election of other city and state officials.[75]

This warning revealed dissatisfaction with reformers' previous attempts at
embedding the system within the city's political structure, but it also suggested a degree of optimism, similar to that expressed by allies, in the possibility of expanding proportional representation beyond the five boroughs.

The 1945 proportional representation elections found a significant increase in overall voter turnout throughout the city and, despite the red-baiting
that followed the victories of Cacchione and Davis in 1943, stronger support
for the Communist Party as well. Greater participation in the 1945 elections
caused the council to expand from 17 seats to 23. Ostensibly, the Democratic
Party found success in the elections, retaining its majority power while
increasing its share of seats in Brooklyn, the Bronx, and Queens. However,
Tammany again suffered the ignominy of not controlling the vote in
Manhattan, as Isaacs, Davis, and American Labor Party member Eugene Connolly joined only two Democrats representing the borough. The most striking
aspect of the 1945 tally, though, rested in the high vote totals earned by non-
Democratic candidates, particularly those on the Left. Communists Cacchione and Davis easily won reelection. Cacchione reached the 75,000-vote
threshold for automatic victory, as did Isaacs (Republican) and Quill (ALP),
and Davis received the second-highest vote in Manhattan. This concentration
of votes continued the trend seen in the 1943 results, with minority coalition
members garnering some of the highest vote tallies in several boroughs.
Rather than weakening following the end of the Second World War, public
support for the Communist council members rose dramatically in November
1945. Unless the electoral laws were changed, the inclusion of radical anti-
Democratic Party voices in the council seemed a reasonable expectation for
the foreseeable future.

City Council Election Results, 1945
(by borough)

Member	Party	Votes Received
BROOKLYN		
Members elected: 8		
Peter V. Cacchione	C	75,000
Joseph T. Sharkey	D	75,000
Anthony J. DiGiovanna	D	72,718
Walter R. Hart	D	69,929
Genevieve B. Earle	R/CNP	64,678
Louis P. Goldberg	L	64,201
Edward Vogel	D	58,614
William M. McCarthy	D	53,152
MANHATTAN		
Members elected: 5		
Stanley M. Isaacs	R	75,000
Benjamin J. Davis Jr.	C	63,498
William A. Carroll	D	61,486
Eugene P. Connolly	ALP	54,208
S. Samuel DiFalco	D	46,892
THE BRONX		
Members elected: 5		
Michael J. Quill	ALP	75,000
Charles E. Keegan	D	67,673
Edward A. Cunningham	D	66,538
Bertha Schwartz	D	43,977
Ira J. Palestin	L	39,052
QUEENS		
Members elected: 4		
James A. Phillips	D	75,000
Hugh Quinn	D	75,000

| Alfred J. Phillips | R | 51,969 |
| L. Gary Clemente | D | 50,364 |

RICHMOND
Members elected: 1

| Frederick Schick | D | 27,272 |

Abbreviations: ALP = American Labor Party; C = Communist; CNP = Citizens Non-Partisan; D = Democratic; L = Liberal; R = Republican.

Source: Annual Report of the Board of Elections in the City of New York for the Year 1945, 29.

The 1945 council results proved unacceptable to most of the local news media. As was the case following the 1943 elections, anti-PR newspapers responded to the 1945 tally by attacking the system; however, the press raised the rhetorical stakes of PR's impact significantly. Similar to the arguments of Simon Sterne and other reformers in the late nineteenth century, their rationale increasingly claimed that the public did not have the mental faculties necessary to properly govern itself. Faced with the great number of votes allotted to Cacchione and Davis, and to a lesser extent the ALP victors Quill and Connolly, press depictions of proportional representation turned explicitly anti-democratic. The *Daily News* ran the headline: "PR Flops, as Usual . . . A Burlesque of Democracy."[76] The editorial bemoaned the reelection of Davis and Cacchione as evidence that the public was too ignorant to utilize PR, as "the majority of voters, as a group, are unorganized, good-natured, and dimly informed as to the merits and politics of each of the multitude of candidates for the Council."[77] According to the *Daily News*, the reelection of two Communists to the council could only be explained by voter ignorance and the surreptitious machinations of the Communist Party.

The paper's broader critique of the local electorate represented a distinct shift from the generally anti-Tammany tone of coverage that had prevailed since the Seabury investigations of the early 1930s. In the years leading up to charter reform in 1936, the city's press portrayed voters as uniformly underrepresented, locked out of positions of power by Tammany's monopoly of political power. With the introduction of proportional representation, and even after New York's first PR election, many of the city's highest-circulation dailies concluded that the system ushered in a new era when voters would actually have the power to elect a representative legislature. At the time, certain critics in the Democratic and Republican parties wondered aloud whether the voters should actually possess such authority. With Cacchione's victory in 1941, the major dailies became increasingly critical of the public's electoral decisions. Also, critics began to redirect criticism of the public's choices to a new argument that PR had actually produced an unrepresentative council—proportional representation had, in effect, become the new Tammany, a system that through confusion and delay controlled its own monopoly of power in city government.

In its front-page coverage of the final PR tally, the *New York Times* explicitly challenged PR's aptness for electing a truly representative council. The *Times* chastised the system for producing "many invalid ballots due to improper marking. It also duplicated the 'bullet' voting [casting ballots for first choices only] of two years ago for Communist candidates, and there was a repetition of the casting of second-choice votes along racial lines, regardless of party designation."[78] Though voters were not required to denote second- or third-choice selections on the PR ballot, opponents frequently asserted that anyone who participated in single-choice voting sought to unfairly manipulate the electoral process.

As demonstrated in this coverage following the 1945 elections, the press expressed palpable fear of popular rule. This sentiment reversed the perspectives of the PR debate from the nineteenth century, when good-government advocates contended that reform required proportional representation to make up for the lack of informed voting on the part of the masses. Elite reformers had argued that the masses backed the political machines of New York City because they were too ignorant to vote effectively; now anti-PR advocates concluded that the election of two Communists confirmed their argument that the majority of voters could not effectively govern themselves. The implications were clear—PR must be eliminated as it threatened to destroy the democratic process in New York City. Voters, according to this narrative, could not decide for themselves who should lead them; moreover, even if they could, PR would push their wishes in a radical direction that would bring the city to the brink of its own demise.

Ironically, given the criticism mounted against PR in New York, the reform community viewed the current political context as amenable to spreading the system throughout the world. Despite the emotional and physical devastation wrought by the Second World War, as well as the strengthening of anti-Communist sentiment against PR in New York City, good-government advocates saw possibilities for global electoral reform that could occur in the war's aftermath. The growing tide of red-baiting offered by Republicans and Democrats against PR did not deter the system's supporters. As leftists benefited from PR in the 1943 and 1945 council elections, the system's more moderate supporters continued their efforts to broaden PR's use. George Hallett, who had long advocated proportional representation at all levels of government throughout the world, argued that the Second World War provided electoral reformers a unique opportunity to entrench the system as part of postwar reconstruction. Hallett petitioned Acting Secretary of State Adolf Berle to aid in these efforts and asserted that Charles Poletti, then implementing US reconstruction policies in Italy, desired to "elect by PR an Italian constituent assembly to draw up a constitution for a democratic Italy and to govern the country . . . until the new constitution is adopted."[79] Poletti had briefly served as Governor of New York State in 1942, following his tenure as lieutenant governor under Herbert Lehman, and had advocated a statewide expansion of PR during the 1938 Constitutional Convention. In 1943, Secretary of War Henry Stimson appointed Poletti to help direct US reconstruction efforts in Italy. Berle, who would soon lead the Liberal Party, had worked for years in New York City government as well as in President Roosevelt's inner circle of advisers, the so-called Brains Trust. Berle retained positions of authority within the Roosevelt and Truman administrations through the end of World War II, serving as assistant secretary of state from 1938 to 1944, before working as US ambassador to Brazil in 1945–1946.[80] As chamberlain of the City of New York in the early 1930s, Berle advocated municipal reform and went so far as recommending that his own position be abolished as a way to make local government more efficient. In 1936, he campaigned for charter reform and proportional representation, endorsing these policies as essential to ending Tammany corruption.

As assistant secretary of state in 1943, though, Berle denied Hallett's request, concluding that, at the national level, "democracy functions best where there is an effective two-party system. PR certainly is not a means to that end."[81] Berle's perception of whether PR enhanced democracy seemed to depend on his political objectives at any given time. Upon his return to city government in the mid 1940s, Berle again found merits in PR when he campaigned to retain the system as a leader of the Liberal Party, especially since his party's prospects depended upon diversity in local representation. However, in the position of assistant secretary of state, Berle characterized PR as a hindrance to democracy because it enabled such a multiplicity of parties to be represented.

The war's impact on the PR movement, both locally and globally, revealed itself in the changing characterizations of the goals expressed by PR advocates in New York City and London. Hallett volunteered to join John H. Humphreys, director of the Proportional Representation Society in London, in crafting PR provisions for areas under Allied control in the war's closing months. Whereas much of Hallett's correspondence with Humphreys during the 1930s focused on campaigns for PR in various American cities, the war brought greater depth to both reformers' rhetoric. The electoral debate in New York City often incorporated arguments that PR was critical to ensuring local security; meanwhile, security was a very real concern for the PRS in London as it literally faced the daily threat of being bombed. In a letter to Hallett, Humphreys declared, "Our chief work for proportional representation is a contribution to the building of a new world that will give more truthful expression to the principles of democracy."[82] He requested that Hallett take over the campaign for PR globally while the London society persevered during the war.

When Allies grew optimistic of an impending victory, advocates on both sides of the Atlantic argued that proportional representation could ensure stability and prevent future conflicts. Edmund Harvey, a member of Britain's Parliament, exalted New York City's experience with PR as evidence for the system's incorporation in British elections. Harvey went so far as to proclaim reform victorious in New York City, asserting that "in America it is this very system which has been used successfully to destroy the corrupt influence of Tammany Hall. The effect in New York has been the purifying of municipal life and the breaking of the terrible power of Tammany."[83] Like the reformers of New York City, Harvey linked municipal reform with global concerns:

> Think of the divisions that will happen in some of the countries that are being liberated or are about to be liberated from Nazi tyranny, of the need for national unity and co-operation, and how that might be helped forward by a just system of Proportional Representation. If we are willing to go forward with such a reform, we shall not only secure a better basis for our own progress in the future, but be able to hand on all those advantages of the civilisation that is past and go forward to build securely the foundations for a nobler civilisation for our children in the days to come.[84]

Echoing PRS President Humphreys in London, as well as Seabury, Hallett, and other PR advocates in New York City, Harvey positioned PR as essential to securing a peaceful global system based upon representative self-government. As expressed by Humphreys, "We are looking forward anxiously to the restoration of democratic government in Europe.... I have a very strong feeling that the liberated countries which have PR in their laws—Belgium, Holland, Denmark, Norway—will adjust themselves more easily to postwar conditions than those countries which do not use a proportional system."[85] In other words, PR offered a critical means of creating a peaceful postwar order based upon a fully representative vision of democracy.

George Hallett perceived the war's conclusion as providing an opportunity for expanding proportional representation as part of global reconstruction efforts. He argued that the proposed United Nations could serve as the perfect mechanism to implement PR worldwide. He petitioned Dana Converse Backus, a former member of the Citizens Union's Executive Committee, who served on the International Secretariat working to structure the United Nations in San Francisco in spring 1945. Hallett proposed a "world parliament," with direct election of representatives by popular vote using the Hare system of PR. Hallett based his proposal upon the example of proportional representation as used in New York City and recalled its use in other countries, as well as its being presented by Norway as the best means of electing delegates to the League of Nations in 1926. Hallett's entreaty didn't get very far, as Backus replied that the US delegates already had "their hands full with existing proposals."[86]

Having faced repeal referenda in 1938 and 1940, the system's supporters in New York City feared another campaign for the system's abolition during the war. Hallett expressed concern as to the prospects of defending PR in this context, without Franklin Roosevelt's name on the ballot as a candidate for reelection, as had been the case in 1936 and 1940. In private correspondence with Samuel Seabury in November 1942, Hallett warned, "The war conditions and a possibility of a very light vote present us with special problems and I have a feeling that we should begin early to make plans to cope with them."[87] Earlier in the year, Hallett emphasized the necessity of buttressing Republican support for PR, declaring to Thomas J. Curran, president of the National Maritime Union, "I have no idea whether the Democrats mean to press their attack on PR this fall, but it seems to me it would be little short of a calamity to take away the representation of large minorities in the country's largest city at a time when democracy is fighting for its life. The responsibility for turning the scales one way or the other in this vital matter may rest in the hands of the Republican party organization."[88] In such terms, Hallett continued the argument that he had utilized in the 1940 campaign that PR served as a bulwark for democracy amid a world war pitting fascism against democracy.

When repeal campaigns did not materialize in the years after Pearl Harbor, Hallett wrote to Humphreys in July 1944, "There are no signs yet of the expected attack on PR here in New York."[89] Hallett suspected that PR's opponents had learned from their defeats in 1936 and 1940 and sought to avoid presenting voters with a PR referendum during the next presidential election in 1944. Hallett's suspicions proved prescient. During the war, a group of PR's most powerful critics developed a strategy to prevent raising the repeal issue on another ballot featuring President Roosevelt. From 1942 to 1946, they avoided the public repeal campaigns that had failed in 1938 and 1940, instead building a rhetorical context within which PR became linked to the successes of Communists. The torrent of criticism directed toward Cacchione and Davis, in particular, relentlessly questioned the legitimacy of the electoral system by which they were victorious. This strategy kept PR and the possibility of repeal in the public mind; it forged a perception that the system threatened democracy at home while New Yorkers fought to secure it abroad. Biding their time until the first off-year election cycle following the war, in 1947, repeal advocates prepared to wage what they hoped would be their final campaign against proportional representation.

6 THE DEMOCRATIC-REPUBLICAN ALLIANCE AND THE REPEAL OF PROPORTIONAL REPRESENTATION

In the midst of Allied victories in World War II in 1945, the national Democratic Party found itself in troubling circumstances. The death of President Franklin Roosevelt in April, shortly after the beginning of his fourth term, presented the party with the problem of recasting itself. This challenge was further compounded by Harry S. Truman's status as a relatively unknown Missouri politician, with little national exposure prior to his selection as Roosevelt's running mate at the 1944 Democratic National Convention. In New York City, Roosevelt's death combined with Mayor La Guardia's decision to avoid another reelection campaign to create a sense of tenuous opportunity for various politicians and party organizations long at odds with Fusion. In August 1944, Attorney General Francis Biddle had reported to Roosevelt that the "ALP hold the balance of power in New York State," a reflection on the American Labor Party's ability to garner pro-Roosevelt support from both major parties, but particularly the Democratic Party and Tammany Hall.[1] However, the president's death, and the leftward move of the ALP, created an opening for Republicans.

The nation's most powerful Democrats privately expressed grave concerns as to the ability of the party to win in the November elections. On June 8, Eleanor Roosevelt wrote Bronx Democratic

Party chair Ed Flynn about her lunch meeting that day with President
Truman:

> [Truman] is very much worried by the Democratic situation in
> New York City and frankly, I am worried about it too. . . . I hardly
> think that the ticket, even with Mr. [William] O'Dwyer to head it,
> can stand up against the Republican ticket. . . . I feel that every Dem-
> ocratic defeat helps [Thomas] Dewey in the State. . . . [E]ven the best
> of Democratic organizations will not win unless we have the com-
> pletely unattached liberals and many of the liberal Republicans with
> us. . . . In addition, we definitely have to hold the colored vote and
> show that the gestures made by Mr. Dewey were not honest-to-
> goodness interests [sic]. . . . Mr. Dewey is capable of playing a clever
> political game and we will not only have to be good politicians but
> really make our party honest, standing for the things which most of
> us as individuals know are right.[2]

Eleanor Roosevelt's comments reveal her continued role in Democratic
Party affairs following her husband's death. They also suggest how the party's leadership defined key voting populations during a period of tremendous upheaval at the close of the Second World War. For Roosevelt, and
perhaps Truman and Flynn, the Democratic Party faced the challenge of
connecting with voters who no longer identified the party with liberalism.
The Republican and Liberal parties provided outlets for liberals disaffected with Tammany Hall. Primarily via his New Deal programs, Franklin
Roosevelt had begun to attract African Americans to the Democratic
Party in significant numbers. Yet, as Eleanor Roosevelt feared, such Democratic gains brought by Franklin could prove temporary if the party did
not continue to develop policies that resonated on a more fundamental
level with voters.

These objectives—to establish Truman as a leader in his own right, to
maintain popular support for the Democratic Party following Franklin
Roosevelt's death, and to provide a party agenda for the postwar/post–New
Deal era—found their unifying theme in the Cold War. Truman and the
Democratic Party utilized the emerging global competition between the for-
merly allied United States and Soviet Union to reinvigorate itself following
World War II. In federal policy, this context produced such objectives as
national health insurance and desegregation of the armed services, as well as

the Marshall Plan and the Truman Doctrine. Anti-Communism provided the glue for these disparate policies.

In New York City, a renewed postwar campaign against proportional representation gave Democrats a chance to remove their Communist and non-Communist opposition in one fell swoop. The party had already built a substantial anti-Communist foundation within which to situate its postwar local and national agendas, constructed through consistent attacks upon both proportional representation and a variety of council members elected by use of the system.

During the war, those opposed to proportional representation feared repeating what they viewed as the failures of previous campaigns—in particular, the timing of repeal efforts to coincide with President Roosevelt's reelection victories in 1936 and 1940 and the congressional elections of 1938. Shortly before the 1943 council results, Parks Commissioner Robert Moses summarized the war's impact on a potential repeal drive in a patronizing letter to Genevieve Earle, "No doubt this is the devil of a time to quarrel with a device which in the past has at least kept one of my favorite characters in public life."[3] Following the 1943 council elections, Moses criticized the election of two Communists via PR, yet stopped short of taking the lead in an immediate repeal effort.[4] Moses wrote to Ferdinand Hermens shortly after the election, "The recent results of PR in New York City have shocked even some of its strongest adherents. I am sure that there will be a real drive for repeal."[5] Yet, Moses and other repeal organizers concluded that Roosevelt's reelection campaign in 1944 posed too great a danger to repeal prospects for another referendum campaign. Instead, they supported another attempt at abolishing PR through the New York State legislature.[6] As was the case in 1938, home rule advocates ultimately overpowered PR's opponents in Albany and the 1944 repeal effort failed.

This context helps explain why Moses concluded in 1944 that the next repeal campaign should take place in 1947 rather than 1944, 1945, or 1946. Bronx Chamber of Commerce president and repeal advocate George F. Mand relayed Moses's sentiments in an attempt to convince Democratic Party boss Ed Flynn that a campaign should be waged against PR in the near future.[7] Mand again raised the issue in June 1945, less than two weeks after Eleanor Roosevelt's correspondence with Flynn about her meeting with President Truman regarding the state of the Democratic Party: "Doubtless you will recall plan the for repeal of 'PR' as worked out with Bob Moses. We put it aside to await the municipal election but I am wondering if the present picture is opportune. Perhaps the Republicans would go along, but not their friends the fusion and liberal groups in my opinion."[8] Mand's letter suggested that he, Moses, and Flynn, the principal architects of earlier repeal campaigns, had already constructed a strategy for repeal; only the timing of implementation needed to be finalized. Mand emphasized the desire to avoid a national election season and wondered whether 1945 provided the best opportunity to attack PR. Moreover, Mand saw the Republican Party, though not reform and liberal elements within it, as potential allies. Flynn responded tersely that he didn't feel "the time is ripe now" for a campaign and cautioned patience for when "conditions change."[9]

With the mayoral campaign on the docket in 1945 and congressional elections slated for 1946, 1947 appeared to be the next opportune time to campaign against PR. No major municipal officers would be elected in that year, including council members, whose terms were extended to four years in 1945. Thus, repeal advocates calculated that their best moment to attack PR would be during the election cycle with the lowest possible voter turnout.

As historian Charles Garrett concludes in his study of reform during the La Guardia years, the repeal struggle of 1947 "was one of the most dramatic and emotionally charged campaigns ever waged in New York City over an issue that did not involve the election of candidates to public office."[10] Advocates for and against repeal produced more than "7,000,000 pamphlets and cards, several thousand street and shop meetings, door-to-door canvassing, [the] use of sound trucks and radio speeches."[11] Advocates of proportional representation faced reduced press support following the election of Communists Cacchione and Davis and escalating international tensions between the Soviet Union and the United States after World War II. The Keep PR Committee included many of the good-government groups that had long advocated electoral reform, including the Citizens Union, City Club, Women's City Club, and the New York City chapter of the League of Women Voters. Added to this core was a collection of organizations representing progressive causes, including the Americans for Democratic Action, the American Veterans Committee, the Commerce and Industry Association, the Federation of Jewish Women's Organizations, the Greater New York Congress of Industrial Organizations (CIO) Political Action Committee, the International Ladies Garment Workers Union, International Workers Orders, the National Association for the Advancement of Colored People (NAACP), the National Council of Jewish Women, the National Lawyers Guild, Progressive Citizens of America, and United Neighborhood Houses.[12] From diverse perspectives and objectives, this coalition saw proportional representation as essential to the cause of progressive legislation at the municipal level. These groups included many long-time proponents of PR as well as several prominent liberal, progressive, and radical organizations that joined the debate once repeal became a distinct possibility.

Pro-PR literature attempted to refocus the debate on the corruption that a revived Tammany Hall would cause if repeal succeeded. The CIO distributed 2 million leaflets entitled "Want Grafters in City Hall?" The cover drawing featured a familiar depiction of a bloated party boss, eager to bilk more public funds for private gain, with money overflowing from his pockets.[13] The Citizens Union charged that the repeal movement was based on the goal of removing political enemies from office rather than a desire to preserve democracy against Communism. In an article entitled "The Red Herring," the group argued, "This year their (anti-PR forces) purpose is the same as in 1940—to do away with any effective minority in the Council [and] restore the near-monopoly they used to enjoy in the Board of Aldermen. . . . But of course that isn't what they say!"[14]

In other pro-PR campaign material, supporters emphasized the authority that proportional representation gave to voters and the threat repeal posed to their political power. The Harlem Citizens Committee in Support of Proportional Representation argued that repeal would prevent independent black candidates from seeking office:

> If PR is repealed, there will not be a single Negro in the Council. True, a Negro clubhouse leader may have the privilege of "naming" the councilmanic candidate, but that leaves the people out in the cold. The Negro clubhouse man would have to name a candidate acceptable to the bosses downtown. And since we have experienced the "racial considerations" of Tammany, we know that the chances of a Negro being named from any of the senatorial districts are small indeed.[15]

Both Communist council members contended that anti-PR leaders were attempting to blind voters to the realities repeal would accomplish. Peter Cacchione declared, "The opponents of PR do not have a leg to stand on. Every one of their arguments is misleading, is a distortion or an outright falsehood. They are resorting to bare-faced lying in order to hoodwink the people."[16] In his autobiography handwritten while in prison for sedition in the 1950s, Ben Davis charged, "[Redbaiters] turn this 'menace' on and off as suits their evil purposes, like manipulating a water-spigot."[17] Echoing earlier critiques against anti-Communism, Davis described opponents to the PR coalition as threats to domestic liberty, "Anti-Communism has its source in the ruling circles of Big Business and domestic fascism within our country."[18] Davis linked classist, racist, and ideological threats to freedom as underpinning the assault on PR, a connection supported by other pro-PR organizations.

The National Association for the Advancement of Colored People endorsed the campaign to keep proportional representation and did so specifically because, according to a press release, "PR is the best method through which minority groups can be assured of satisfactory leadership and representation in the City Council."[19] The Keep PR Committee of Jamaica, Queens, echoed the NAACP and charged that the Democratic-Republican coalition sought to monopolize local government power at the expense of electing a legislature "truly representative of the different political parties and national groups."[20] The Queens-based organization received support from several prominent black community members, including Captain Hugh Mulzac and author Shirley Graham, who served as honorary chairs, and honorary sponsor singer/actress Lena Horne. Both of the quotations cited here show a clear connection between PR and minority representation that galvanized African American activists in 1947.

In an invitation to Councilman Stanley Isaacs, Sarah Margaret Freid of the Progressive Citizens of America linked the fate of PR with that of progressive social programs in the city. Freid insisted:

> We would, however, very much appreciate your interlocking the question of PR with the other [policy] topics of the evening to the extent that proper representation for us in the city is most important if we wish to secure for ourselves a positive city program for a controlled cost of living, extensive unsubsidized public housing, [and] a continuation of the five cent subway fare.[21]

Peter Cacchione also addressed the immediate policy implications of repeal. He urged voters, "Do not fall into the trap set by reactionaries of making Proportional Representation an issue of communism. The issue is corrupt machine boss rule vs. people's rule. . . . The issue is high cost of living vs. rolling back prices, rationing and price control. The issue is maintaining rent control."[22] With the diverse representation resulting from PR, progressive programs had a chance of passage. Without it, such legislation appeared practically impossible.

Pro-PR activists developed counterarguments that explicitly recognized the dominant tropes of the repeal campaign. Genevieve Earle repeated the claim that anti-PR forces intended "to panic voters into killing PR on the 'Red Issue.'"[23] In preparing its speakers for public discussions about proportional representation, the League of Women Voters outlined several arguments usually levied against the system: PR "emphasizes racial discrimination," "[is] responsible for the elevation of Hitler to power," "fails to provide for genuine local representation," "creates minorities and minority bloc voting, thwarting the will of [the] majority," "[is] un-American," and leads to "invalid votes," "[presents] too many candidates," "[allows] extremists," and "[leads to] Communists [controlling] City Hall." The document incorporated point-by-point suggestions for counterarguments, which framed PR as beneficial to democracy through its ability to properly represent minority opinions.[24] This campaign material also demonstrates the recognition of the primary rhetorical devices marshaled in the PR campaign. Rather than being blindsided by the use of anti-Communist assertions about PR, its defendants realized the importance of such arguments to the repeal effort and attempted to specifically address them.

The League of Women Voters and other women's organizations that had been longtime supporters of proportional representation saw an increase in the arguments stressing the repeal referendum's merits. After a contentious session, the New York City Federation of Women's Clubs, which represented 50,000 members in nearly 200 clubs citywide, passed a resolution supporting repeal.[25] The Women's City Club of New York, a proponent of PR since its founding, renewed its endorsement of the system but only after overcoming objections from one of its directors. The group agreed to lend its name and membership list to the Keep PR Committee and helped fund the campaign to retain PR.[26]

Many prominent members of the Keep PR Committee contributed to the anti-Communist rhetorical atmosphere that threatened proportional representation. Herbert Pell, a former New York congressman, minister to Portugal and Hungary, and New York State chairman of the Democratic Party, eagerly provided his services to help save the system. Yet one of Pell's central contributions to the campaign, his article "PR and the Communists," emphasized the heightened threat that Communists would pose if proportional representation was repealed.

Pell began his piece by accepting opponents' central contention on its face, "that [repeal] will automatically exclude the Communist Party from direct representation in the City Council."[27] Ignoring the ill effects that repeal would likely cause for other leftist and moderate groups in New York City politics, Pell focused on justifying PR as bringing about the lesser of

two evils. According to Pell, PR actually prevented Communists from gaining greater authority in the legislature. In fact, Pell asserted, the system's removal would dramatically increase Communist influence and power in city
politics. How could PR limit Communist authority? Pell posited that
Communists possessed about one-tenth of the total city vote, a generous
assumption at best, and the "great advantage of Proportionate Representation [as he labeled the system] is that it reduces these pressure groups to
their proper proportion." Thus, "organized minorities cannot club an assembly elected by Proportionate Representation, as they can the leader of a
District or of a State desirous of building up a majority made of a good
many discordant elements."[28] Without PR, Pell argued, Communists and
their ilk would run amok and seek to be the deciding influence in city- and
statewide elections, in effect exhibiting political power far beyond their
actual numbers:

> Obviously, [the Communist bloc of votes] would not be decisive in
> every vote at every primary, but the percentage working regularly
> would inevitably and fairly rapidly pick off one office after another.
> A District leadership here and there, an occasional alderman, some-
> times a member of the Assembly, possibly a minor judge or two, would
> be Communistic or sympathetic to the Communist cause. These
> men, influential in the selection of candidates, would work for the
> nomination of others who agreed with them and eventually, although
> a small minority, they could control important positions and legisla-
> tive boards which they never could have done under Proportionate
> Representation.[29]

Pell's version of what later became known as the domino theory perceived
Communist strength without PR expanding like a snowball rolling down a
mountain, toppling opponents with increasing ease as its momentum increased. He closed the article by describing the certainty with which these
events would occur and pondering, for dramatic effect, why they had not
begun already "in many parts of the country."[30]

Repeating the core of repeal advocates' arguments against PR, Pell exaggerated the Communist presence in New York City and perpetuated stereo-
types of Communist Party members abusing the democratic system to gain
power on a citywide, then statewide, then, perhaps, nationwide basis. Framing proportional representation as a protection against Communist rule only

further strengthened the belief that Communists indeed endangered the future of democratic government.

As in previous years, PR's supporters, particularly among good-government groups unaffiliated with the Communist Party, attempted to distance themselves from that party, perhaps in response to assertions such as from the *Daily News* that labeled all PR advocates Communists. In this tenuous environment, anti-Communist PR advocates struggled to maintain stable footing from which to defend PR against anti-Communist charges. Nathan Straus, president of the WMCA radio station and former administrator of the US Housing Authority, criticized Communists and repeal advocates in his call for PR's retention in late October. Straus declared, "I have no use for Communists or others who would substitute any totalitarian regime for our American democratic system. That is why I think the propaganda of the forces for repeal of PR [is] so dangerous. They are playing directly into the hands of the Communists by bedeviling and confusing the issue."[31] Echoing Straus's advocacy of PR as a patriotic duty, Father John A. Ryan linked the system to the most American of traditions, "PR is as American as the hot dog, as native as baseball on a Sunday afternoon."[32]

The Liberal Party approached proportional representation from a more complicated standpoint. While the organization benefited greatly from PR, the system also helped gain representation for the party's foes in the American Labor and Communist parties. Ben Davidson, the Liberal Party's executive director, and much of the party's founding board, including labor leaders Alex Rose and David Dubinsky, had opposed the American Labor Party's leftist leadership since they bolted from the ALP over its decision to ally with the Communist Party in the late 1930s. Balancing disdain for Communism with arguments in favor of PR proved a delicate task for the newly formed party. Adolf Berle, chair of the Liberal Party from 1947 until 1955, argued for PR's retention as a symbol of democracy necessary to confront the spread of Soviet-sponsored totalitarianism. Berle, a former New York City chamberlain and State Department official in the Roosevelt and Truman administrations, positioned the Liberal Party as New Yorkers' only option for liberal anti-Communist policies.

In several public addresses, Berle declared his opposition to congressional Taft-Hartley labor restrictions, offered support for public housing and civil rights, and characterized PR as the centerpiece to ensuring liberal representation in local government. He asserted that New Yorkers must see themselves as part of a growing global war against Communism, since "an imperialist foe of the United States would make New York a principal target of its propaganda and bombs."[33] In Berle's vision of the Cold War, the battlefront pitted New Yorkers, democracy, and proportional representation against Communism, the Soviet Union, and the municipal party machines. In one address concerning voter registration, Berle implicated Soviet spies in local politics to a bemused audience:

> The Russian agents . . . know that New York wants liberal, forward-thinking measures; and equally wants American, not Russian, leadership. This time, your registration and your vote is your protection. You are on the firing line. . . . In this year of world crisis, Republican and Democratic bosses . . . want, Lord forgive us, to kill [PR] and give us back—the old Board of Aldermen. You are laughing, but that is exactly what is happening. . . . Vote against repeal of [PR].[34]

Berle championed PR's role in thwarting "reactionary" Republicans and corrupt "Democratic bosses," and he charged that the American Labor Party, perhaps PR's greatest beneficiary, must also be defeated. In fact, Berle later recalled, the ALP represented the domestic arm of a global Communist threat that had positioned New York in its crosshairs:

> The clear plan [of the ALP's local registration drive] was to rig up political machinery capable of paralyzing American political action during the year in which Soviet imperialism is to make its big push. The chief effort is being made in New York because New York is probably the key state in next year's national elections.
>
> After all, Hitler and the Nazis tried exactly the same thing in 1940, with Communist help.
>
> This misbegotten plan, sparked by anti-American foreign powers, could only succeed if a large number of New Yorkers, who are liberal in their thinking, joined the American Labor Party. In blunt fact, the American Labor Party was to be the instrument by which Russian foreign policy was to be served.[35]

Weaving together New Yorkers' recent memory of the war against Germany with a vision of an impending confrontation with the Soviet Union, Berle depicted liberal anti-Communist representation in municipal government as crucial to national security. In so doing, he straddled a very fine line between supporting PR, opposing Communism, and at the same time opposing the former foes of good government, namely, Tammany Hall and its borough allies. While Berle castigated Communist sympathizers, he simultaneously justified the charge repeatedly made against leftists by Democrats and Republicans.

Following this rationale, Berle and the Liberal Party based their campaign against repeal on the assertion that Democrats and Republicans were willing to bargain with Communists and therefore not to be trusted in such perilous times:

> Our Republican and Democratic friends . . . urge you to vote to repeal [PR] because they say it favors Communism. A cynical piece of business; for while they are saying it, the Republicans angled for and got the support of the pro-Communist [American Labor Party] for their candidate for Judge just as the local Democratic machine traded for and got that support last year. . . . Vote to keep PR on its merits—and forget the agonized cries of some political bosses who trade with pro-Communist votes with their left hand while urging the repeal of PR with the other. It just happens that the Liberal Party is the No. 1 enemy of the Communists; and that we alone in the city have steadily declined to trade for Communist votes.[36]

Lest anyone oppose PR because the system aided the election of Communist and American Party candidates, Ben Davidson, the Liberal Party's executive director, suggested that Communists must be countered openly to avoid an underground movement. He argued that the best way to defeat Communism was "through education, more effective organization, [and] presenting positive and constructive solutions to problems," and he characterized the charge that PR must be eschewed to prevent Communist electoral victories as "throwing out the baby with the dirty water."[37] More directly, Davidson echoed Berle's argument that Democrats utilized anti-Communism as a smokescreen to end PR and ensure a Democratic "monopoly in the City Council."[38]

The Liberal Party carefully fused the struggle for PR with its municipal, national, and global reform agenda in the postwar era. Davidson urged party spokespeople to link PR with such issues as "prices, rents, housing, the Taft-Hartley Anti-Labor Act, Palestine, [and the] Marshall Plan."[39] The Liberal Party argued for global interventionism against the Soviet Union, with PR situated as the critical ingredient to ensuring that these policies could be secured in the postwar era.

While the supporters of proportional representation attempted to maintain a coalition that didn't fissure along the seam of Communism, the system's detractors marshaled their resources behind a campaign that centered on

Communism as its primary theme. Backed by veterans groups and the city's financial elite, the Democratic and Republican party establishments spearheaded the movement to repeal PR. This coalition included the American Legion, Catholic War Veterans, Disabled American War Veterans, Veterans of Foreign Wars, the New York Board of Trade, several borough Chambers of Commerce, the Veterans Democratic League, and, of course, New York City Parks commissioner Robert Moses.[40] In the months leading to the autumn of 1947, Moses wrote nationally syndicated newspaper articles concluding that the Soviet Union attempted to infiltrate the West German zones of occupation through PR-type elections. He also made personal, pro-repeal recommendations to Roy W. Howard, the chairman of Scripps-Howard Newspapers, which controlled the *New York World-Telegram*, and to editors at the *New York Times*. Howard sympathized with Moses's criticism of PR and privately declared his support for repeal while anticipating a difficult campaign, "Getting rid of this damned thing, which we helped inflict upon New York, is going to be a rough, tough, shin-kicking job."[41]

The leader of Tammany Hall, Frank J. Sampson, campaigned against PR in terms that suggested a particular vision of urban democracy. He declared, "Proportional representation is un-American, undemocratic, cumbersome, expensive and foreign to our American two-party system, and should be abolished."[42] According to Sampson, PR's undemocratic nature was best seen in its weakening of majority rule. He lamented the inability to remove opposition legislators, either through elections or via some other means, "Under PR, there is no way to take them out of office. Under PR, the majority cannot vote against a minority candidate. The only way to get them out of office is to repeal PR."[43] PR's evil, from Sampson's perspective, rested precisely in its encouragement of minority representation in government. In his more extravagant rhetorical flourishes, though, Sampson derided PR as a facilitator of subversion and a threat to domestic security. He positioned repeal as a solution to both municipal problems and national dangers: "It is time to reassert our patriotism and Americanism—time to deal a death blow to subversive elements by voting Yes on the PR [repeal] proposition."[44]

As outlandish as they may have appeared to PR's supporters, such attacks clearly affected with them, spurring an immediate response. Stanley Isaacs and Simon Gerson commiserated over the repeal arguments that named PR a catalyst for the expansion of global fascism and Communism. Despite the controversy caused by Gerson's affiliation with the Communist Party that began in 1939, the pair continued their correspondence for years. For

Tammany Hall to call PR an "importation from the Kremlin" and a "Stalin Frankenstein" caught Gerson's attention to such an extent that he "took occasion to disabuse Brother [Frank] Sampson of that notion" in a speech Gerson sent to Isaacs. Isaacs responded the following day with details from a debate he engaged in with Brooklyn Democratic council member Walter Hart in which Hart "asserted quite soberly that if it had not been for PR World War II would never have started. He regards it as responsible for the success of both Hitler and Mussolini; worse than that, what he said was accepted and allowed by most of those present at the Board of Trade meeting."[45] While Gerson suggested that Isaacs might have been "amused" by such seemingly outlandish characterizations of PR, the promptness of their responses to each other and to the sources of such rhetoric underscored the perceived power carried by these attacks. As Isaacs noted, the charge that PR singularly caused the Second World War resonated with the influential Board of Trade. In the context of mounting anti-Communist rhetoric in the postwar era, the argument that the Soviet Union now supported PR as part of its global expansionist mission apparently didn't stretch the bounds of credulity.

Republican Party leaders recognized that repeal would likely diminish minority party power and that anti-Communism was the primary tool with which to advocate PR's destruction. In an uncommon demonstration of public unity, Republicans joined Democrats in the repeal campaign. Democratic and Republican leaders had often colluded privately to ensure the perpetuation of their status as the city's two most powerful parties at the expense of any other political organization. But, they rarely demonstrated their affinity for mutual control over municipal affairs so explicitly as during the repeal campaign. In one radio debate in late October, Adolf Berle and Stanley Isaacs found themselves debating the merits of PR with Daniel J. Riesner, secretary of the New York County Republican Committee, and Abraham Kaplan, chair of the Speakers Bureau of the New York County Democratic Committee. According to the *Times*, the pair of Manhattan major-party leaders "argued that PR had given the Communist party representation in the City Council that was entirely out of proportion with its voting strength."[46] While the pro-PR coalition suffered from trying to maintain cohesion while its members debated the merits of Communism, repeal advocates did not have similar concerns. Republicans eagerly joined with Democrats to castigate Communists, PR, and anyone who could be connected with either interest.

The city's major newspapers ran increasingly grave articles about proportional representation in the days leading to the election, usually providing more column inches to the system's critics than to its supporters. Pro-repeal editorials appeared alongside daily news stories that implicitly connected local Communist activity, abetted by PR, to an international Red Menace emerging in 1947. In addition to not challenging Tammany leader Sampson's assertions about PR as a Soviet front, the *Times* ran Sampson's comments under the explosive headline, "Sampson Likens PR to Hitler Law."[47] In another article, the *Times* prominently positioned Sampson's declaration that voters should "throw out this Stalin Frankenstein on Election Day."[48] Encouraging New Yorkers to "throw PR to the wolves," the *Daily News*, the city's highest circulation daily, answered its rhetorically phrased headline "Who Are PR's Best Friends" with a sweeping attack against the system's advocates. According to the *News*, "The loudest and most fervent of them are the local Communists and their fellow travelers. It is easy to see why. . . . The Communists have benefitted heavily, having two avowed members on the Council and a couple of followers of the party line. Naturally, the Reds hate to have this setup threatened with repeal."[49] The paper painted PR's supporters in broad, red-baiting strokes, providing readers with the assumption that virtually any proponent of PR was either a Communist or sympathizer. Amid the burgeoning Cold War, the piece defined repeal as a potent method of confronting Communist expansion, with the removal of the Communist legislators soon to follow, "If PR goes, the Communists . . . will in all probability follow it into innocuous desuetude as soon as the voters can give them the boot."[50]

The *World-Telegram*, directed by Roy Howard, who was personally lobbied by Moses to criticize PR, published the editorial, "PR Godsend to Commies," which concluded:

> Commies and their fellow travelers are bent on capturing key city offices, whether appointive or elective. On the appointive side they do it with Communist-run unions. On the elective side they use any available device to outwit other parties and voters at the polls. In this city and for this purpose PR has proved a veritable godsend to the Communist party. There could be few stronger reasons for voting PR's end.[51]

Further underscoring the ties between repeal advocates and the press, the Citizen's Committee to Repeal Proportional Representation, already privately advised by Moses, clipped and redistributed the editorial as part of its campaign efforts. The editorial also signified the *World-Telegram*'s reversal of its support for charter reform and PR in 1936 and 1940.[52] Following the retention of PR in 1940, the *World-Telegram* had even proclaimed, "The successful defense of PR stands as one high mark for unbossed, progressive, fair-minded democracy."[53] The election of Communists in 1941, 1943, and 1945, the rightward turn of the paper under Howard, and the lobbying of Moses and other repeal advocates resulted in the publication's dramatic attacks against the system in 1947.

Of the city's highest circulation dailies, only the *Herald-Tribune* and the *Post* endorsed PR in 1947. The *Herald-Tribune's* continuing support of PR concerned repeal advocates, as referenced in correspondence between Hermens and Mand from September 1947.[54] In several editorials published during the summer and fall of 1947, the *Post* argued that while PR certainly was not perfect, the Democratic and Republican political machines had yet to prove to voters that they were prepared to lead without corruption. In effect, the *Post* concluded that no better system had yet been devised to implement good government—and the last thing voters needed was a return to Tammany domination. By November 3, 1947, though, the day before voters would decide PR's fate, the paper offered more criticism than praise for the system: "Although we heartily dislike many aspects of Proportional Representation, we think the best way to deal with this proposal that it should be abolished, for reasons already discussed, is to Vote NO."[55] For readers unfamiliar with the publication's previous editorials from May and August, this verdict may have confused more than it clarified. Rather than offering a cogent justification for why New Yorkers should protect PR, the paper's editors opted to avoid the polarized debate and play both sides of the issue.[56]

Joining the *Herald-Tribune* and the *Post* in backing PR was a cohort of smaller publications, including the liberal afternoon paper *PM*, the Communist Party-affiliated *Daily Worker*, the daily *Bronx Home News*, and two weekly black-operated journals: the *Amsterdam News* and the *People's Voice*. Every other major daily and weekly paper throughout the five boroughs opposed PR. According to political scientists Belle Zeller and Hugh A. Bone, pro-repeal papers garnered a daily circulation of 4,845,955, nearly six times the print run of the daily pro-PR press, which produced 813,325 copies. Sunday publication margins proved even greater, with 8,347,520 pro-repeal papers printed—more than eight times the pro-PR total of 979,850.[57]

This imbalance reflected a shift among the local journals, most of which had endorsed PR in connection with charter reform in 1936. The *Times*, the most prominent publication to reverse editorial course, officially proclaimed its opposition to PR in April 1947, after publishing several critical pieces following the elections of Cacchione and Davis in previous years. This announcement

Newspaper Circulation Figures (1940, unless noted)

New York Daily News	1,880,370 (D); 3,383,435 (S)
New York Times	474,277 (D); 788,997 (S)
New York World-Telegram	412,586 (D)
New York Herald-Tribune	346,783 (D); 527,759 (S)
New York Sun	295,807 (D)
New York Post	235,625 (D)
Bronx Home News	106,198 (D) (1941)
Brooklyn Daily Eagle	93,244 (D) (1941)
Jamaica Long Island Press	92,967 (D) (1942)
Daily Worker	48,601 (D) (1941)
Long Island City Star and Journal	40,867 (D)
Brooklyn Citizen	30,426 (D) (1943)
Staten Island Advance	27,943 (D)

Selected Papers Organized by Editorial Stance toward PR in 1947 (1940 Circulation Figures, unless noted)

Pro

New York Herald-Tribune	346,783 (D); 527,759 (S)
New York Post	235,625 (D)
Bronx Home News	106,198 (D) (1941)
Daily Worker	48,601 (D) (1941)

Anti

New York Daily News	1,880,370 (D); 3,383,435 (S)
New York Times	474,277 (D); 788,997 (S)
New York World-Telegram	412,586 (D)
New York Sun	295,807 (D)
Brooklyn Daily Eagle	93,244 (D) (1941)
Jamaica Long Island Press	92,967 (D) (1942)
Long Island City Star and Journal	40,867 (D)
Brooklyn Citizen	30,426 (D) (1943)
Staten Island Advance	27,943 (D)

Abbreviations: D = Daily; S = Sunday.

Source: Circulation figures recorded by Luce Press Clippings in PRL Papers clippings files, CURB.

likely buttressed PR opponents still deciding whether to support another repeal campaign. On four consecutive days during the week before the election, the *Times* ran column-length editorials arguing for the system's abolition.[58] The paper declared that PR had misrepresented the will of the people and produced a series of councils that accomplished little and embarrassed the city. The *Times* quoted earlier criticisms by Mayor La Guardia, who actually supported the system, and longtime PR opponent Hermens that focused on Tammany's ability to elect council majorities despite La Guardia's victories. The paper's references to La Guardia, who had argued that PR should have elected councils more sympathetic to his political objectives, provided a liberal critique of PR to suit its more conservative charge that PR had "fostered splinter parties, seating Communists and other radicals who could not, by normal majority and district voting methods, have hoped to become members and giving them an official sounding-board for views shared by only a meager fraction in the electorate."[59] In effect, the *Times* chastised proportional representation, and by fiat the public, for electing both Tammany hacks and "un-American" leftists. Apparently ignoring the continued strength of the Democratic machine at the district level, the *Times* assured readers that council elections by state senate districts posed "little danger of a return to the old Aldermanic abuses."[60]

The nexus of support for PR's demise among politicians and the press was best demonstrated by the attention paid to Robert Moses's official entry into the repeal campaign shortly before Election Day. After planning with repeal leaders to wait until after Labor Day to officially join the Citizens Committee to Repeal PR, Moses announced his alliance with the organization in a press conference on October 27, 1947—less than two weeks before Election Day.[61] Having planned for this "atomic bomb of the campaign," as Mand foresaw it, to garner widespread media attention, repeal advocates welcomed two lengthy stories in the *Times* concerning Moses's announcement.[62] Entitled "Moses Opposes PR as Communist Arm" and "Moses Asserts PR Harms Democracy," the stories presented the commissioner's views as omniscient and concluded that the case for PR was dead.[63] As the *Times's* editorial attitude became more critical of PR, Moses's rhetoric proved increasingly dire as well, not only concerning the consequences posed by its continued use, but also in his descriptions of the system's supporters. In a letter published by the *Times* days before the referendum, Moses mockingly cast himself and his allies as angelic figures pitted in a holy war against fanatics:

If we have finally concluded that PR is an abject failure and a great political menace, not even Judge [Samuel] Seabury has warrant to relegate us to the forces of darkness and evil and to endow us with horns, cloven hooves and a faint aroma of burning sulfur. Gabriel, as well as the electorate, may decide that we are on the side of the angels. . . . [Why must we endure this] grotesque procedure with its fantastic list of candidates, splinter party endorsements, confusion, wasted votes, irresponsibility, multiplication of racial and religious issues, and its invitation to Communists and radicals to bore from within and bedevil our government? And if we are going the whole hog, why not go along with the Communists and elect all our State officials and legislators and our Congressmen by PR and give the revolutionaries and pressure groups a real field day?[64]

Though he reiterated many long-standing arguments against PR, Moses's letter reflected the broader shift in repeal advocates' rhetoric—to attack all of PR's supporters as essentially being pro-Communist.

The combination of red-baiting and the off-year election cycle overwhelmed support for PR. Just over a decade after passing proportional representation by a margin of 923,186 to 555,217 in 1936, New York City voters abolished the system in a nearly inverse tally of 935,222 to 586,170 in 1947.[65] Beyond the impressive reversal in voter attitudes toward PR between 1936 and 1947, the striking feature of these results rested in the similar total number of votes. It may seem surprising that in the 1947 off-year referendum, 42,989 more votes were counted than for the count held on the day of

1947 Referendum to Abolish PR

	Yes	No
Manhattan	193,054	135,964
Bronx	178,988	150,215
Kings	298,111	217,842
Queens	237,832	75,806
Richmond	27,237	6,343
Citywide	935,222	586,170

"Proposition No. 4: Shall the proposed amendment to the New York City Charter abolishing the proportional representation system of electing Councilmen and providing for the election of one Councilman from each Senate District, be approved?"

Source: Annual Report of the Board of Elections in the City of New York for the Year 1947, 60–61.

President Roosevelt's reelection in 1936. The city's growth over the past decade meant more eligible voters in the five boroughs, and the more than 1.5 million New Yorkers who participated in this referendum underscored the concern they placed upon determining their preferred mechanism of democracy.

The results were not ambiguous, as every borough voted against PR. Queens registered the largest margin against the system, while the Bronx held the smallest. The boroughs with Communist representation, Brooklyn and Manhattan, fell in the middle. Every borough but Richmond (Staten Island) had voted for PR in 1940, but every one, including Richmond, voted against the system in 1947. Brooklyn, which gained representation with reapportionment under the charter reform provisions of 1936, voted more than 62 percent in favor of PR in 1936; in 1947, nearly 62 percent of Brooklynites voted against the system.

The 1947 election revealed the degree to which anti-Communist propaganda influenced local political discourse. However, despite repeal's wide majority, more than half a million New Yorkers endorsed an electoral system explicitly connected to Communism at the dawn of the Cold War. This support for PR occurred after the immersion of anti-Communist propaganda into New York City's political culture—propaganda that implicated growing tensions between the United States and the Soviet Union into municipal policy debates, as well as red-baiting tactics apparent in attacks against PR, Communist council members, and Communism itself begun years earlier.

For the *New York Times*, repeal meant that the "cause of sound government [had] been served."[66] The paper admonished Democrats specifically that they "have had sufficient warning in recent years to know that an aroused electorate, vigorously led, can turn them out of office in elections held on the old-fashioned majority basis, and keep them out for years, for failing to behave in the people's interest. That interest requires able men and women, and not party hacks, as nominees for the Council."[67]

Supporters of proportional representation were not so optimistic. For good-government reformers, repeal meant a staggering reversal of fortune that compelled their reassessment of PR's place within their platform for structural change in municipal governance. For the Communist, Liberal, and American Labor parties, repeal likely meant the end of their elected representation in the governing council of the largest city in the United States. Less than one week after repeal, council member Peter Cacchione—the first Communist Party representative elected via proportional representation in the

United States—suffered a heart attack and died. Federal authorities soon incarcerated council member Ben Davis, declaring that he sought to forcibly overthrow the US government, thereby violating the Smith Act. Council member Genevieve Earle decided that she likely would not win reelection without PR and refused to run for a sixth term in 1949. George Hallett, PR's most vociferous champion, vowed to battle on to bring the system back by the end of the decade. Seemingly alone in his conception of the political possibilities of the late 1940s, Hallett professed to be undeterred by the political landscape wrought by repeal and the evolving Cold War.

Echoing arguments presented by Davis and other leftists, council member Stanley Isaacs objected to the postwar encroachment on civil liberties by the Truman administration and strengthened by numerous state and local restrictions. As presented in the summer of 1947, Isaacs's argument fused the federal anti-Communist campaigns with the Democratic-Republican movement to repeal PR and end progressive representation in New York City government: "The recent proposals menace these rights. We dare not allow bitter hostility to Communist activities be made an excuse for proper protection. We cannot allow those who like to restrict the liberties and hamper the freedom of individual citizens to take advantage of the anti-Communist sentiment to gain their ends."[68] His assertion spoke to the importance of the representation enabled by PR and hindered by its repeal. In the months following repeal, Isaacs gauged the state of political culture in New York City and the country as a whole. What he described encapsulated the dramatic alteration of the city's, and the nation's, political culture with the onset of the Cold War: "I believe that we are suffering from hysteria in this country, based on fear of communist aggression; and plans are being made which are the product of such fear and such hysteria rather than the product of far-sighted wisdom. These are troubled days."[69] The Cold War narrowed the political spectrum, and, according to Isaacs, fostered the creation of policies destined to perpetuate conflict and fear. In New York City, the basic elements of this anti-Communist discourse had been developing for years, with their fruition in PR's repeal.

EPILOGUE

REPEAL'S AFTERMATH

The vision of democracy championed by the advocates of proportional representation in New York City ended with the first city council elections after PR was repealed in 1949, when the council returned to Democratic Party dominance. Democrats received 52.6 percent of votes cast in 1949, yet controlled 24 of 25 seats in the legislature. In the next election in 1953, Democrats won 23 of 25 seats with 51.7 percent of the vote.[1] By 1950, Stanley Isaacs stood as the only member of the PR-elected minority coalition to remain in the council. Genevieve Earle's departure at the end of 1949 marked the end of an unprecedented period for women in New York City politics. Prior to Earle, only one woman had won election to the council (then the board of aldermen) in the city's history. In the PR elections held between 1937 and 1945, four women were elected to the council. As the political culture shifted with more women serving, two more women were appointed, without elections, as temporary replacements for council members who departed in the middle of their terms. Following repeal, the council did not seat a new female member until 1965. Although opponents of PR had vilified Communists and radicals as the system's chief beneficiaries, repeal doomed the representative participation of people based on gender, ideology, and party affiliation for decades.

The Democratic Party used the Cold War as rationale to justify anti-populist and anti-democratic measures in the aftermath of repeal. No more acute example of this occurred than the decision by a Democratic judge to prevent a Communist Party representative from replacing Peter Cacchione on the city council. Cacchione's death shocked the political Left in New York City, which immediately called for his replacement with another member of the Communist Party. The city charter stipulated, "Any vacancy which may occur among the councilmen shall be filled by election, by a majority of all the councilmen, of a person who must be of the same political party as the councilman whose place has become vacant if such a councilman was elected as the candidate of a political party and who must be a resident of the borough from which such councilman was elected."[2] The council even passed Ben Davis's resolution on February 19, 1948, permitting Communist Simon Gerson to assume Cacchione's position on the council.[3] Gerson's initial success occurred despite the fact that his profile in city politics stemmed largely from his controversial appointment as an assistant to Stanley Isaacs during Isaacs's tenure as Manhattan borough president.[4] However, certain anti-Communists viewed Cacchione's death as creating an opportunity to remove one of the legislature's two Communists without needing to wait until the first post-PR elections in 1949. Jarring Cacchione's allies and, albeit briefly, his enemies, advocates sued to prevent the seating of another Communist in Cacchione's place. Instead, they contended that the Communist Party did not constitute a legal political party as defined by New York State election law. Justice James McNally, who ran for his judgeship on the Democratic ticket in 1945, wrote the opinion that prevented Gerson's placement on the council.

The debate over Gerson's appointment continued for months, with the courts ruling in July 1948 that the Communist Party did not in fact have standing as a legal party and therefore the council was not required to seat Cacchione's replacement with another Communist. The court cited an earlier challenge to the party's status in New York State, which held that, in order to be considered a legal political party, its gubernatorial candidate needed to have received at least 50,000 votes in the most recent election.[5] Vito Marcantonio, the American Labor Party's only representative in the US Congress, argued that the minimum-vote requirement only pertained to state election law and that the New York City Charter permitted a variety of designations not recognized at the state level.[6] Ignoring such legal arguments, and the decision of Brooklynites to elect a Communist in 1945, the city's judicial establishment effectively removed any legal rights previously held by the Communist Party.

The victory of repeal and the refusal to replace Cacchione with a fellow Communist signified an emerging Red Scare in New York City that sought to narrow democratic representation, remove leftists and their allies from government, and frame dissenters as threats to domestic security. In 1948, Mayor William O'Dwyer removed 150 city employees who were members of the American Labor Party.[7] Similar purges occurred in increasing numbers in cities across the country, as well as in the federal government, in the late 1940s and early 1950s. According to historian Richard Fried, the rhetoric forged to kill proportional representation in New York City inspired similar attacks in other urban areas. In the largest municipality with PR still in use, Cincinnati, repeal advocates argued that the system threatened to bring Communist legislators to that city.[8]

In perhaps the most powerful symbol of the Red Scare's impact on the practice of municipal democracy, Communist Ben Davis ran for reelection to the council in 1949 from a jail cell. Davis retained an endorsement from the American Labor Party, in spite of his conviction on charges that he violated the Smith Act through his criticism of US policy. After he was declared an enemy of the state and imprisoned in 1949, Davis used the campaign to frame President Truman's Cold War policies as a threat to black empowerment and the reconstruction of urban America. Davis underscored the connection between politics, economy, and culture in demanding that the city council address civil rights legislation. In addition to campaigning for greater employment opportunities for black veterans, Davis advocated the integration of major league baseball.[9] Following the violence that had erupted in Harlem in 1943 and his own ongoing battle to defend himself against government-sponsored political discrimination, Davis concluded that the American political and economic elite approved of killing black Americans in war and enjoying their labor as entertainment, while refusing to provide equal powers under the law.

In privately discussing the Davis campaign and the movement of Harlemites to support local Republican and American Labor Party candidates, Eleanor Roosevelt argued that the Democratic Party must increase the number of African American appointees as a means of quelling black defections to other parties. She asserted to Democratic Party leader Ed Flynn, "The Negroes are very conscious of this type of recognition and while I do think it is easier to get a following for people like Ben Davis among the poorer Negroes, the educated ones would be able to keep the balance if they could show real gains in recognition for their race."[10] Roosevelt made clear her perception that concerns over race- and class-centered policies contributed to Davis's support, but she also implied that wooing wealthy, "educated" black New Yorkers with patronage appointments would provide a better path to increasing Democratic popularity than shifting the party's policies to the left.

The American Labor Party, which endorsed Davis for the council and US House member Vito Marcantonio for mayor, fused local and national policies in its 1949 municipal campaign materials. The leftist organization framed the battle over municipal politics in the postwar era as an essential component of the Cold War, with the voting public deciding whether their neighborhoods, their city, and their nation would endorse local and federal anti-Communists' agenda. The ALP explicitly cast New Yorkers as potential victims of Cold War militarism, with arms expenditures favored over local investment in health care, education, housing, and infrastructure. The vision of urban peril, and potential prosperity, crafted by Davis and the ALP distilled PR's essential contribution to democracy in New York City and American politics—the system enabled the election of public officials who advocated policies that contrasted, often radically, with those of their counterparts in government. In the aftermath of PR's repeal, diversity in representation declined significantly.[11]

The political discourse that contributed to the downfall of proportional representation in New York City produced far-reaching consequences for the municipal reform movement in the United States. Many of the organizations that had championed PR for generations rescinded their endorsements. The Women's City Club of New York, which experienced tumultuous internal debates over whether to endorse the system in 1947, opted against supporting a campaign for its return in 1948.[12] Perhaps the best example of this shift occurred within the National Municipal League (NML). The NML had merged with the Proportional Representation League in 1932, bringing PR's central advocates, including George Hallett, into its organizational structure. For decades, the NML had published hundreds of articles supporting PR's use in the United States and globally. However, by 1954, the organization had begun to seriously question whether to continue its official endorsement of the system.[13] Objections to PR raised by NML members focused more on the public relations liability of supporting a system linked with Communism than on any particular flaw within PR itself.

In 1962, the NML revised its Model State Constitution and proposed replacing PR with elections by single-member districts (similar to the format installed after repeal in New York City). For Hallett, the move represented a troubling departure from the NML's decades-long endorsement of PR as an electoral model, as well as a final assault on the system's use in the United States. He wrote the group's executive committee and council, arguing that hope still existed for PR to be adopted in New York City and state, with opportunities also available in other cities and states throughout the country. Asserting that "although we have currently only Cambridge (Mass.) in the PR fold in American cities, the record of [PR's] experience here is a long and honorable one," Hallett struggled to resurrect the NML's support for the system. Fifteen years after repeal in New York City, Hallett immersed himself once more in arguments about the causes of PR's abolition. He explained, "We would almost surely still have PR in New York City if it were not for the large vote that was temporarily polled here for Communist candidates during World War II, when the United States and Russia were friendly allies, resulting in the strictly proportionate election of two Communists in a total of 23." Again seeking to distance the mechanics of PR from the results it enabled, Hallett emphasized that "no Communists would any longer have the slightest chance of confusing the issue by getting elected here" and, without much evidence, assured the NML that there was a "good chance" that proportional representation would be renewed in New York City in the near future. Hallett concluded his letter with an explication of his understanding of democracy represented by PR, "A model system of representation should assure not only majority rule but a sizeable opposition in the legislative body, at least whenever there is any sizeable opposition in the electorate. This can only be assured in general by some plan for representing minorities." For Hallett, democracy required minority representation and influence in government. Without such representation, according to Hallett, democracy could not exist. The impact of one of the nation's most influential government-reform organizations dropping its endorsement of his life's work was likely not lost on Hallett either. He ended his letter by castigating the "evils of the single-member district plan" and admonishing the NML that its disapproval of PR "will forfeit any just claim to moral or intellectual leadership in the basic field of representation."[14]

Between 1937 and 1949, proportional representation brought dramatic change to the meaning and practice of democracy in America's largest city. Coalitions for and against the system considered it crucial to a fundamentally new conception of urban politics that challenged the boundaries of who could be elected, what interests could be represented, and ultimately what policies could be addressed by municipal government. Its repeal reversed an expansion of democratic rights and protected Democratic and Republican Party hegemony in New York City politics. Activists on both sides struggled to define democracy by fusing local, national, and international political discourses. PR held the fate of a progressive vision of government that thrived during the Depression and World War II—an ideal Democrats and Republicans defeated by fueling an urban Cold War defined by fear of diverse representation in government.

NOTES

INTRODUCTION

1. Democracity papers in folder 7, "Theme Building—Democracity," box 137, New York World's Fair 1939 and 1940 Incorporated Records (NYWF), Manuscripts and Archives Division, New York Public Library, New York City (NYPL).
2. Robert D. Kohn, "Building the World of Tomorrow," RadioTalk interview broadcast on W2XR, 6:30 P.M., December 17, 1936, folder "Henry Dreyfuss #2," box 135, NYWF, NYPL.
3. Sources differ as to how precisely to punctuate the abbreviation for proportional representation. All references in this manuscript have been changed to "PR" for consistency. The name of New York City's legislative branch of government has changed over the centuries. Prior to being known as the board of aldermen in the early twentieth century, the city legislature was called the municipal assembly, and before that the common council, a term dating to the colonial era. In 1937, the city council replaced the board of aldermen and has remained in existence ever since. For the purposes of this manuscript, the term "council" refers strictly to the post–1936 city council and not to the earlier common council. See Edward O'Donnell, "Common Council," *The Encyclopedia of New York City*, ed. Kenneth T. Jackson (New Haven: Yale University Press, 1995), 267–268.
4. See Chapter 43, "Election of Councilmen by Proportional Representation," in Laurence A. Tanzer, *The New York City Charter: Adopted November 3, 1936 . . .* (New York: Clark Boardman, 1937), 462–472.
5. In his examination of the evolution of public perceptions of totalitarianism from the end of World War I to the Cold War, Benjamin L. Alpers argues that a changing, but consistently influential, vision of totalitarianism in American public culture emerged with the rise of Fascist and Communist dictatorships in Europe during the 1920s. Alpers's perspective informs my understanding of the ways in which anti-fascist rhetoric evolved into and ultimately strengthened anti-Communist attacks on PR in the late 1930s and 1940s. See Alpers, *Dictators, Democracy, and American Public Culture:*

Envisioning the Totalitarian Enemy, 1920s–1950s (Chapel Hill: University of North Carolina Press, 2003). For a complementary, trans-Atlantic interpretation, see Marc J. Selverstone, *Constructing the Monolith: The United States, Great Britain, and International Communism, 1945–1950* (Cambridge, MA: Harvard University Press, 2009).

6. Thomas Kessner, *Fiorello H. La Guardia and the Making of Modern New York* (New York: McGraw-Hill, 1989), 427; and Charles V. Hamilton, *Adam Clayton Powell, Jr.: The Political Biography of an American Dilemma* (New York: Atheneum, 1991), 115.

7. Glenn Fowler, "Dr. George Hallett of Citizens Union," *New York Times*, July 4, 1985, A12.

8. For a comprehensive history of voting rights struggles in the United States, see Alexander Keyssar, *The Right to Vote: The Contested History of Democracy in the United States* (New York: Basic Books, 2000).

9. In these three instances, US officials endorsed the list model of proportional voting, which allotted parliamentary seats according to the percentage of votes cast for lists of political parties and individual candidates. In preparation for the 2005 elections in Iraq, female candidates were spaced to appear on every third ballot line, as organizers hoped to ensure that women would win at least twenty-five percent of the parliamentary seats. See Kenneth Katzman, *Congressional Research Service Report: RS21968; Iraq: Elections, Government, and Constitution* (Washington, DC: Library of Congress, 2006).

CHAPTER 1

1. Mary P. Ryan, *Civic Wars: Democracy and Public Life in the American City during the Nineteenth Century* (Berkeley: University of California Press, 1997), 11 and 121.

2. Leslie M. Alexander, *African or American? Black Identity and Political Activism in New York City, 1784–1861* (Urbana: University of Illinois Press, 2008), n23, 182. Also see George E. Walker, *The Afro-American in New York City, 1827–1860* (New York: Garland, 1993), 112–115.

3. Alexander, *African or American?* 103. According to Alexander, black political activism emerged in the 1840s specifically to gain male suffrage.

4. *Debates and Proceedings in the New York State Convention for the Revision of the Constitution* (Albany: n.p., 1846), 785; quoted in Alexander, 118. Alexander argues that white politicians feared the impact of black political participation at the municipal and state levels.

5. David Quigley, *Second Founding: New York City, Reconstruction, and the Making of American Democracy* (New York: Hill and Wang, 2004), 55.

6. Richard L. McCormick, *From Realignment to Reform: Political Change in New York State, 1893–1910* (Ithaca: Cornell University Press, 1981), 52–55. State constitutional conventions proved critical to later attempts at restructuring city government to either limit or expand voting rights as part of so-called reform campaigns.

7. Edwin G. Burrows and Mike Wallace, *Gotham: A History of New York City to 1898* (New York: Oxford University Press, 1999), 823.

8. Ibid., 823–825; Sean Wilentz, *Chants Democratic: New York City and the Rise of the American Working Class, 1788–1850* (New York: Oxford University Press, 1984), 315–316; and Frank Vos, "Tammany Hall," *The Encyclopedia of New York City*, 1149–1151.

9. Burrows and Wallace, *Gotham*, 825.

10. Burrows and Wallace, *Gotham*, 830.

11. Burrows and Wallace, *Gotham*, 835–836.

12. Burrows and Wallace, *Gotham*, 837.

13. Burrows and Wallace, *Gotham*, 890–895. Also see Lisa Keller, *Triumph of Order: Democracy and Public Space in New York and London* (New York: Columbia University Press, 2009), 159–164.

14. Quigley, *Second Founding*, 9.

15. The Union League Club organized in 1863 to direct city support to the Union war effort. See Quigley, *Second Founding*, 33.

16. Quigley, *Second Founding*, 39.

17. Burrows and Wallace, *Gotham*, 917–922.

18. See Burrows and Wallace, *Gotham*, 927; and Ryan, *Civic Wars*, 271–282.

19. Burrows and Wallace, *Gotham*, 928.

20. Burrows and Wallace, *Gotham*, 1002.

21. Ryan, *Civic Wars*, 274.

22. Burrows and Wallace, *Gotham*, 1008–1010.

23. Ryan, *Civic Wars*, 271–282.

24. See Ryan, *Civic Wars*, 274 and 279; and Charles Garrett, *The La Guardia Years: Machine and Reform Politics in New York City* (New Brunswick, NJ: Rutgers University Press, 1961), 21–22.

25. Samuel Tilden, letter dated February 28, 1868, box 6, Samuel J. Tilden Papers, NYPL; quoted in Quigley, *Second Founding*, 63. Tilden didn't officially break with Tammany until the investigations of 1871. See Quigley, *Second Founding*, 99–100.

26. See Chapter 9 in Clarence Gilbert Hoag and George Hervey Hallett Jr., *Proportional Representation* (New York: Macmillan, 1926).

27. Hoag and Hallett, *Proportional Representation*.

28. Howard Lee McBain, "Proportional Representation in American Cities," *Political Science Quarterly* 37 (June 1922): 284.

29. McBain, "Proportional Representation," 284–285. As discussed in later chapters, the charge that limited voting prevented anti-candidate voting became a key argument against PR in the twentieth century.

30. Hoag and Hallett, *Proportional Representation*, 45.

31. David C. Hammack, *Power and Society: Greater New York at the Turn of the Century* (New York: Columbia University Press, 1987), 110.

32. Burrows and Wallace, *Gotham*, 1027. Also see Kevin P. Murphy, *Political Manhood: Red Bloods, Mollycoddles, and the Politics of Progressive Era Reform* (New York: Columbia University Press, 2008), 45–47.

33. Garrett, *The La Guardia Years*, 21–22.

34. *Report of the Commission to Devise a Plan for the Government of Cities in the State of New York* (Tilden Commission) (New York: Evening Post Steam Presses, 1877), 28.

35. Hammack, *Power and Society*, 201.

36. "The Week," *Nation* 25 (25 October 1877): 248.

37. "The Government of Cities," *New York Times*, 6 June 1877, 2.

38. "The Government of Cities."

39. "The Government of Cities."

40. "The Government of Cities."

41. Quigley, *Second Founding*, 160.

42. Quoted in Quigley, *Second Founding*, n35, 208–209.

43. Garrett, *The La Guardia Years*, 21–22.

44. Burrows and Wallace, *Gotham*, 1184.

45. Garrett, *The La Guardia Years*, 23–24.

46. Garrett, *The La Guardia Years*, 25.

47. McCormick, *From Realignment to Reform*, 52–55.

48. McCormick, *From Realignment to Reform*, 53–54.

49. McCormick, *From Realignment to Reform*, 117.

50. Richmond is the county name for the borough of Staten Island. Although Staten Island has become the more popular designation, historical sources frequently referred to this entity as Richmond, and both titles are used in this book.

51. Simon Sterne, "Some Reflections on Recent Change and Proposed Reforms in Legislation Affecting the City of New York," address before the Constitution Club, January 21, 1885, Simon Sterne Papers, NYPL; in Hammack, *Power and Society*, 201.

52. Hammack, *Power and Society*, 200.

53. Simon Sterne, president, and M. N. Fortney, secretary and treasurer, Proportional Representation Society of New York, "An Address to Members of the Constitutional Convention of the State of New York," 1894, Manuscripts and Special Collections, New York State Library, Albany, New York (NYSL).

54. Sterne and Fortney, "An Address."

55. Hammack, *Power and Society*, 200–201.

56. Hammack, *Power and Society*, 205.

57. Hammack, *Power and Society*, 216–223.

58. Hammack, *Power and Society*, 228.

59. Hammack, *Power and Society*, 206.

60. See Records of the New York State Constitutional Convention, 1915, New York State Archives, Albany, New York (NYSA).

61. Wagner testimony, June 30, 1915, *State of New York, In Convention, Record No. 39*, 543 and 537, box 2, Records of the New York State Constitutional Convention, 1915, NYSA.

62. See Garrett, *The La Guardia Years*, 85, and the Records of the New York State Constitutional Convention, 1915, NYSA.

63. Lawrence H. Chamberlain, *Loyalty and Legislative Action: A Survey of Activity by the New York State Legislature, 1919–1949* (Ithaca: Cornell University Press, 1951), 48. The Socialist group included Louis Waldman, who later campaigned for, then against, PR as a member of the American Labor and Liberal parties.

64. Chamberlain, *Loyalty and Legislative Action*, 13–14.

65. Frederick Shaw, *The History of the New York Legislature* (New York: Columbia University Press, 1954), 132.

66. Garrett, *The La Guardia Years*, 26–28.

67. For a summary of proportional representation's use in the United States and internationally by the mid-1920s, see Hoag and Hallett, Chapter 10, "Proportional Representation with the Single Transferable Vote at Work," in *Proportional Representation*, 196–271. Adoption dates for American cities on 275.

68. Hoag and Hallett, *Proportional Representation*, 193.

69. Hoag and Hallett, *Proportional Representation*, 200.

70. Hoag and Hallett, *Proportional Representation*, 201–202.

71. *Wattles ex rel. Johnson v. Upjohn*, 211 Mich. 514 (1920), 179 N.W. 335; quoted in Hoag and Hallett, *Proportional Representation*, 468. Also see "Minority or Proportional Representation," *Columbia Law Review* 21:2 (February 1921): 182–186.

72. *Wattles ex rel. Johnson v. Upjohn* (1920); quoted in Hoag and Hallett, *Proportional Representation*, 472.

73. *Wattles ex rel. Johnson v. Upjohn* (1920).

74. *Wattles ex rel. Johnson v. Upjohn* (1920).

75. The *Columbia Law Review* characterized the Michigan Supreme Court's ruling as a "misuse of judicial power" that threatened the constitutional viability of the Hare system in other states. The journal warned that PR's fate "must ultimately depend upon the power of its supporters to overcome the possible prejudices of the tribunal against any new electoral plan of minority representation." See "Minority or Proportional Representation," 185–186.

76. Hoag and Hallett, *Proportional Representation*, 204–205.

77. *People ex rel. Devine v. Elkus*, 59 Cal. A396, 211 Pac. 34 (1922); quoted in Hoag and Hallett, *Proportional Representation*, 468.

78. See "Decision against Proportional Voting System Will Stand," *Sacramento Bee* (December 22, 1922), clipping in folder "California Supreme Court—Constitutionality of PR," box 7, Proportional Representation League (PRL) Papers, Rare Book and Manuscript Library, Columbia University, New York City (CURB). Also see telegram from Devlin and Devlin to Albert H. Maris, November 2, 1922, concerning the Superior Court's approval of PR, also in box 7, PRL Papers.

79. Hoag and Hallett, *Proportional Representation*, 207.
80. Robert D. Johnston, *The Radical Middle Class: Populist Democracy and the Question of Capitalism in Progressive Era Portland, Oregon* (Princeton: Princeton University Press, 2003), 141–145.
81. See folder "Ohio–Constitutionality of PR," box 55, PRL Papers, CURB.
82. In later years, the New York City Democratic Party focused its campaign against PR on the charge that the election of several representatives for a single district unconstitutionally prevented voters from deciding upon every candidate in their given district.
83. George Hallett to Irvin Engler, November 11, 1922, folder "California Supreme Court—Constitutionality of PR," box 7, PRL Papers, CURB.
84. Albert Sprague Bard to Walter T. Arndt, Secretary of the Citizens Union, December 20, 1921, folder "Correspondence, 1916–1921," box 133, series XIII, Proportional Representation Committee, 1913–1947, Albert Sprague Bard Papers, NYPL.
85. Franklin W. M. Cutcheon, "Appendix B—Opinion of Franklin W. M. Cutcheon concerning the Possibility of a System of Proportional Representation under the Existing Constitution of the State of New York," *Report of the New York Charter Commission to the Legislature with a Draft of Charter for the City of New York* (New York: M. B. Brown, 1923), 340.
86. George Hallett to Isaac Adler, January 21, 1927, folder 54-1A, "NYS Correspondence," box 54, PRL Papers, CURB. Adler was a lawyer in Rochester.
87. For correspondence between the PRS and PRL, see PRL Papers, CURB, and the PRS Papers, McDougall Trust Library, London.
88. H. G. Wells, "The PR Parliament," pamphlet published by the PRS, London (undated, 1924?), folder 22-11B, box 22, PRL Papers, CURB. This article was reprinted in the United States as "H. G. Wells Believes ...," *Detroit Times*, May 31, 1924, clipping also in box 22, PRL Papers.
89. Wells, "The PR Parliament."
90. Fritz Kauffmann to John H. Humphreys, January 11, 1925, folder "Germany Correspondence," box 25, PRL Papers, CURB. For a history of the PRS and the movement for PR in Britain, see Jenifer Hart, *Proportional Representation: Critics of the British Electoral System, 1820–1945* (New York: Oxford University Press, 1992).

CHAPTER 2

1. Herbert Mitgang, *The Man Who Rode the Tiger: The Life and Times of Judge Samuel Seabury*, 2nd ed. (New York: Fordham University Press, 1996), 165.
2. Quoted in Mitgang, *The Man Who Rode the Tiger*, 175.
3. Mitgang, *The Man Who Rode the Tiger*, 180.
4. Mitgang, *The Man Who Rode the Tiger*, 178–215.
5. Mitgang, *The Man Who Rode the Tiger*, 218–219.
6. Mitgang, *The Man Who Rode the Tiger*, 228–234.

7. Mitgang, *The Man Who Rode the Tiger*, 253.

8. Samuel Seabury, "Address of Samuel Seabury at City Charter Committee Dinner, Hotel Sinton, Cincinnati, Ohio," February 26, 1932, folder 48-2B, "NYC Printed Documents, 1920–1930," box 48, PRL Papers, CURB.

9. George Hallett to Paul Blanshard, February 18, 1932, folder 48-1, "NYC Correspondence, 1931–1939," box 48, PRL Papers, CURB.

10. In a 1935 speech, Seabury emphasized the crucial role he anticipated the public playing in the fate of charter reform and proportional representation, arguing that the reformers must better tailor their message to garner a broader audience. See "Address by Samuel Seabury before the Proportional Representation League, Baltimore, Maryland," November 25, 1935, folder 25A-5A, "PRL Meetings, 1929–1935," box 25A, PRL Papers, CURB.

11. Richard S. Childs to George Hallett, February 4, 1932, folder 48-1, "NYC Correspondence, 1931–1939," box 48, PRL Papers, CURB. Hallett agreed with Childs, a former director of the PR League, and posited, "It is, of course, true that not many New Yorkers can explain the details of PR." See George Hallett to Richard S. Childs, February 8, 1932, also in box 48, PRL Papers.

12. George Hallett to James Marshall, April 6, 1932, folder 48-1, "NYC Correspondence, 1931–1939," box 48, PRL Papers, CURB.

13. George Hallett to Franklin Delano Roosevelt, February 19, 1932, folder 54-1, "NYS Correspondence," box 54, PRL Papers, CURB. In an earlier letter to State Senator Thomas C. Desmond, Hallett wrote that Roosevelt had "indicated his cordial approval" of PR's use in New York State. See George Hallett to Thomas C. Desmond, September 12, 1931, also in box 54, PRL Papers.

14. Samuel Seabury, *In the Matter of the Investigation of the Departments of the Government of the City of New York, etc., pursuant to Joint Resolutions adopted by the Legislature of the State of New York. Final Report to Hon. Samuel H. Hofstadter, Chairman, New York (State) Legislature, Joint Committee on Affairs of the City of New York* (New York, 1932), 2–3, hereafter cited as Seabury Report.

15. Quoted in Seabury Report, 7. Roosevelt's quotation appeared in his gubernatorial message to the state legislature on December 9, 1932.

16. Seabury Report, 8.

17. Seabury Report, 9.

18. Seabury Report.

19. Seabury Report, 10.

20. Seabury Report.

21. Seabury Report, 10–12.

22. Seabury Report, 12–13.

23. "The Seabury Plan," *Nation* 136 (January 11, 1933): 32. See Chapter 1 for discussion of the *Nation's* endorsement of reform at the end of Reconstruction.

24. See "Proportional Representation," a 1933 report for the Proportional Representation League, box 25A, PRL Papers, CURB. According to records from the

1932 Annual Meeting of the PRL, the group planned campaigns for PR in cities, counties, and states throughout the country, as well as for use in national presidential elections. See "1932 Annual Meeting Correspondence," folder 25A-5A, "PRL Meetings, 1929–1935," box 25A, PRL Papers, CURB.

25. Shaw, *The History of the New York Legislature*, 54–55.
26. Charles Brecher, "Mayoralty," *The Encyclopedia of New York City*, 739.
27. Joseph McGoldrick, "Now that Election Is Over," *Nation* 137 (November 22, 1933): 591.
28. McGoldrick, "Now that Election Is Over," 592.
29. W. A. Warn, "Estimate Board May Get Power La Guardia Seeks; Mayor at Capitol Today," *New York Times*, January 10, 1934, 1.
30. Warn, "Estimate Board." This rhetoric echoed Tammany's earlier attacks against then-governor Roosevelt for his support of the Seabury hearings. By 1934, Roosevelt's local and national opposition used similar, anti-dictatorial terms to criticize his New Deal programs.
31. Garrett, *The La Guardia Years*, 221.
32. Lucille Buchanan, secretary of Municipal Affairs for the New York City League of Women Voters, "New York Charter Commission of 1934," December 1934, *Volume 3*, Records of the Charter Revision Commission, 1935–1936, Arthur W. Diamond Law Library, Columbia University, New York City (CULL).
33. Editorial, "The Latest Charter Plan," *New York Times*, August 2, 1934, 16.
34. "Smith and Seabury Quit as Foes Block Charter Reform," *New York Times*, August 3, 1934, 1.
35. Quoted in "Text of Smith's Appeal to Public in Fight to Bring About Charter Reform," *New York Times*, August 7, 1934, 8. Smith's speech was broadcast on WMCA radio.
36. W. A. Warn, "New Charter Bill Voted Unanimously at Albany; Mayor to Pick Board of 9," *New York Times*, August 16, 1934, 1.
37. Full citation is New York City Charter Revision Commission Act, Chapter 867 of Laws, 1934. Full text of the act included in *Matter of Mooney v. Cohen*, 272 NY 33, in *New York Court of Appeals, Cases and Briefs, September 28–October 23, 1936, Volume 199*, 29–34, Record Series: Cases and Briefs on Appeal, 1847–1993, NYSA.
38. Quoted in "Smith for Law to Create New Charter Body Named by Mayor or Governor," *New York Times*, August 7, 1934, 1.
39. "Seabury Demands Lehman Take Lead in Charter Fight," *New York Times*, August 9, 1934, 1.
40. Shaw, *The History of the New York Legislature*, 158.
41. New York City Charter Revision Commission Act, Chapter 867 of Laws, 1934, 31–32.
42. Shaw, *The History of the New York Legislature*, 156.
43. In fact, as a backup plan in case the proportional representation referendum failed, the eventual charter proposal contained alternate regulations for undertaking

council elections in single-representative senatorial districts rather than borough-wide tallies under PR. Repeal advocates later used this point to underscore the simplicity of removing the system.

44. "Mayor Seeks Board with Views like His," *New York Times*, August 16, 1934, 13.

45. Historian Frederick Shaw argues that Tammany saw the courts as a way to scuttle charter reform and proportional representation without openly campaigning for either. Shaw concludes that the Democratic Party underestimated both popular and judicial support for reform and PR. See Shaw, *The History of the New York Legislature*, 171.

46. Quoted in "Mayor Seeks Board with Views like His," *New York Times*, August 16, 1934, 13.

47. Quoted in "Mayor Seeks Board with Views like His."

48. "La Guardia Names New Commission to Draft Charter," *New York Times*, January 13, 1935, 1.

49. Tanzer, *The New York City Charter: Adopted November 3, 1936*, 5. See also "La Guardia Names New Commission to Draft Charter."

50. "La Guardia Names New Commission to Draft Charter."

51. Editorial, "A New Charter Commission," *New York Times*, January 14, 1935, 14.

52. "A New Charter Commission."

53. "La Guardia Names New Commission to Draft Charter," *New York Times*.

54. "Deutsch Holds Up City Charter Fund," *New York Times*, January 26, 1935, 19.

55. Kessner, *Fiorello H. La Guardia and the Making of Modern New York*, 404–405. Also see "Changes to the City Charter, 1653–1989," compiled by Edward T. O'Donnell, *The Encyclopedia of New York City*, 203–207.

56. See New York (City) Charter Revision Commission, *Records of Public Hearings and Minutes of Executive Meetings: February 18, 1935–August 14, 1936*, 4 vols., NYPL; quote in New York (City) Charter Revision Commission, *Records of Public Hearings and Minutes of Executive Meetings, Volume 1, February 18–May 17, 1935*, 1.

57. Objecting to the board of estimate's equal distribution of powers by borough regardless of population size, the US Supreme Court ultimately declared the board unconstitutional. See *Board of Estimate v. Morris*, 489 US 688 (1989).

58. W. P. Vogel Jr., "Tammany Due to Shift Attack on Proportional Representation," *New York Herald-Tribune*, March 3, 1937.

59. League of Women Voters of the City of New York (NYCLOWV), "Recommendations: From the New York City League of Women Voters to the Committee on Proportional Representation, New York City Charter Commission," July 3, 1934, *Volume 4*, Records of the Charter Revision Commission, 1935–1936, CULL.

60. New York (City) Charter Revision Commission, *Records of Public Hearings and Minutes of Executive Meetings, Volume 1, February 18–May 17, 1935*, 3. Testimony of Dorothy Straus on February 18, 1935.

61. Charter Revision Commission, *Records of Public Hearings, Volume 1*, 4. Testimony of George Hallett on February 18, 1935.

62. Price, Waldman, Guggenheimer, and Dreier testified in favor of PR on the first day of testimony, February 18, 1935. Dayton offered his support for PR on March 5, 1935, and Deutsch in May 1935. See Charter Revision Commission, *Records of Public Hearings, Volume 1.*

63. Quoted in Mitgang, *The Man Who Rode the Tiger*, 347.

64. Quoted in Mitgang, *The Man Who Rode the Tiger.*

65. "Address by Samuel Seabury before the Proportional Representation League, Baltimore, Maryland," November 25, 1935, folder 25A-5A, "PRL Meetings, 1929–1935," box 25A, PRL Papers, CURB.

66. Charter Revision Commission, *Records of Public Hearings, Volume 1*, 37. Testimony of George U. Harvey on April 15, 1935.

67. Harvey Testimony, Charter Revision Commission, *Records of Public Hearings*, 38.

68. Many of PR's Republican supporters switched to oppose the system as soon as minority-party council members outnumbered Republicans following the 1937 PR tally. Republican opposition to PR increased with every council election under the system.

69. Charter Revision Commission, *Records of Public Hearings, Volume 1*, 38.

70. Charter Revision Commission, *Records of Public Hearings, Volume 1.*

71. Charter Revision Commission, *Records of Public Hearings, Volume 1*, 39.

72. Charter Revision Commission, *Records of Public Hearings, Volume 1*, 39–42; quote on 39.

73. See James J. Lyons testimony on April 17, 1935, in Charter Revision Commission, *Records of Public Hearings, Volume 1.*

74. Charter Revision Commission, *Records of Public Hearings, Volume 1*, 11. Alfred E. Smith testimony on May 28, 1935.

75. Charter Revision Commission, *Records of Public Hearings, Volume 1*, 5. Alexander U. Mayer (incorrectly listed as "Alexander Uman" in CRC records) testimony on February 18, 1935.

76. Charter Revision Commission, *Records of Public Hearings, Volume 1*. Alexander U. Mayer testimony.

77. New York (City) Charter Revision Commission, *Records of Public Hearings and Minutes of Executive Meetings, Volume 2, May 24–September, 24, 1935*. Alexander U. Mayer testimony on July 17, 1935. Mayer also sent a letter containing his testimony to George McCaffrey—civic activist, Secretary of the Civic Conference of New York City, prominent member of the Merchants' Association of the City of New York, and proponent of PR. See Alexander U. Mayer to G. H. McCaffrey, July 17, 1935, folder "July 1935," box 3, Genevieve B. Earle Papers, CURB.

78. Charter Revision Commission, *Records of Public Hearings, Volume 2*. Mayer testified on July 17, 1935.

79. Charter Revision Commission, *Records of Public Hearings, Volume 2.*

80. George Hallett to Alfred J. Gray, September 18, 1935, PRS Papers, MTL. At the time, Gray served as the assistant secretary of the PRS, based in London.

81. Tanzer, *The New York City Charter*, 5–6.

82. Minutes of CRC executive meeting, March 31, 1936, *Volume 11*, Records of the CRC, CULL.

83. Kessner, *Fiorello H. La Guardia and the Making of Modern New York*, 214 and 405.

84. See New York (City) Charter Revision Commission, *Preliminary Report and Draft of the Proposed Charter for the City of New* York, published April 27, 1936, 11.

85. Charter Revision Commission, *Public Hearings, May 7–22, 1936*, 2. Testimony of James J. Lyons on May 14, 1936.

86. Charter Revision Commission, *Public Hearings, May 7–22, 1936*, 2–3.

87. Charter Revision Commission, *Public Hearings, May 7–22, 1936*, 3.

88. See Eric Holmberger, *The Historical Atlas of New York City: A Visual Celebration of Nearly 400 Years of New York City's History* (New York: Henry Holt, 1994), 136–137; Chris McNickle, *To Be Mayor of New York: Ethnic Politics in the City* (New York: Columbia University Press, 1993), 48–51; and Stanley Nadel, "Germans," *The Encyclopedia of New York City*, 463–464.

89. Charter Revision Commission, *Public Hearings, May 7–22, 1936*, 7.

90. Charter Revision Commission, *Public Hearings, May 7–22, 1936*, 3.

91. Charter Revision Commission, *Public Hearings, May 7–22, 1936*, 8–9.

92. Civil Service Branch, Communist Party, "FLASH! We OPPOSE The New Proposed Charter," in Vertical Files, folder "NYC Charter Revision, 1936," City Hall Library, New York City (CHL).

93. Civil Service Branch, Communist Party, "FLASH!"

94. Communist Party, "FLASH!"

95. Communist Party, "FLASH!"

96. Eugene Connolly to George Hallett, September 19, 1936, folder 47-1A, "NYC Proposed Charter, 1936," box 47, PRL Papers, CURB.

97. For further information on home rule, see Chapter 1.

98. The borough presidents served on the HRL's executive committee, which included Thomas Keogh, Samuel Levy, Albert D. Phelps, and Edward J. Mooney. John Munholland chaired the group, whose vice-chairmen included Waldman and George F. Mand, chair of the Bronx Chamber of Commerce and leader of the repeal movement in 1947. Membership list provided on Home Rule League against Proposed Charter letterhead, A. W. Barrett to Louis Waldman, October 26, 1936, folder "General Correspondence, City Charter Revision, 1936," box 1, Louis Waldman Papers, NYPL.

99. HRL letterhead, Waldman Papers, NYPL.

100. Once Communist Party representatives won election to the council in 1941, anti-PR rhetoric shifted the foreign menace eastward, to the Soviet Union.

101. Home Rule League against Proposed Charter, "Defeat a Bad Charter: Vote NO without Fail," in Vertical Files, folder "NYC Charter Revision, 1936," CHL.

102. Home Rule League against Proposed Charter, "Defeat a Bad Charter."

103. Home Rule League against Proposed Charter, "Defeat a Bad Charter."

104. Home Rule League against Proposed Charter, "Defeat a Bad Charter."
105. Home Rule League against Proposed Charter, "Defeat a Bad Charter."
106. As discussed in Chapter 3, arguments against PR on the basis of cost in both time and money emerged during the considerable delays incurred during the city's first PR tally in 1937.
107. See *Matter of Mooney v. Cohen*. Kings County ruling reprinted in *Matter of Mooney v. Cohen*, Section 1, 46–52.
108. *Matter of Mooney v. Cohen*, Section 1, 50.
109. Mooney's original petition reprinted in *Matter of Mooney v. Cohen*, Section 1, 15–28.
110. The three-member board of elections included Heffernan, David B. Costuma, and Jacob A. Livingston. As a delegate to the New York State Constitutional Convention in 1938, Heffernan voted to prohibit PR on a statewide basis.
111. Respondents Points, reprinted in *Matter of Mooney v. Cohen*, 13. Italics in original.
112. Respondents Points, reprinted in *Matter of Mooney v. Cohen*, 26.
113. Respondents Points, reprinted in *Matter of Mooney v. Cohen*.
114. Windels's brief reprinted in *Matter of Mooney v. Cohen*, Section 2.
115. State constitution quoted in Paul A. Windels, Appellant's Brief, *Matter of Mooney v. Cohen*, Section 2, 16–17, ellipses in original.
116. For examples of political cartoon depictions of Tammany, see "Do You Want to Vote for This?" *New York World-Telegram*, October 29, 1936; and "The Best Argument for the New Charter," *New York World-Telegram*, October 31, 1936, clippings in Vertical Files, folder "NYC Charter Revision, 1936," CHL.
117. Proportional Representation Campaign Committee pamphlet, "PR Means Proportional Representation; It also Means People's Rule," 1936, in Vertical Files, folder "NYC Proportional Representation," CHL.
118. Citizens Charter Campaign Committee pamphlet, "Charter Catechism!" 1936, in Vertical Files, folder "NYC Charter Revision, 1936," CHL.
119. "Charter Revision," WHN radio broadcast, 7:15 P.M., December 28, 1935, folder III-1, "Publicity," box 5, Earle Papers, CURB.
120. Mrs. H. Edward Dreier to Genevieve Earle, July 23, 1935, folder IV-1, "Proportional Representation," box 5, Earle Papers, CURB.
121. See "Charter Revision Urged by 11 Women Paraders," *New York Herald-Tribune*, October 2, 1936, 3; and NYCLOWV, "A Primer on Charter Revision and Proportional Representation" 1936, in Vertical Files, folder "NYC Charter Revision, 1936," CHL.

CHAPTER 3

1. "Proportional Representation with Ballots; for the Fifth, Sixth, and Seventh Grades; Teacher, or President of Civic Club in Charge," undated, folder "Political Papers: Citizens Non-Partisan Committee, 1940–45," box 23, Richard Welling Papers, NYPL.

2. "Proportional Representation with Ballots (based on the rules for electing Members of the City Council of Cincinnati); Eighth Grade and High School," undated, folder "Political Papers: Citizens Non-Partisan Committee, 1940–45," box 23, Welling Papers, NYPL.

3. As discussed in Chapter 4, anti-PR activists later charged that radicals used these lectures to deceive the city's youth into supporting PR.

4. Proportional Representation Joint Committee pamphlet, "John Q. Voter Gets a Break," 1937, PRS Papers, MTL; also in Vertical Files, folder "NYC Proportional Representation," CHL.

5. From "Opinion of Church, J.," *New York Law Journal* 97 (March 17, 1937): 1323; reprinted in *Matter of Bowe v. Cohen*, 274 NY 411, *New York Court of Appeals, Cases and Briefs, April 19–April 30, 1937, Volume 103*, 72–92, Record Series: Cases and Briefs on Appeal, 1847–1993, NYSA. Quote on 78–79.

6. From "Opinion of Church, J.," 89.

7. Quoted in "New Voting Plan Declared Invalid," *New York Times*, March 24, 1937, 22.

8. Tanzer, *The New York City Charter*, 14–15.

9. "New Election Law Fought as Invalid; Suit Calls It 'Lottery' with Luck Determining the Selections at Polls," *New York Times*, February 21, 1937, 21. Cyrus Miller and petitioner John F. Collins were also members of the scuttled 1934 commission that opposed PR. As discussed later in this chapter, many delegates to the 1938 convention historically opposed PR but voted for the system as a defense of city home rule.

10. See *Matter of Bowe v. Cohen*. Also see "Democrats Fight Proportional Vote; Five Borough Organizations Join in Suit Attacking Its Constitutionality," *New York Times*, February 26, 1937, 2.

11. Petitioners' brief, *Matter of Bowe v. Cohen*.

12. Petitioners' brief, *Matter of Bowe v. Cohen*.

13. See Section 1007, Chapter 43, in Tanzer, *The New York City Charter*.

14. George Hallett, "An Explanation of 'PR,'" letter to the editor, *New York Times*, February 17, 1937, 20; quoted in appellants' "Statement," *Matter of Bowe v. Cohen*.

15. William C. Chanler, "Reply Brief for Respondents," in *Matter of Bowe v. Cohen*.

16. John R. Crews and Kenneth F. Simpson, "Brief," in *Matter of Bowe v. Cohen*.

17. Crews and Simpson, "Brief."

18. Quoted in Tanzer, *The New York City Charter*, 544. Also see "Proportional Vote Wins in High Court," *New York Times*, June 3, 1937, 1.

19. Quoted in Tanzer, *The New York City Charter*, 543–544.

20. Quoted in Tanzer, *The New York City Charter*, 543.

21. Quoted in Tanzer, *The New York City Charter*, 546.

22. Quoted in Tanzer, *The New York City Charter*, 552 and 559.

23. George Hallett, Citizens Union Press Release, December 16, 1936, PRS Papers, MTL.

24. Hallett, Citizens Union Press Release.

25. "8-Hour Day for PR Ordered by Mayor," *New York Times*, November 11, 1937, 20.

26. Editorial, *New York World-Telegram*, November 24, 1937; quoted by William J. Schieffelin in "The Result of the PR Election for Councilmen," broadcast on WHN, November 26, 1937, folder IV-2, "Proportional Representation," box 5, Earle Papers, CURB.

27. Editorial, "Tammany and the Council," *New York Times*, November 17, 1937, 22.

28. Editorial, "Tammany and the Council."

29. See Kenneth Waltzer, "The American Labor Party: Third-Party Politics in New Deal-Cold War New York, 1936–1954," PhD diss., Harvard University, 1977.

30. "Morris, an Athlete, Heads City Council," *New York Times*, November 3, 1937, 13.

31. "Aldermanic Minority Headed by Curran; Board Picks Morris as Baldwin Successor," *New York Times*, August 25, 1934, 14.

32. Editorial, *New York Daily News*, undated (early 1938?), clipping in folder 46-1B, "New York City under PR," box 46, PRL Papers, CURB.

33. Out of the 2,300,200 ballots cast in the 1937 mayoral election, La Guardia totaled 1,344,630 and Democrat Jeremiah T. Mahoney received 890,756, with 64,834 distributed among other candidates. See "Mayoralty," *The Encyclopedia of New York City*, 739.

34. Immediately after the victory of proportional representation in 1936, the City Club of New York's Board of Trustees agreed that the system's success required voting machines. See *Minutes of the Board of Trustees (Volume 1935–1940)*, November 23, 1936, City Club of New York Papers, New-York Historical Society Manuscript Collection, New York City.

35. "Another Snipe at PR," *New York World-Telegram*, January 16, 1939, clipping in folder 46-1B, "New York City under PR," box 46, PRL Papers, CURB.

36. George Hallett to Louis Cohen, June 20, 1938, folder 53-1B, "NYS Constitutional Convention, 1938," box 53, PRL Papers, CURB.

37. Susan Jenkins, "Report on New York City Council by the Civic Education Group, Henry Street Settlement," January 31, 1938, folder IV-2, "Proportional Representation," box 5, Earle Papers, CURB. Jenkins served as executive secretary of the settlement's Civic Education Group. Also see Schieffelin, "The Results of the PR Election for Councilmen"; Sophia A. Olmstead, "Remarks on the PR Election," interview broadcast on WEVD, December 1, 1937; and George Hallett, "PR Has Accomplished Its Purpose," broadcast on WEVD, December 1, 1937. Above sources also in box 5, Earle Papers.

38. Jenkins, "Report on New York City Council."

39. The Brooklyn Republican Party's ineptitude in PR elections increased in 1939 and 1941, when the election of Brooklyn Communist Peter V. Cacchione precipitated the party's official turn against the system.

40. Lawson H. Brown, "Observations on the [*New York*] *Herald-Tribune* Tabulation of Results of the Election by PR for Brooklyn Councilmen, 1937," December 10, 1937, folder IV-2, "Proportional Representation," box 5, Earle Papers, CURB. Brown served as secretary to Brooklyn Borough president Ingersoll.

41. Brown, "Observations on the [*New York*] *Herald-Tribune* Tabulation."

42. "PR at Work: How Progressive Unity Could Have Won—and Can Win," *State of Affairs* 4 (July–August 1939), published by the Legislative and Research Bureau of the New York State Communist Party.

43. "PR at Work," *State of Affairs* 4 (July–August 1939).

44. "PR at Work," *State of Affairs* 4 (July–August 1939).

45. "Deadlock in the City Council," *New Masses* (January 18, 1938): 3–6, clipping in folder IV-2, "Proportional Representation," box 5, Earle Papers, CURB. Italics in original.

46. Jenkins, "Report on New York City Council," Earle Papers, CURB.

47. Quoted in "New Fusion Rule Starts in the City; Many Jobs Filled," *New York Times*, January 2, 1938, 1.

48. See folder 1, "Biographical Material," in box 1, Genevieve B. Earle Papers, La Guardia and Wagner Archives, La Guardia Community College, City University of New York, New York City (LGWA). Other repositories of Earle's papers include the Columbia University Rare Book and Manuscript Collection and the Municipal Archives. After attaining her first term in the city council in 1937, Earle won reelection in 1939, 1941, 1943, and 1945. Earle died in a home fire in 1956. See "Mrs. Earle, Former Councilman, Dies in Blaze at Home," *New York Times*, March 7, 1956, 35.

49. Genevieve B. Earle, Reminiscences, 1949–1950, 46, Columbia Center for Oral History, Columbia University, New York City (CCOH).

50. Earle, Reminiscences, 43–45.

51. Quoted in "Mrs. Earle Shuns Appeal to Women in Campaign," October 28, 1937, *New York Journal-American* (?), clipping in scrapbook three, Earle Papers, LGWA.

52. Quoted in "Use Political Power, Woman Leader Urges," *New York Daily News*, January 17, 1937, clipping in folder 7, "Clippings 2," box 1, Earle Papers, LGWA.

53. Quoted in "Mrs. Earle Chides Women on Votes; Only One of Sex Elected to New City Council Says They Neglect Opportunities," *New York Times*, November 29, 1937, 2. Italics added.

54. O. R. Pilat, "Men, Beware Ballot, There's Feminine Chicanery Afoot; It's All a Plot to Elect Mrs. Earle to the Council on Second-Hand Votes," *New York Post*, August 31, 1937, clipping in scrapbook 3, Earle Papers, LGWA.

55. Pilat, "Men, Beware Ballot."

56. Council members James A. Burke and Williams N. Conrad, the so-called insurgents, ran against the Democratic Party leadership in Queens. In the initial weeks of the council, though, Burke and Conrad strayed from the minority coalition and voted mostly with the Democratic majority. In later months, certain Republican Party council members left the minority's ranks as well, voting with Democrats as opposed to Fusionists, Laborites, and, eventually, Communists.

57. Newbold Morris, in collaboration with Dana Lee Thomas, *Let the Chips Fall: My Battles against Corruption* (New York: Appleton-Century-Crofts, 1955), 124.

58. Quoted in Morris, *Let the Chips Fall*, 124.

59. Morris, *Let the Chips Fall*, 125.
60. "Cashmore Ousted; Burke Is Elected to Council Post," *New York Times*, January 26, 1938, 1.
61. Morris, *Let the Chips Fall*, 125–127.
62. Morris, *Let the Chips Fall*, 128.
63. Morris, *Let the Chips Fall*.
64. Morris, *Let the Chips Fall*.
65. Russell Owen, "'SRO' Out at City Hall; Our New City Council Offers a Varied Cast and a Drama with Highlights of Comedy," *New York Times*, January 30, 1938, 122. SRO stood for Standing Room Only, connoting the entertainment quality and popularity of council sessions.
66. Untitled, *New York World-Telegram*, January 24, 1938, photocopy of artwork in Reuben A. Lazarus Papers, LGWA.
67. Morris's term, see *Let the Chips Fall*, 128.
68. "The First PR Council," *Searchlight*, published by the Citizens Union, 29 (October 1939): 3-4, folder "Political Papers: City Council Election Campaign," box 23, Welling Papers, NYPL.
69. Morris contended that the majority contrived to create these disturbances and delays as a way of discrediting the minority and the council president. See Morris, *Let the Chips Fall*, 123.
70. Municipal Affairs Committee, New York City League of Women Voters, "Highlights of the League's Program in the First City Council," September 15, 1939, folder "Citizens Union—PR—City Council," box R-1, Citizens Union Papers, CURB.
71. Wyona Dashwood, "Visions of a Great City; B. Charney Vladeck, Who Fled Russia to Find His Democratic Ideal, and Whose Office Overlooks New York's Un-Ideal Slums, Speaks as a Councilman upon the Defeat of Machine Politics," *Christian Science Monitor*, March 9, 1938, clipping in folder "City Council, 1937–1938," box 4, Vladeck Addendum, series 4, B. Charney Vladeck Papers, Tamiment Library and Robert F. Wagner Labor Archives, New York University, New York City (TLWA).
72. "B. C. Vladeck Dies; City Councilman," *New York Times*, October 31, 1938, 1.
73. For resolutions filed by the minority under Vladeck's leadership, see folder "City Council, 1937–1938," box 4, Vladeck Addendum, series 4, Vladeck Papers, TLWA. As discussed in Chapter 1, Wagner had advocated PR and municipal reform at the New York State Constitutional Convention of 1915.
74. "B. C. Vladeck Dies; City Councilman," *New York Times*.
75. Quoted in a Citizens Non-Partisan Committee report, by George Hallett and Margaret I. Tanzer, Campaign Manager and Assistant Campaign Manager, respectively, for the CNPC, Fall 1939 (?), folder VII-2, "Political Reform, 1939–1941," box 7, Earle Papers, CURB.

76. Quoted in Citizens Non-Partisan Committee report, by George Hallett and Margaret I. Tanzer.
77. "Democrats Elect Council Majority," *New York Times*, December 1, 1937, 1. This article revised the tally reported one week earlier showed Cacchione losing by only 245 votes. Cacchione argued that this revision, along with the transfer process in the later counts, pointed to a conspiracy against his election. See "Surpless Elected by Narrow Margin; Communist, Nosed Out as PR Tally Ends in Brooklyn, May Ask Recount," *New York Times*, November 28, 1937, 1.
78. For an examination of La Guardia's struggles with both the Republican and Democratic parties at the city and state levels, see Kessner, *Fiorello H. La Guardia and the Making of Modern New York*.
79. Memorandum by Reuben Lazarus, April 21, 1938, folder 56, "Corporation Counsel—William C. Chanler, 1938–1939," box 3, Lazarus Papers, LGWA.
80. Address by Newbold Morris, "Committee on Cities, Their Organization, Government, and Powers," June 3, 1938, folder 53, "Charter Revision—1939 (3), June 1938," box 3, Lazarus Papers, LGWA.
81. Testimony of Louis M. Killeen, *State of New York, In Convention, Record No. 69*, August 19, 1938, 3284, folder 53-1A, "NYS Constitutional Convention, 1938," box 53, PRL Papers, CURB, hereafter cited as *1938 Convention Record*. Transcript of 1938 Convention Record also in NYSA.
82. Testimony of Louis M. Killeen.
83. Testimony of Louis M. Killeen. As discussed in Chapter 2, Mayor La Guardia initially expressed similar concerns that PR had actually diminished progressive support in the city council.
84. The first proposal to amend Article II (Suffrage) of the New York State Constitution by prohibiting PR passed 96 to 35. The subsequent vote to accept Article II as amended passed by an even larger margin of 112 to 38. See *1938 Convention Record*, 3290 and 3300.
85. Testimony of Joseph C. Baldwin, *1938 Convention Record*, 3291.
86. "The First PR Council," *Searchlight*.
87. Testimony of Joseph V. McKee, *1938 Convention Record*, 3291.
88. Testimony of Abbot Low Moffat, *1938 Convention Record*, 3292.
89. Abbott Low Moffat to Kenneth F. Simpson, May 11, 1938, folder "Legislature, Its Organization . . . ," box 5, Series 0095, Records of the New York State Constitutional Convention, 1938, NYSA.
90. Testimony of Louis M. Killeen, *1938 Convention Record*, 3292–3293.
91. Testimony of James A. Foley, *1938 Convention Record*, 3294.
92. Testimony of Helen Z. M. Rodgers, *1938 Convention Record*, 3295. Rodgers chaired the convention's Committee on Suffrage.
93. Testimony of James A. Foley, *1938 Convention Record*, 3295.
94. Moffat's amendment failed by a 94 to 38 margin.

95. Quoted in "State Lawmakers Warned by Mayor," *New York Times*, August 24, 1938, 1. La Guardia's speech was broadcast on WABC at 7 P.M.

96. Quoted in "State Lawmakers Warned by Mayor."

97. Editorial, "The Bold Deal to Kill 'PR,'" *Brooklyn Eagle*, August 24, 1938, clipping in folder 52-5, "NYS Constitutional Convention, 1938, Proposed Ban on PR," box 52, PRL Papers, CURB.

98. "The Bold Deal to Kill 'PR.'"

99. See also Editorial, "Home Rule Defied in PR Defeat," *Brooklyn Eagle*, August 26, 1938, clipping in folder 52-5, "NYS Constitutional Convention, 1938, Proposed Ban on PR," box 52, PRL Papers, CURB.

100. Editorial, "Amendment Number Seven: Prohibiting 'PR,'" *Brooklyn Eagle*, October 27, 1938, clipping in folder 52-5, "NYS Constitutional Convention, 1938, Proposed Ban on PR," box 52, PRL Papers, CURB.

101. Opening comments by subcommittee chair, Rep. Joe Starnes (Alabama), on September 15, 1938, in House of Representatives Subcommittee of the Special Committee to Investigate Un-American Activities, *Investigation of Un-American Propaganda Activities in the United States: Hearings before a Special Committee on Un-American Activities . . . , Volume 2, September 15–October 22, 1938* (Washington, DC: United States Government Printing Office, 1938), 981.

102. References included in New York City testimony, *Investigation of Un-American Propaganda Activities . . .* , 981–1106. Following two unsuccessful bids for the council, Cacchione won a seat in 1941 and gained reelection in 1943 and 1945.

103. Simon W. Gerson, *Pete: The Story of Peter V. Cacchione, New York's First Communist Councilman* (New York: International Publishers, 1976), 24–25.

104. New York City testimony, *Investigation of Un-American Propaganda Activities . . .* , 1063.

105. Editorial, "PR as a Trojan Horse," *New York Sun*, October 25, 1938. Hermens wrote several anti-PR texts, most notably "The Trojan Horse of Democracy," *Social Research* 5 (1938): 397–423; *Democracy and Proportional Representation*, Public Policy Pamphlet Number 31 (Chicago: University of Chicago Press, 1940); and *Democracy or Anarchy? A Study of Proportional Representation* (Notre Dame, IN: Review of Politics, 1941).

106. "PR as a Trojan Horse."

107. "PR as a Trojan Horse."

108. Peter V. Cacchione, "Defeat the Kelly-Tammany Machine," radio address, October 29, 1938, microfilm, Peter V. Cacchione Papers, TLWA.

109. See "Republicans Quit Plan to Ban PR," and "Democratic Chiefs Ask Plank for PR," *New York Times*, September 29, 1938, 19 and 20.

110. Editorial, *Staten Island Advance*, November 20, 1938, clipping in folder 46-1B, "New York City under PR," box 46, PRL Papers, CURB. The Staten Island (Richmond) press, in alliance with the borough's Republican and Democratic

leadership, uniformly opposed PR. The 1938 tally provided the only instance when the borough backed PR; Richmond voted against PR in the 1936, 1940, and 1947 elections. Given that the borough's voting population did not reach the 50,000 quota for electing a council member, the city charter required that Richmond elect at least one representative to the legislature. In essence, this requirement guaranteed disproportionate representation for Richmond in the council.

111. Editorial, *Staten Island Advance*, November 20, 1938.
112. "The Council Majority," *New York Herald-Tribune*, December 1, 1938, clipping in folder 46-1A, "New York City under PR," box 46, PRL Papers, CURB.
113. "Mayor to Demand County Reforms," *New York Times*, November 30, 1938, 1.
114. "Council Kills County Job Bills after Stormy All-Night Session," *New York Times*, December 22, 1938, 1.
115. "Cashmore Ousted; Burke Is Elected to Council Post," *New York Times*, January 26, 1938, 1.
116. "Council Kills County Jobs Bills after Stormy All-Night Session," *New York Times*.
117. Morris, *Let the Chips Fall*, 129.
118. Quoted in "Council Kills County Job Bills after Stormy All-Night Session," *New York Times*.
119. "Council Kills County Job Bills after Stormy All-Night Session"; and Morris, *Let the Chips Fall*, 129.
120. Quoted in Editorial, "The Real Trouble," *Daily Worker*, December 27, 1938, clipping in folder 52-5, "New York State Constitutional Convention, 1938, Proposed Ban on PR," box 52, PRL Papers, CURB.
121. "The Real Trouble."
122. "The Real Trouble."
123. "Tammany Asks for It!" *New York World-Telegram*, December 28, 1938, clipping in folder 46-1B, "New York City under PR," box 46, PRL Papers, CURB.
124. George Hallett to Genevieve Earle, November 17, 1938, folder VII-1, "Political Reform, 1939–1941," box 7, Earle Papers, CURB.
125. Elsie Parker to John H. Humphreys, May 24, 1939, PRS Papers, MTL. At the time, Parker served as secretary for the National Municipal League in New York City; Humphreys directed the Proportional Representation Society in London.
126. After working as a Progressive organizer during the early 1910s, Pell joined the Democratic Party, served a term in Congress beginning in 1919, and led the New York Democratic Committee from 1921 until 1926. Pell worked in several diplomatic positions under President Roosevelt during the 1930s and 1940s, including tenure as minister to Portugal and Hungary.
127. Herbert Pell to Stanley Isaacs, March 4, 1939, folder "Isaacs, Stanley M.," box 10 (General Correspondence, Ho-Ja), Herbert C. Pell Papers, Franklin D. Roosevelt Presidential Library, Hyde Park, New York (FDRL).

CHAPTER 4

1. John H. Humphreys to George Hallett, September 25, 1939, PRS Papers, MTL.
2. John H. Humphreys to George Hallett, June 5, 1940, PRS Papers, MTL.
3. John H. Humphreys to George Hallett, January 29, 1941, PRS Papers, MTL.
4. "Communist Appointed to City Post; Communist Named to Staff by Isaacs," *New York Journal-American*, December 22, 1937, 1.
5. "Can He Serve Two Masters," *Brooklyn Eagle*, February 10, 1938, folder "Confidential Examiner for Stanley Isaacs, Clippings," Simon Gerson Papers, TLWA.
6. "Hurray for Stalin," *New York World-Telegram*, March 1, 1938; and "Isaacs Puts the Red Smear on a Liberal Administration," *New York World-Telegram*, March 2, 1938, both in folder "Confidential Examiner for Stanley Isaacs, Clippings," Gerson Papers, TLWA.
7. Rollin Kirby to Nathan Greene, March 8, 1938, folder, "Correspondence: O'Dwyer, Paul," Gerson Papers, TLWA.
8. Rollin Kirby to Simon Gerson, May 6, 1939, folder, "Correspondence: O'Dwyer, Paul," Gerson Papers, TLWA.
9. Remarks of William J. Schieffelin introducing Stanley Isaacs at the Citizens Union annual dinner, March 18, 1938, folder "1938," box 1, Stanley M. Isaacs Papers, CURB.
10. Remarks of William J. Schieffelin.
11. See Criminal Alien Information Bureau reports in the mayoral papers of Fiorello H. La Guardia, Municipal Archives, New York City (NYMA).
12. Kessner, *Fiorello H. La Guardia and the Making of Modern New York*, 492.
13. Alien Squad Report, August 2, 1939, in subject files "Communist Party," microfilm reel 150, La Guardia Papers, NYMA.
14. Ferdinand A. Hermens to Fiorello La Guardia, November 3, 1939, in subject files "PR, 1936–1940," microfilm reel 193, La Guardia Papers, NYMA.
15. Hermens to La Guardia, November 3, 1939.
16. Hermens, *Democracy or Anarchy? A Study of Proportional Representation*, 397.
17. George Hallett, "The New Book Against PR," *National Municipal Review* 31 (May 1942): 293.
18. O. Garfield Jones, "Book Reviews: *Democracy or Anarchy? A Study of Proportional Representation*, by F. A. Hermens," *Journal of Politics* 3 (November 1941): 534.
19. Hermens to La Guardia, November 3, 1939.
20. Fiorello H. La Guardia, Press Release, February 18, 1940, in subject files "PR 1936–1940," microfilm reel 193, La Guardia Papers, NYMA.
21. Charles Krumbein, "Report for the State Committee to the Tenth New York State Convention," *Proceedings, Tenth Convention, Communist Party, New York State* (New York: New York State Committee, Communist Party, 1938), 11 and 27, Reference Center for Marxist Studies, New York City (RCMS). Following the RCMS's closure, the center's collection, along with the papers of the Communist

Party of the United States of America, were donated to the Tamiment Library at New York University in 2006.

22. Krumbein, "Report for the State Committee," 29.

23. Krumbein, "Report for the State Committee," 88–89.

24. "A Political Manual for Harlem," issued by the Harlem Division of the Communist Party, USA, September 1939," 105–116, personal collection of Professor Robin D. G. Kelley, University of Southern California.

25. "Four Red Candidates Are Ruled Off Ballot for City Council on Legal Technicality," *New York Times*, October 14, 1939, 1.

26. "Complete Tables Showing Counting of PR Vote for Councilmen in All Boroughs," *New York Times*, November 18, 1939, 10. The transfer of Cacchione's votes occurred on the 42nd of 45 counts.

27. "Cashmore Offers Truce," *Brooklyn Eagle*, November 18, 1939, clipping in folder, "City Council Campaign—1939: Newspaper Clippings, ALP," box 27, Harry Laidler Papers, TLWA.

28. "The Cat That Ate the Canary," *New York Daily News*, November 14, 1939. For another critical interpretation of Tammany's electoral success under PR, see "PR— Meaning Power Racket," *Saturday Evening Post*, January 27, 1940, 26.

29. Quoted in "New Deal Termed Threat to Liberty; Platform of Westchester Young Republicans Scores 'Dictatorship Trend,'" *New York Times*, January 21, 1940, 32.

30. Quoted in "New Deal Termed Threat to Liberty."

31. "PR Should Be Repealed; Experiment Is Unimpressive," *Brooklyn Eagle*, November 3, 1940, clipping in folder 49-4B, "NYC Clippings, 1940," box 49, PRL Papers, CURB. Also see "PR Again Proved to Be a Failure," *Brooklyn Citizen*, November 13, 1941; "NY City Should Be Educated to Kill Its Big Lottery, PR," *Brooklyn Eagle*, November 23, 1941; and "Political Truce Ought to Doom PR," *Brooklyn Eagle*, December 13, 1941, clippings in folder 50-3A, "NYC Clippings, 1941," box 50, PRL Papers, CURB.

32. "Heffernan Says: PR Advocates and the Tammany Scarecrow," *Brooklyn Eagle*, December 17, 1941, clipping in folder 50-3C, "NYC Clippings, 1941," box 50, PRL Papers, CURB.

33. Stanley Isaacs to David Dubinsky, June 26, 1941, folder "Correspondence, 1941," box 1, Isaacs Papers, CURB.

34. Stanley Isaacs to Bruce Bliven, September 26, 1941, folder "Correspondence, 1941," box 1, Isaacs Papers, CURB.

35. Stanley Isaacs to John A. Lyon, December 27, 1939, folder "Correspondence, 1939," box 1, Isaacs Papers, CURB.

36. Simon Gerson to Stanley Isaacs, September 27, 1940, folder "Correspondence, 1940," box 1, Isaacs Papers, CURB.

37. Charles Belous to Fiorello La Guardia, February 2, 1940, in subject files, "American Labor Party," microfilm reel 183, La Guardia Papers, NYMA.

38. Unauthored letter regarding the history of Democratic Party opposition to PR, October 29, 1940, folder 45-1A, "New York City, 1940," box 45, PRL Papers, CURB.

39. Louis Cohen, "PR Unmasked," 1940, Vertical Files, folder "NYC Proportional Representation," CHL.

40. Louis Cohen to Robert Moses, October 28, 1940, folder "C," box 13, Robert Moses Papers, NYPL.

41. Ferdinand Hermens to Robert Moses, October 22, 1940, folder "C," box 13, Moses Papers, NYPL.

42. In 2007, the author participated in a conference titled "Robert Moses and the Modern City: New Perspectives on the Master Builder"; sponsored by Columbia University, the Queens Museum of Art, and the Museum of the City of New York. The conference was dedicated to reevaluating Moses's impact on New York City.

43. Robert A. Caro, *The Power Broker: Robert Moses and the Fall of New York* (New York: Vintage, 1974). For a generally more sympathetic critique of Moses and his influence on New York City, see Hilary Ballon and Kenneth T. Jackson, eds., *Robert Moses and the Modern City: The Transformation of New York* (New York: W. W. Norton, 2007).

44. Paul Goldberger, "Robert Moses, Master Builder, Is Dead at 92," *New York Times*, July 30, 1981, A1. Among his various titles, Moses directed the Triborough Bridge Authority. This position afforded him the power to manage the collection of tolls throughout the city, which he used to fund building projects at his discretion.

45. "A Proposal: To Change the Method of Electing the New York City Board of Aldermen; That Every Party May Receive Its Fair Share of Representation," submitted by the Proportional Representation League to the New York City Charter Commission, October 1922, folder 45-3, "NYC Election Figures," box 45, PRL Papers, CURB.

46. Caro, *The Power Broker*, 133–140.

47. See Moses's comments during the December 4, 1941, council hearing examined at the end of this chapter.

48. Raymond Ingersoll to George Hallett, December 14, 1933, folder 48-1, "NYC Correspondence, 1931–1939," box 48, PRL Papers, CURB.

49. Robert Moses to Ferdinand Hermens, with a copy to Louis Cohen, October 24, 1940, folder "C," box 13, Moses Papers, NYPL.

50. Robert Moses to Louis Cohen, May 23, 1940, folder "C," box 13, Moses Papers, NYPL.

51. Moses to Hermens, October 24, 1940.

52. See Moses's correspondence with publisher Roy Howard examined in Chapter 5.

53. Hermens to Moses, October 22, 1940.

54. Moses to Hermens, October 24, 1940.

55. Hermens to Moses, October 22, 1940.

56. Moses to Hermens, October 24, 1940.

57. "The Threat to the City Council," *New York Herald-Tribune*, October 17, 1940, clipping in Vertical Files, folder "NYC Proportional Representation," CHL. Also see Editorial, "Remember to Save PR," *New York Herald-Tribune*, October 21, 1941, in folder 49-4A, "NYC Clippings, 1940," box 49, PRL Papers, CURB.

58. Quoted in "Morris Denounces Fight against PR; Effort to Defeat It, He Says, Is Made by Reactionary Politicians of City; Tammany's Hand Is Seen . . . ," *New York Times*, October 30, 1940, 26.

59. Editorial, "Vote No and Save PR," *New York Times*, November 4, 1940, 18. For another example of the argument by the *Times* that Tammany endorsed repeal strictly as a means of preserving its power in city government, see Editorial, "To Save PR: Vote No," *New York Times*, October 21, 1940, 16.

60. "Counter Thrust on to Save City's PR; La Guardia, Morris and Civic Groups Open Fight," *New York Times*, November 3, 1940, 51.

61. Editorial, "Don't Let Them Kick Out PR," *New York World-Telegram*, October 28, 1940, in folder 49-4B, "NYC Clippings, 1940," box 49, PRL Papers, CURB.

62. George Hallett, "PR Should Not Be Repealed," radio address on WBNX, October 16, 1940, folder 45-1A, "New York City 1940," box 45, PRL Papers, CURB.

63. Hallett, "PR Should Not Be Repealed."

64. George Hallett to Editor of the *New York Sun*, July 10, 1940, folder 45-1A, "New York City 1940," box 45, PRL Papers, CURB.

65. See "Stalin Urges U.S., Britain to Open 2D Fighting Front," and "Boro Red Up Front in Early PR Count," *Brooklyn Eagle*, November 6, 1941, 1.

66. "Nine from Borough Are Elected to City Council," *Brooklyn Eagle*, November 12, 1941, 1.

67. "What a Contraption!" *Brooklyn Eagle*, November 14, 1941, 14.

68. "Defend PR—Or Back to Tin Boxes," *Daily Worker*, November 17, 1941, in folder 50-3A, "NYC Clippings, 1941," box 50, PRL Papers, CURB. Also see Max Frimmel, "Tammany Wars on PR Ballot, Seeks Absolute Machine Grip," *Daily Worker*, October 27, 1941, folder 50-3B, "NYC Clippings, 1941," box 50, PRL Papers, CURB.

69. *Proceedings of the Council of the City of New York, from July 1 to December 30, 1941, Second Council, Second Session, Volume II* (New York, 1942), 283–284.

70. "The Communist Councilman," *New York Daily News*, November 21, 1941, in folder 50-3A, "NYC Clippings, 1941," box 50, PRL Papers, CURB.

71. "Gavel Is Hurled at Hearing on PR; Cohen Lets It Fly at Critic, Rushes at Him—Missile Hits Mrs. Casey's Foot," *New York Times*, December 5, 1941, 25.

72. "Excerpt from Stenographic Record of a Public Hearing on PR by the Committee on State Legislation, Privileges and Elections of the City Council, Held in the Councilmanic Chamber, City Hall," December 4, 1941, folder "H," box 15, Moses Papers, NYPL.

73. "Excerpt from Stenographic Record."

74. "Zealots of the Burning Eye," *New York Sun*, December 8, 1941, in folder 50-3A, "NYC Clippings, 1941," box 50, PRL Papers, CURB.

CHAPTER 5

1. John Edgar Hoover, Memorandum for (Excised), March 28, 1941, Subject File, Peter V. Cacchione, File Number NY 100-8339, Federal Bureau of Investigation. File attained by author via Freedom of Information and Privacy Act (FOIPA) request, with file contents unclassified on October 23, 2003.
2. Richard M. Fried, *Nightmare in Red: The McCarthy Era in Perspective* (New York: Oxford University Press, 1990), 51.
3. Fried, *Nightmare in Red.*
4. Fried, *Nightmare in Red*, 53–54.
5. Fried, *Nightmare in Red*, 104.
6. Kessner asserts, "In New York City [La Guardia] had formed a supersecret 'sabotage squad,' whose existence was unknown even to the FBI and army intelligence, composed of 180 specially trained police officers selected to infiltrate and report on potentially subversive groups." See Kessner, *Fiorello La Guardia and the Making of Modern New York*, 492.
7. D. M. Ladd, "Memorandum to the Director," November 13, 1941, Cacchione FBI File.
8. John Edgar Hoover to Special Agent in Charge (New York, NY), December 5, 1941, Cacchione FBI File.
9. E. E. Conroy to the Director, FBI, "Re: Peter V. Cacchione; Internal Security," November 12, 1943, Cacchione FBI File.
10. See the Alien Squad reports of the New York City Police Department in the mayoral papers of Fiorello H. La Guardia in the NYMA (New York City), the records of the State Police task force assigned to investigate un-American activities in the NYSA (New York State), and the FBI files of Cacchione and Davis (federal).
11. Campaign scrapbooks, Cacchione Papers, TLWA.
12. "Laidler Off ALP Ticket: Council Redesignation Denied because of His Isolationism" (paper not listed, perhaps the *New York Post*), September 10, 1941, clipping in folder "City Council Campaign—1941: Newspaper Clippings," box 27, Harry W. Laidler Papers, TLWA.
13. "NEW YORK: Harlem's First," *Time*, January 12, 1942.
14. "NEW YORK: Harlem's First."
15. Hamilton, *Adam Clayton Powell, Jr.*, 115.
16. Gerald Horne, *Black Liberation/Red Scare: Ben Davis and the Communist Party* (Newark, DE: University of Delaware Press, 1994), 30–31.
17. Mark D. Naison, "Herndon Case," *Encyclopedia of the American Left*, ed. Mari Jo Buhle, Paul Buhle, and Dan Georgakas (Urbana: University of Illinois Press, 1992), 307.
18. Du Bois, "As the Crow Flies," *Amsterdam News*, March 23, 1940, in David Levering Lewis, *W. E. B. Du Bois: The Fight for Equality and the American Century, 1919–1963* (New York: Henry Holt, 2000), 464. Also see Horne, *Black Liberation/Red Scare*, 83–84.

19. Lewis, *W. E. B. Du Bois*, 538–539.
20. Michael Denning, *The Cultural Front: The Laboring of American Culture in the Twentieth Century* (New York: Verso, 1997), 23–24.
21. "Smaller and Redder," *New York World-Telegram*, November 12, 1943, folder 50-4, "1943 PR Election," box 50, PRL Papers, CURB. Also see "Communist Gains in Council Bring New Attack on PR," *New York World-Telegram*, November 29, 1943; and "Plan Unity Drive to Abolish PR: Moses Asserts Public Awakened to Peril by Red Gains," *New York Journal-American*, November 23, 1943, also in box 50, PRL Papers.
22. George Hallett to Kyle A. Vandergrift, June 11, 1941, folder "Correspondence, 1937," box 1, Isaacs Papers, CURB. [The 1941 letter has evidently been placed incorrectly in the 1937 folder.]
23. "Association Reaffirms Support of Proportional Representation," *Commerce & Industry Association of New York Bulletin* 7 (September 1947): 1, Vertical Files, folder "NYC Proportional Representation," CHL.
24. Laurence Arnold Tanzer, Reminiscences, 1949, 38, CCOH.
25. Communist Party leaflet, "Don't Let Your Country Down . . . You Lose Two Votes," 1943, microfilm reel 3, Cacchione Papers, TLWA.
26. See "Democracy: Victory at Home; Victory Abroad," *Pittsburgh Courier*, February 7, 1942. The *Courier* was one of the most influential African American newspapers of the day, and the Double-V became a cultural icon for progress in the struggle against racism in the United States.
27. "Summary Report," March 15, 1947, Subject File, Benjamin J. Davis Jr., File Number NY 100-23825, Federal Bureau of Investigation. File attained by author via FOIPA request, with file contents previously unclassified. The meeting referenced in the report occurred at the time of Davis's election to the council in November 1943.
28. Cheryl Lynn Greenberg, *Or Does It Explode? Black Harlem in the Great Depression* (New York: Oxford University Press, 1991), 211.
29. See Frederick Woltman, "Reds' Gains in Council Laid to Racial Drives," *New York World-Telegram*, November 11, 1943; and "Racial Tunes Played by Reds for Quill, Davis," *New York World-Telegram*, November 12, 1943, in folder 50-4, "1943 PR Election," box 50, PRL Papers, CURB.
30. Earle, Reminiscences, 72–73 and 124.
31. Benjamin J. Davis, "Autobiography," 745, microfilm reel 3, Benjamin J. Davis Jr. Papers, Schomburg Center for Research in Black Culture, New York Public Library, New York City (SC). Davis's autobiography was later published as *Communist Councilman from Harlem: Autobiographical Notes Written in a Federal Penitentiary* (New York: International Publishers, 1969).
32. Earle, Reminiscences, 81.
33. Earle, Reminiscences, 79–80.
34. Earle, Reminiscences, 79.

35. Stanley Isaacs to Col. Edward S. Greenbaum, September 14, 1942, folder "Correspondence, 1943–1945," box 2, Isaacs Papers, CURB.

36. Stanley Isaacs to Natalie and Ted Davison, March 27, 1942, folder "Correspondence, 1943–1945," box 2, Isaacs Papers, CURB.

37. Stanley Isaacs to Harriet Borchard, December 10, 1942, folder "Correspondence, 1930–1942," box 1, Isaacs Papers, CURB.

38. "Vote for O'Dwyer for Mayor; Re-elect Ben Davis for City Council," flyer issued by the Negro Labor Victory Committee,1945, part IV, microfilm reel 2, National Negro Congress (NNC) Papers, SC.

39. Davis, "Autobiography," 738.

40. Shaw, *The History of the New York Legislature*, 224.

41. Terry S. Ruderman, "Stanley M. Isaacs: The Conscience of New York," PhD diss., City University of New York, 1977, 159–160.

42. Davis, "Autobiography," 792.

43. Davis, "Autobiography," 812; and Shaw, *The History of the New York Legislature*, 224.

44. Quoted in Davis, "Autobiography," 63. Italics added.

45. Quoted in Davis, "Autobiography."

46. "Record of Ben Davis in the City Council, 1944–45," flyer issued by the New York County Communist Party Election Campaign Committee, 1945, microfilm reel 2, NNC Papers, SC.

47. "Record of Ben Davis in the City Council, 1944–45."

48. See Shaw, *The History of the New York Legislature*, chap. 12, "A Three-Ring Circus," 211–228.

49. "New City Council to Serve 4 Years," *New York Times*, November 4, 1945, 5.

50. Citizens Committee to Re-Elect Councilman Peter V. Cacchione, "Here's What You Vote for When You Vote No. 1 for Peter V. Cacchione," 1945, microfilm reel 3, Cacchione Papers, TLWA.

51. See "The Correct Way to Vote" and "Vote this Way," 1945, issued by the Citizens Committee to Re-Elect Councilman Peter V. Cacchione, microfilm reel 3, Cacchione Papers, TLWA.

52. "Vote this Way," 1945, part IV, microfilm reel 2, NNC Papers, SC.

53. "Artists' Committee Presents: All Star Victory Show to Re-elect Benjamin J. Davis Jr.," 1945, part IV, microfilm reel 2, NNC Papers, SC.

54. Denning, *The Cultural Front*, 334.

55. "They Are Voting for Benjamin J. Davis, Jr.," flyer issued by the New York County Communist Party Election Campaign Committee, 1945, part IV, microfilm reel 2, NNC Papers, SC. Also see Edward G. Perry to Duke Ellington, October 9, 1945, part IV, microfilm reel 2, NNC Papers, SC.

56. "Memorandum: Subject: Election Campaign," 1945, part IV, microfilm reel 2, NNC Papers, SC.

57. Robert L. Bobrick and Minna Pologe, Lower West Side Club, ALP, to Fellow ALP Voter, May 24, 1943, folder "Political Papers: American Labor Party," box 23, Welling Papers, NYPL.

58. Adolf A. Berle and Joseph V. Leary to Harry Truman, September 11, 1947, folder "1947 Exec. Dir.," box 7, Liberal Party (LP) Papers, NYPL.

59. "Liberal Party Program Submitted to the Statewide Convention," May 19–20, 1944, by the Committee on Program and Platform, Dr. John L. Childs, Chairman; folder "Political Papers: American Labor Party," box 23, Welling Papers, NYPL.

60. "Why the Liberal Party? Outline Submitted by Ben Davidson for Women's Division Course on the 'Know-How of Politics,'" undated, folder "Women's Division," box 2, LP Papers, NYPL.

61. George Bernstein, Speakers' Bulletin No. 3, "Why Trade Unionists Should Enroll in the Liberal Party," September 1947, folder "1947 Exec. Dir.," box 7, LP Papers, NYPL.

62. Bernstein, Speakers' Bulletin No. 3.

63. "Why the Liberal Party? Outline Submitted by Ben Davidson for Women's Division Course on the 'Know-How of Politics,'" undated, folder "Women's Division," box 2, LP Papers, NYPL.

64. "Why the Liberal Party? Outline Submitted by Ben Davidson."

65. "Manhattan's Labor Candidate: Benjamin F. McLaurin, Liberal-Republican Candidate for City Council," pamphlet, 1945, part IV, microfilm reel 2, NNC Papers, SC.

66. Press Release, July 27, 1945, Liberal Party of New York State, folder "Municipal–City Council," box 4, LP Papers, NYPL.

67. Press Release, July 27, 1945, Liberal Party of New York State.

68. Press Release, July 27, 1945, Liberal Party of New York State.

69. Charles A. Collins to Benjamin McLaurin, August 1, 1945, letter reprinted as press release issued by the Negro Labor Victory Committee, part IV, microfilm reel 2, NNC Papers, SC.

70. "Excerpt from Statement Read before State Executive Committee, December 12, 1945, by Dr. John L. Childs, on the Municipal Election and the Future of the Liberal Party," marked "Private and Confidential," folder "Councilmen," box 6, LP Papers, NYPL.

71. "Excerpt from Statement Read before State Executive Committee."

72. "Excerpt from Statement Read before State Executive Committee."

73. Daniel J. Link, "'Every Day Was a Battle': Liberal Anticommunism in Cold War New York, 1944–1956," PhD diss., New York University, 2006.

74. "Proportional Representation," August 27, 1945, folder "Proportional Representation," box 4, LP Papers, NYPL.

75. "Proportional Representation," August 27, 1945.

76. Editorial, "PR Flops, as Usual," *New York Daily News*, November 15, 1945, 31.

77. Editorial, "PR Flops, as Usual."

78. "Democrats Hold Firm Council Grip as Vote Count Ends," *New York Times*, November 18, 1945, 1.

79. George Hallett to A. A. Berle, August 20, 1943, PRS Papers, MTL.
80. See Adolf A. Berle Jr. Papers, FDRL.
81. A. A. Berle to George Hallett, August 25, 1943, PRS Papers, MTL.
82. John H. Humphreys to George Hallett, January 29, 1941, PRS Papers, MTL. The organization's headquarters were bombed during the Blitz, and one of its chief officials died in combat in Europe.
83. Edmund Harvey, Member of Parliament, "House of Commons; Extract from the Official Report," October 10, 1944, speech before the House of Commons, folder 22-11A, "England–Pamphlets, Clippings, Memos," box 22, PRL Papers, CURB.
84. Harvey, speech in the House of Commons, October 10, 1944.
85. John H. Humphreys to Elsie Parker, October 4, 1944, PRS Papers, MTL.
86. George Hallett to Major Dana Converse Backus, May 7, 1945, and Backus to Hallett, May 1, 1945, PRS Papers, MTL. Quotation in untitled and undated attachment authored by Hallett.
87. George Hallett to Samuel Seabury, November 6, 1942, folder 45-1B, "New York City, 1940," box 45, PRL Papers, CURB.
88. George Hallett to Thomas J. Curran, July 3, 1942, folder 45-1B, "New York City, 1940," box 45, PRL Papers, CURB.
89. George Hallett to John H. Humphreys, July 31, 1944, PRS Papers, MTL.

CHAPTER 6

1. Francis Biddle to Franklin Roosevelt, August 30, 1944, in Office Files, folder 670, "Tammany Hall 1933–1944," FDRL.
2. Eleanor Roosevelt to Ed Flynn, June 8, 1945, folder "FIR-FLY," box 3288, Anna Eleanor Roosevelt Papers, Part II, 1945–1952, FDRL. In 1949, Flynn served as Democratic Party leader for the Bronx, a position he held from 1922 until 1953. Flynn chaired the Democratic National Committee from 1940 through 1943 and retained considerable influence in the Democratic Party through his Bronx office.
3. Robert Moses to Genevieve Earle, October 27, 1943, folder "H," box 17, Moses Papers, NYPL.
4. "Moses Declines to Lead Fight for PR Repeal," *Brooklyn Eagle*, November 14, 1943, clipping in scrapbook 4, 1938–1939, Earle Papers, LGWA. While Moses refused to lead a repeal campaign, he continued to criticize PR and supported its repeal. See "Plan Unity Drive to Abolish PR: Moses Asserts Public Awakened to Peril by Red Gains," *New York Journal-American*, November 23, 1943, clipping in folder 50-4, "1943 PR Election," box 50, PRL Papers, CURB.
5. Robert Moses to Ferdinand Hermens, November 12, 1943, folder "H," box 17, Moses Papers, NYPL.
6. "Democrats Move to Kill PR Voting; City Organizations Inspire a Move at Albany along Two Legislative Lines," *New York Times*, January 16, 1944, 1.

7. See January 28, 1944, and June 27, 1944, letters of George Mand to Edward Flynn and June 25, 1944, response from Flynn to Mand, folder "Mand, George A., 1935–1950," box 17, Edward J. Flynn Papers, FDRL. In January 1950, Mand cited his leadership in the PR repeal movement in an unsuccessful attempt to convince Flynn to arrange his appointment as US Marshall. See handwritten note from Mand to Flynn, dated January 3, 1950, and Flynn's negative reply, dated January 6, 1950, also in box 17, Flynn Papers.

8. George Mand to Edward Flynn, June 21, 1945, folder "Mand, George A., 1935–1950," box 17, Flynn Papers, FDRL.

9. Flynn to Mand, June 25, 1945.

10. Garrett, *The La Guardia Years*, 242.

11. "Proponents of PR to Open Big Drive; Thousands of Street and Shop Meetings to Be Held before Nov. 4 to Fight Repeal," *New York Times*, October 27, 1947, 22.

12. Belle Zeller and Hugh A. Bone, "American Government and Politics: The Repeal of PR in New York City—Ten Years in Retrospect," *American Political Science Review* 42 (December 1948): 1130.

13. Committee to Save PR, "Want Grafters in City Hall?" 1947, microfilm reel 3, Cacchione Papers, TLWA. The CIO's support for PR is described in Warren Moscow, "Moses Asserts PR Harms Democracy; Holds It Fosters Bloc System that Is a Threat to Our Form of Government," *New York Times*, October 28, 1947, 20.

14. "The Red Herring," *Citizen Union News* (May 1947), Vertical Files, folder "NYC Proportional Representation," CHL. For similar position papers published by the Communist Party and the League of Women Voters, see "The Fight to Save PR," published by the Legislative Bureau, New York State Committee, Communist Party; and "PR Defense Organizes," published by the Keep PR Committee of the League of Women Voters, July 6, 1947, microfilm reel 3, Cacchione Papers, TLWA.

15. *Amsterdam News*, November 1, 1947, quoted in Zeller and Bone, "American Government and Politics," 1138. This excerpt echoed the argument offered in the Communist Party's "Political Manual for Harlem" from 1939, discussed in Chapter 4.

16. Peter V. Cacchione, "U.S. Largest Cities Choose PR Voting," *Daily Worker*, October 15, 1947, 4.

17. Davis, "Autobiography," 738.

18. Benjamin J. Davis, *Why I Am a Communist* (New York: New Century Publishers, 1947), 6.

19. Press Release, "New York Branches Urge PR Retention," Undated, National Association for the Advancement of Colored People (NAACP) Records, Part II, Branch File: 1940–1955, folder "New York State Conference, 1943–1952," box II:C133, Manuscript Division, Library of Congress, Washington, DC (LOC). For a comprehensive examination of civil rights activism in New York City following World War II, see Martha Biondi, *To Stand and Fight: The Struggle for Civil Rights in Postwar New York City* (Cambridge, MA: Harvard University Press, 2003).

20. Joyce Turner, Secretary of the Keep PR Committee of Jamaica, "Vote 'No' at the End of the Row," October 16, 1947, NAACP Records, Part II, Branch File: 1940–1955, folder "Jamaica, 1940–1950," box II:C121, LOC.

21. Sarah Margaret Freid to Stanley Isaacs, October 3, 1947, folder "Progressive Citizens of America, 1947," box 14, Isaacs Papers, NYPL. Freid's full title was Chairman, Program and Education Committee, Washington Heights—Inwood Chapter, Progressive Citizens of America. For a similar argument that repeal threatened minority parties, see "New Yorkers Face Vote on PR . . . Repeal Aimed at Minority Parties," PM, June 19, 1947.

22. Peter V. Cacchione, "Untitled," 1947, microfilm reel 3, Cacchione Papers, TLWA.

23. Genevieve B. Earle, "Let's Look at the Record," November 1, 1947, Vertical Files, folder "NYC Proportional Representation," CHL.

24. "Fact Sheet to Accompany Discussion Outline: PR," September 1947, folder "Apportionment; Proportional Representation; League Files and Material, 1932–1947," box 10, NYCLOWV Papers, CURB.

25. "Women's Club Delegates against PR 3 to 1; Three Counts Are Taken at Stormy Session," New York Times, November 1, 1947, 9.

26. Minutes of Board of Directors Meetings, 1947, Women's City Club of New York (WCCNY) Papers, microfilm, Bobst Library, New York University, New York City (BL).

27. Herbert C. Pell, "PR and the Communists," undated (circa 1947), 1, folder "Proportional Representation, 1947," box 23, Pell Papers, FDRL.

28. Pell, "PR and the Communists," 5.

29. Pell, "PR and the Communists," 4.

30. Pell, "PR and the Communists," 6.

31. Nathan Straus, "Statement on Proportional Representation," October 27, 1947, folder "Apportionment; Proportional Representation; League Files and Material, 1932–1947," box 10, NYCLOWV Papers, CURB.

32. Quoted in "Supporters of PR Redouble Battle," New York Times, October 23, 1947, 52.

33. A. A. Berle, "Speech, Public Meeting of the Liberal Party," September 26, 1947, folder "Speeches, 1947," box 147, Berle Papers, FDRL.

34. A. A. Berle, "Liberal Unity for a Liberal America," October 6, 1947, speech aired on WMCA radio from 8:45 P.M. to 9:00 P.M., folder "Speeches, 1947," box 147, Berle Papers, FDR Library.

35. Berle, "Liberal Unity for a Liberal America."

36. A. A. Berle, address on WNBC radio, November 3, 1947, folder "Speeches, 1947," box 147, Berle Papers, FDRL.

37. Ben Davidson, "Speakers' Bulletin #4: The Case for Proportional Representation," September 1947, folder "1947, Exec. Dir.," box 7, LP Papers, NYPL.

38. Davidson, "Speakers' Bulletin #4."

39. Ben Davidson, "Speakers' Bulletin #1: Questions Dealing with the Objectives of the 1947 Enrollment and Election Campaign of the Liberal Party," September 1947, folder "Exec. Dir.," box 7, LP Papers, NYPL.
40. Zeller and Bone, "American Government and Politics," 1130.
41. See Robert Moses to Roy W. Howard, May 16, 1947; Roy W. Howard to Robert Moses, May 19, 1947; and Robert Moses to Lester Markel, Sunday editor of the *New York Times*, May 13, 1947, folder "Proportional Representation," box 30, Moses Papers, NYPL. Howard quotation in letter to Moses dated May 19, 1947, also in box 30, Moses Papers.
42. Quoted in "Sampson Likens PR to Hitler Law," *New York Times*, November 1, 1947, 9.
43. Quoted in "Sampson Likens PR to Hitler Law."
44. Quoted in Ray Ghent, "Repeal of PR by More than 2 to 1 Predicted," *New York World-Telegram*, October 31, 1947, 3.
45. Simon Gerson to Stanley Isaacs, October 8, 1947, and reply dated October 9, 1947, folder "1947—Gerson, S. W.," box 14, Isaacs Papers, NYPL.
46. "Impellitteri Asks Voters to Kill PR; Supporters of Law Censure Legion Stand—Communist Rally Backs Statute," *New York Times*, October 30, 1947, 2. The debate was broadcast on WQXR.
47. "Sampson Likens PR to Hitler Law," *New York Times*.
48. "Heads of Tammany Join Fight on PR; Kill 'Stalin Frankenstein' Project at the Balloting on Nov. 4, Voters Urged," *New York Times*, October 8, 1947, 21.
49. "Who Are PR's Best Friends," *New York Daily News*, September 17, 1947, clipping in folder "Apportionment; Proportional Representation; League Files and Material, 1932–1947," box 10, NYCLOWV Papers, CURB.
50. "Who Are PR's Best Friends."
51. Editorial, "PR Godsend to Commies!" *New York World-Telegram*, September 9, 1947, clipping in Vertical Files, folder "NYC Proportional Representation," CHL.
52. For endorsements of charter reform and PR in 1936, see "Charter and PR," *New York World-Telegram*, October 20, 1936, 22; "Gangway for Charter Plus PR," *New York World-Telegram*, October 26, 1936, 18; "Five Safe, Sound 'Yeses,'" *New York World-Telegram*, October 27, 1936, 20; and "Why Women Should Be for New Charter and PR," *New York World-Telegram*, November 2, 1936, 32. Other pro-repeal editorials included "Poisonous Fruits of PR," *New York World-Telegram*, October 30, 1947, 34; and "Amendments and Propositions," *New York World-Telegram*, October 31, 1947, 26. The latter column concluded that "for city voters [the repeal] issue tops all others in the election."
53. "PR Wins," *New York World-Telegram*, November 6, 1940, folder 49-4A, "NYC Clippings, 1940," box 49, PRL Papers, CURB.
54. George Mand to Ferdinand Hermens, September 6, 1947, folder "PR," box 29, Moses Papers, NYPL.
55. Editorial, "Tomorrow's Voting," *New York Post*, November 3, 1947, 37.

56. For earlier *Post* editorials concerning PR, see "Proportional Representation," *New York Post*, May 12, 1947, 21; and "Bad vs. Worse," *New York Post*, August 5, 1947, 21.

57. Zeller and Bone, "American Government and Politics," 1131.

58. See editorials "The Record on PR—I," *New York Times*, October 27, 1947, 20; "The Record on PR—II," *New York Times*, October 28, 1947, 24; "The Record on PR—III," *New York Times*, October 29, 1947, 26; and "The Record on PR—IV," *New York Times*, October 30, 1947, 24.

59. "The Record on PR—I." For analysis of La Guardia's criticism of PR following the 1937 council elections, see Chapter 3.

60. "The Record on PR—III."

61. George Mand to Ferdinand Hermens, with a copy to Robert Moses, July 27, 1947, folder "H," box 29, Moses Papers, NYPL; and Press Release for the Citizens Committee to Repeal PR, October 22, 1947, in folder "Proportional Representation," box 30, Moses Papers. The other members of the Citizens Committee included George F. Mand, chairman and president of the Bronx Chamber of Commerce; Maude E. Ten Eych, Republican assemblywoman for the First District; M. D. Griffith, executive vice-president of the New York Board of Trade; Arthur J. Duffy, American Legion; and James Carberry, Veterans of Foreign Wars.

62. George Mand to Robert Moses, July 31, 1947, folder "Proportional Representation," box 30, Moses Papers, NYPL.

63. "Moses Opposes PR as Communist Arm; Letter Asserts Russians Use It, as the Nazis Did, to Seize Power in Germany," *New York Times*, October 20, 1947, 5; and "Moses Asserts PR Harms Democracy; Holds It Fosters Bloc System that Is a Threat to Our Form of Government," *New York Times*, October 28, 1947, 20.

64. Robert Moses, "Against PR," letter to the editor, *New York Times*, November 3, 1947, 22.

65. *Annual Report of the Board of Elections in the City of New York for the Year 1947* (New York, 1948), 60–61.

66. "PR Is Repealed," *New York Times*, November 5, 1947, 26.

67. "PR Is Repealed."

68. Stanley Isaacs to Edward Reese, June 5, 1947, Isaacs Papers, NYPL; quoted in Ruderman, "Stanley M. Isaacs: The Conscience of New York," 165.

69. Stanley Isaacs to Abraham Schargel, American Veterans Committee, March 22, 1948, folder "Correspondence, Ca. 1943–1945," box 2, Isaacs Papers, CURB.

EPILOGUE

1. Shaw, *The History of the New York Legislature*, 254.

2. James McNally, *New York Law Journal*, July 22, 1948, folder "Electoral Democracy 'Gerson Re: Seating of Communist by New York City Council,'" box 49, Vito Marcantonio Papers, NYPL.

3. "Petition of Bertha Melzer, resident of Brooklyn, to the City Council," July 1, 1948, folder "Electoral Democracy 'Gerson Re: Seating of Communist by New York City Council," box 49, Marcantonio Papers, NYPL.

4. See Chapter 4.

5. *Amter v. Flynn*, 275 NY 396 (1937).

6. Vito Marcantonio, "Legal Argument in Support of Resolution to Elect a Communist Councilman," January 14, 1948, folder "Electoral Democracy 'Gerson Re: Seating of Communist by New York City Council,'" box 49, Marcantonio Papers, NYPL.

7. Fried, *Nightmare in Red*, 109–110.

8. Fried, *Nightmare in Red*, 110.

9. Posters such as "They fought for DEMOCRACY; now they want JOBS" starkly characterized the need for government policies to ensure that black Americans could participate equally in the postwar economy. In advocating professional baseball's integration, Davis released "Good enough to DIE . . . but not good enough to PITCH!" an image both sobering and inflammatory. The poster showed a dead black soldier lying face down with a checkmark covering the scene, juxtaposed with a picture of a black baseball pitcher placed behind a large X. For Davis campaign literature, see microfilm reel 4, Davis Papers, and microfilm reel 2, NNC Papers, SC.

10. Eleanor Roosevelt to Ed Flynn, November 5, 1949, folder "Roosevelt, Franklin and Eleanor, 1931–1962," box 15, Flynn Papers, FDRL. In 1949, Flynn served as Democratic Party leader for the Bronx, but he retained considerable influence in national party decisions following his tenure as Democratic National Committee chair from 1940 to 1943.

11. The poster "No War! Peace!" contained two contrasting depictions of the purpose of postwar America. The upper half featured an updated interpretation of the party boss long used in anti-Tammany cartoons—a skeleton, with bloated belly and adorned with top hat and tuxedo, carrying money bags in each arm as he straddled an atomic bomb. The caption read, "That ATOM BOMB that the Democrat, Republican, and Liberal bosses want to start a new war with . . . costs $2,000,000,000." In the lower half lay the victim of the skeleton's treachery—an idyllic urban community that populated a public housing development, with residents strolling through a park under partly cloudy skies. The accompanying caption stated, "$2,000,000,000, will build 50 housing projects—homes for 2 million people!" American Labor Party campaign poster, 1949, microfilm reel 4, Davis Papers, SC. Beset by the continuing anti-Communism of the Cold War, the ALP disbanded in 1956.

12. Minutes of Board of Directors Meetings, 1947, WCCNY Papers, BL.

13. "The National Municipal League and Proportional Representation," February 4, 1954, folder "Model City Charter," box 10, Series III, PRL Papers, CURB.

14. George Hallett to the Executive Committee and Council of the National Municipal League, October 22, 1962, folder "Model City Charter," box 10, Series III, PRL Papers, CURB. Hallett wrote as executive secretary of the Citizens Union.

BIBLIOGRAPHY

PRIMARY SOURCES
Manuscript and Archival Collections

Arthur W. Diamond Law Library, Columbia University, New York City (CULL)
New York City Charter Revision Commission, 1935–1936 (CRC)

Brooklyn Collection, Brooklyn Public Library (BPL)
Brooklyn Daily Eagle
Ingersoll, Raymond V.

City Hall Library, New York City (CHL)
Vertical Files

Franklin D. Roosevelt Presidential Library, Hyde Park, New York (FDRL)
Berle, Adolf A. Jr.
Cuneo, Ernest
Flynn, Edward J.
Pell, Herbert C.
Roosevelt, Anna Eleanor
Roosevelt, Franklin D. (Papers as New York State Senator, Office of the Governor of New
   York Papers, Office Files)
Tugwell, Rexford
Vertical Files

La Guardia and Wagner Archives, La Guardia Community College, City University of
   New York, Long Island City, New York (LGWA)
Earle, Genevieve B.
Lazarus, Reuben A.
Morris, Newbold

Manuscript Collection, New-York Historical Society, New York City (NYHS)
City Club of New York (CCNY)

Manuscript Division, Library of Congress (LOC)
  National Association for the Advancement of Colored People (NAACP)

Manuscripts and Archives Division, New York Public Library, New York City (NYPL)
  Bard, Albert Sprague
  Isaacs, Stanley M.
  Liberal Party
  Lloyd, Lola Maverick
  Marcantonio, Vito
  Moses, Robert
  National Civic Federation
  New York World's Fair 1939 and 1940 Incorporated (NYWF)
  Schiff, Dorothy
  Schwimmer, Rosika
  Sterne, Simon
  Tilden, Samuel J.
  Waldman, Louis
  Welling, Richard

Manuscripts and Special Collections, New York State Library, Albany, New York
  (NYSL)

Manuscripts, Archives, and Rare Books Division, Schomburg Center for Research in
  Black Culture, New York Public Library, New York City (SC)
  Davis, Benjamin J. Jr.
  National Negro Congress (NNC)

McDougall Trust Library, London (MTL)
  Proportional Representation Society (PRS)

Microfilm Collection, Elmer Holmes Bobst Library, New York University, New York
  City (BL)
  Women's City Club of New York (WCCNY)

Municipal Archives, New York City (NYMA)
  Earle, Genevieve B.
  Impellitteri, Vincent R.
  La Guardia, Fiorello H.
  O'Dwyer, William P.

New York State Archives, Albany, New York (NYSA)
  New York Court of Appeals, Cases and Briefs on Appeal, 1847–1993
  New York State Police Non-Criminal Investigation Files, 1940–1970
  Records of the Joint Legislative Committee to Investigate Seditious Activities (Lusk Com-
    mittee)
  Records of the Joint Legislative Committee to Investigate the State Education System
    (Rapp-Coudert Committee)

Records of the New York State Constitutional Convention, 1915
Records of the New York State Constitutional Convention, 1938

Rare Book and Manuscript Library, Columbia University, New York City (CURB)
Citizens Union
Earle, Genevieve B.
Isaacs, Stanley M.
League of Women Voters of the City of New York (NYCLOWV)
McAneny, George
Minor, Robert
Proportional Representation League (PRL)

Reference Center for Marxist Studies, New York City (RCMS); Collection donated to TLWA in 2006
Pamphlet Collection

Special Collections and University Archives, Rutgers, State University of New Jersey, New Brunswick, New Jersey (RUSC)
American Labor Party

Tamiment Library and Robert F. Wagner Labor Archives, New York University, New York City (TLWA)
Cacchione, Peter V.
Gerson, Simon W.
Laidler, Harry W.
Quill, Michael J.
Vertical Files
Vladeck, B. Charney

Oral Histories

Columbia Center for Oral History, Columbia University, New York City (CCOH)
Childs, Richard S.
Earle, Genevieve B.
Isaacs, Stanley M.
Marcantonio, Vito
Morris, Newbold
New York Political Studies, Part A: Brooklyn Politics, 1930–1950
New York Political Studies, Part C: New York Election of 1949
New York Political Studies, Part III, 1949
No Ivory Tower
Schieffelin, William Jay
Socialist Movement
Tanzer, Laurence Arnold

The Oral History of the American Left, TLWA

Government Documents

Annual Reports of the Board of Elections in the City of New York for the Years 1936–1949. New York, 1936–1949.

Individual Case Files. Federal Bureau of Investigation, U.S. Department of Justice. Records for Peter V. Cacchione and Benjamin J. Davis.

Hill, Robert A., ed. *The FBI's RACON: Racial Conditions in the United States during World War II.* Boston: Northeastern University, 1995.

Katzman, Kenneth. *Congressional Research Service Report: RS21968; Iraq: Elections, Government, and Constitution.* Washington, DC: Library of Congress, 2006.

House of Representatives Subcommittee of the Special Committee to Investigate Un-American Activities. *Investigation of Un-American Propaganda Activities in the United States: Hearings before a Special Committee on Un-American Activities. . . , Vol. 2, Sept. 15–Oct. 22, 1938.* Washington, DC: United States Government Printing Office, 1938.

New York (City) Charter Revision Commission. *Preliminary Report and Draft of the Proposed Charter for the City of New York.* New York, 1936.

New York (City) Charter Revision Commission. *Public Hearings, May 7–22, 1936.* New York, 1936.

New York (City) Charter Revision Commission. *Records of Public Hearings and Minutes of Executive Meetings: February 18, 1935–August 4, 1936.* 4 vols. New York, 1936.

Proceedings of the Board of Aldermen and Municipal Assembly, Aldermanic Branch, 1935–1937. New York, 1935–1937.

Proceedings of the Council of the City of New York, 1938–1949. New York, 1938–1949.

Report of the Commission to Devise a Plan for the Government of Cities in the State of New York (Tilden Commission). New York: Evening Post Steam Presses, 1877.

Report of the New York Charter Commission to the Legislature with a Draft of Charter for the City of New York. New York: M. B. Brown, 1923.

Reports of the New York State Constitution Convention Committee, Vols. 1–12. New York: Burland Printing, 1938.

Seabury, Samuel. *In the Matter of the Investigation of the Departments of the Government of the City of New York, etc., pursuant to Joint Resolutions adopted by the Legislature of the State of New York. Final Report to Hon. Samuel H. Hofstadter, Chairman, New York (State) Legislature, Joint Committee on Affairs of the City of New York.* New York, 1932.

Tanzer, Laurence A., *The New York City Charter: Adopted November 3, 1936. . . .* New York: Clark Boardman, 1937.

Periodicals: Contemporary Journals and Magazines

American City
Atlantic Monthly
Commonweal
Forum

Journal of Politics
Life
Literary Digest
Nation
National Municipal Review
New Outlook
New Republic
Newsweek
Searchlight
Survey
Time

Periodicals: Newspapers

Amsterdam News
Bronx Home News
Brooklyn Daily Eagle
Brooklyn Tablet
Daily Worker
New York Daily News
New York Herald-Tribune
New York Journal-American
New York Post
New York Sun
New York Times
New York World-Telegram
People's Voice
Saturday Evening Post
PM
Sacramento Bee
Staten Island Advance

SECONDARY LITERATURE

Adams, Katherine H., and Michael L. Keene. *Alice Paul and the American Suffrage Campaign*. Chicago: University of Chicago Press, 2008.

Adler, Leslie Kirby. "The Red Image: American Attitudes toward Communism in the Cold War Era." PhD diss., University of California, Berkeley, 1970.

Alexander, Leslie M. *African or American? Black Identity and Political Activism in New York City, 1784–1861*. Urbana: University of Illinois Press, 2008.

Alpers, Benjamin L. *Dictators, Democracy, and American Public Culture: Envisioning the Totalitarian Enemy, 1920s–1950s*. Chapel Hill: University of North Carolina Press, 2003.

Anderson, Kristi. *After Suffrage: Women in Partisan and Electoral Politics before the New Deal*. Chicago: University of Chicago Press, 1996.

Appy, Christian G. *Cold War Constructions: The Political Culture of United States Imperialism, 1945–1966*. Amherst: University of Massachusetts Press, 2000.

Baker, Jean H., ed. *Votes for Women: The Struggle for Suffrage Revisited*. New York: Oxford University Press, 2002.

Ballon, Hilary, and Kenneth T. Jackson, eds. *Robert Moses and the Modern City: The Transformation of New York*. New York: W. W. Norton, 2007.

Barber, Kathleen, ed. *Proportional Representation and Election Reform in Ohio*. Columbus: Ohio State University Press, 1995.

Barry, Francis S. *The Scandal of Reform: The Grand Failures of New York's Political Crusaders and the Death of Nonpartisanship*. New Brunswick, NJ: Rutgers University Press, 2009.

Barson, Michael, and Steven Heller. *Red Scared! The Commie Menace in Propaganda and Popular Culture*. San Francisco: Chronicle Books, 2001.

Bederman, Gail. *Manliness and Civilization: A Cultural History of Gender and Race in the United States, 1880–1917*. Chicago: University of Chicago Press, 1995.

Bender, Thomas. "Book Review: *The Populist Persuasion: An American History*." *Nation* 260 (March 13, 1995): 350.

Berg, Bruce F. *New York City Politics: Governing Gotham*. New Brunswick, NJ: Rutgers University Press, 2007.

Biondi, Martha. *To Stand and Fight: The Struggle for Civil Rights in Postwar New York City*. Cambridge, MA: Harvard University Press, 2003.

Blake, Angela M. *How New York Became American, 1890–1924*. Baltimore: Johns Hopkins University Press, 2006.

Bloom, Nicholas Dagen. *Public Housing That Worked: New York in the Twentieth Century*. Philadelphia: University of Pennsylvania Press, 2008.

Bone, Hugh A. "Political Parties in New York City." *American Political Science Review* 40:2 (1946): 272–282.

Boone, Gloria Marie. "The Reform Rhetoric of Samuel Seabury of New York: The Battle against Tammany Hall and Municipal Corruption." PhD diss., Ohio University, 1982.

Bouton, Terry. *Taming Democracy: "The People," the Founders, and the Troubled Ending of the American Revolution*. New York: Oxford University Press, 2007.

Boyer, Paul. *By the Bomb's Early Light: American Thought and Culture at the Dawn of the Atomic Age*. Chapel Hill: University of North Carolina Press, 1994.

Brinkley, Alan. "AHR Forum: The Problem of American Conservatism," *American Historical Review* 99 (April 1994): 409–429.

Brown, Elsa Barkley. "Womanist Consciousness: Maggie Lena Walker and the Independent Order of Saint Luke." In *Unequal Sisters*, edited by Ellen Carol DuBois and Vicki L. Ruiz. New York: Routledge, 1990.

Buhle, Mari Jo, Paul Buhle, and Dan Georgakas. *The Encyclopedia of the American Left*. Urbana: University of Illinois Press, 1992.

Burnham, Robert A. "Reform, Politics, and Race in Cincinnati: Proportional Representation and the City Charter Committee, 1924–1959." *Journal of Urban History* 23 (January 1997): 131–163.

Burrows, Edwin G., and Mike Wallace. *Gotham: A History of New York City to 1898*. New York: Oxford University Press, 1999.

Canning, Kathleen. "Feminist History after the Linguistic Turn: Historicizing Discourse and Experience." *Signs* 19 (Winter 1994): 368–404.

Capeci, Dominic J. *The Harlem Riot of 1943*. Philadelphia: Temple University Press, 1977.

Carleton, Don E. *Red Scare! Right-wing Hysteria, Fifties Fanaticism, and Their Legacy in Texas*. Austin: Texas Monthly, 1985.

Caro, Robert A. *The Power Broker: Robert Moses and the Fall of New York*. New York: Vintage, 1974.

Carter, Robert Frederick. "Pressure from the Left: The American Labor Party, 1936–1954." PhD diss., Syracuse University, 1965.

Chamberlain, Lawrence H. *Loyalty and Legislative Action: A Survey of Activity by the New York State Legislature, 1919–1949*. Ithaca: Cornell University Press, 1951.

Cohen, Lizabeth. *Making a New Deal: Industrial Workers in Chicago, 1919–1939*. Cambridge, UK: Cambridge University Press, 1990.

Countryman, Vern. *Un-American Activities in the State of Washington: The Work of the Canwell Committee*. Ithaca: Cornell University Press, 1951.

Cumings, Bruce. *The Origins of the Korean War. Vol. 2, The Roaring of the Cataract, 1947–1950*. Princeton: Princeton University Press, 1990.

———. "'Revising Postrevisionism,' or The Poverty of Theory in Diplomatic History." *Diplomatic History* 17 (Fall 1993): 539–560.

Cuordileone, K. A. "Politics in an Age of Anxiety: Cold War Political Culture and the Crisis of American Masculinity, 1949–1960." *Journal of American History* 87 (September 2000): 515–545.

Dabel, Jane E. *A Respectable Woman: The Public Roles of African American Women in 19th Century New York*. New York: New York University Press, 2008.

Davis, Benjamin J. *Communist Councilman from Harlem: Autobiographical Notes Written in a Federal Penitentiary*. New York: International Publishers, 1969.

———. *Why I Am a Communist*. New York: New Century Publishers, 1947.

Denning, Michael. *The Cultural Front: The Laboring of American Culture in the Twentieth Century*. New York: Verso, 1997.

Dewey, Donald. *The Art of Ill Will: The Story of American Political Cartoons*. New York: New York University Press, 2007.

Dudziak, Mary L. *Cold War Civil Rights: Race and the Image of American Democracy*. Princeton: Princeton University Press, 2000.

Dunn, John. *Democracy: A History*. New York: Atlantic Monthly, 2005.

Edwards, Rebecca. *Angels in the Machinery: Gender in American Party Politics from the Civil War to the Progressive Era*. New York: Oxford University Press, 1997.

Enstad, Nan. "Fashioning Political Identities: Cultural Studies and the Historical Construction of Political Subjects." *American Quarterly* 50 (December 1998): 745–782.

Fein, Michael R. *Paving the Way: New York Road Building and the American State, 1880–1956*. Lawrence: University Press of Kansas, 2008.

Fine, Nathan. *The Collapse of the Seabury Investigation.* New York: Rand School, 1932.

Finegold, Kenneth. *Experts and Politicians: Reform Challenges to Machine Politics in New York, Cleveland, and Chicago.* Princeton: Princeton University Press, 1995.

Fousek, John Howard. "To Lead the Free World: American Nationalism and the Ideological Origins of the Cold War, 1945–1960." PhD diss., Cornell University, 1994.

Fraser, Steve, and Gary Gerstle, eds. *The Rise and Fall of the New Deal Order, 1930–1980.* Princeton: Princeton University Press, 1989.

Freedman, Estelle. "Separatism as Strategy: Female Institution Building and American Feminism, 1870–1930." *Feminist Studies* 5 (Fall 1979): 512–529.

Freeland, Richard M. *The Truman Doctrine and the Origins of McCarthyism: Foreign Policy, Domestic Politics, and Internal Security, 1946–1948.* New York: Knopf, 1972.

Freeman, Joshua B. *In Transit: The Transport Workers Union in New York City, 1933–1966.* New York: Oxford University Press, 1989.

———. *Working Class New York: Life and Labor since World War II.* New York: New Press, 2000.

Fried, Richard M. *Nightmare in Red: The McCarthy Era in Perspective.* New York: Oxford University Press, 1990.

———. *The Russians Are Coming! The Russians Are Coming!* New York: Oxford University Press, 1998.

Gaddis, John Lewis. *We Now Know: Rethinking Cold War History.* New York: Oxford University Press, 1997.

Galie, Peter J. *Ordered Liberty: A Constitutional History of New York.* New York: Fordham University Press, 1996.

Garrett, Charles. *The La Guardia Years: Machine and Reform Politics in New York City.* New Brunswick, NJ: Rutgers University Press, 1961.

Gellhorn, Walter, ed. *The States and Subversion.* Ithaca: Cornell University Press, 1952.

Gerson, Simon W. *Pete: The Story of Peter V. Cacchione, New York's First Communist Councilman.* New York: International Publishers, 1976.

Gilfoyle, Timothy J. *City of Eros: New York City, Prostitution, and the Commercialization of Sex, 1790–1920.* New York: W. W. Norton, 1992.

———. *A Pickpocket's Tale: The Underworld of Nineteenth-Century New York.* New York: W. W. Norton, 2006.

Ginzberg, Lori D. *Untidy Origins: A Story of Woman's Rights in Antebellum New York.* Chapel Hill: University of North Carolina Press, 2005.

Goodman, James. *Stories of Scottsboro.* New York: Vintage, 1994.

Goyens, Tom. *Beer and Revolution: The German Anarchist Movement in New York City, 1880–1914.* Urbana: University of Illinois, 2007.

Gratz, Roberta Brandes. *The Battle for Gotham: New York in the Shadow of Robert Moses and Jane Jacobs.* New York: Nation Books, 2010.

Greenberg, Cheryl Lynn. *Or Does It Explode? Black Harlem in the Great Depression.* New York: Oxford University Press, 1991.

Gregory, Steven. *Black Corona: Race and the Politics of Place in an Urban Community.* Princeton: Princeton University Press, 1998.

Griffin, Robert, and Athan Theoharis. *The Specter: Original Essays on the Cold War and the Origins of McCarthyism*. New York: New Viewpoints, 1974.

Hallett, George H. Jr. *Proportional Representation: The Key to Democracy*. Washington, DC: National Home Library Foundation, 1937.

Hamilton, Charles V. *Adam Clayton Powell, Jr.: The Political Biography of an American Dilemma*. New York: Atheneum, 1991.

Hammack, David C. *Power and Society: Greater New York at the Turn of the Century*. New York: Columbia University Press, 1987.

Hart, Jenifer. *Proportional Representation: Critics of the British Electoral System, 1820– 1945*. New York: Oxford University Press, 1992.

Heale, M. J. *McCarthy's Americans: Red Scare Politics in State and Nation, 1935–1965*. Athens: University of Georgia, 1998.

Hermens, F. A. *Democracy and Proportional Representation*, Public Policy Pamphlet Number 31. Chicago: University of Chicago, 1940.

———. *Democracy or Anarchy? A Study of Proportional Representation*. Notre Dame, IN: Review of Politics, 1941.

———. "The Trojan Horse of Democracy." *Social Research* 5 (1938): 397–423.

Hoag, Clarence Gilbert, and George Hervey Hallett Jr. *Proportional Representation*. New York: Macmillan, 1926.

Hofstadter, Richard. *The Paranoid Style in American Politics and Other Essays*. Cambridge, MA: Harvard University Press, 1996.

Hogan, Michael J. *A Cross of Iron: Harry S. Truman and the Origins of the National Security State, 1945–1954*. Cambridge, UK: Cambridge University Press, 1999.

Holmberger, Eric. *The Historical Atlas of New York City: A Visual Celebration of Nearly 400 Years of New York City's History*. New York: Henry Holt, 1994.

Holmes, Thomas Michael. "The Specter of Communism in Hawaii, 1947–1953." PhD diss., University of Hawaii Press, 1975.

Horne, Gerald. *Black Liberation/Red Scare: Ben Davis and the Communist Party*. Newark: University of Delaware Press, 1994.

———. *Black and Red: W. E. B. Du Bois and the Afro-American Response to the Cold War, 1944–1963*. Albany: State University of New York Press, 1986.

Horowitz, Daniel. *Betty Friedan and the Making of "The Feminine Mystique": The American Left, the Cold War, and Modern Feminism*. Amherst: University of Massachusetts Press, 1998.

Hunt, Michael H. *Ideology and U.S. Foreign Policy*. New Haven: Yale University Press, 1987.

Hunter, Allen, ed. *Rethinking the Cold War*. Philadelphia: Temple University Press, 1998.

Irons, Peter H. "America's Cold War Crusade: Domestic Politics and Foreign Policy, 1942–1948." PhD diss., Boston University, 1972.

Isaacs, Edith S. *Love Affair with a City: The Story of Stanley M. Isaacs*. New York: Random House, 1967.

Jackson, Kenneth T. *Crabgrass Frontier: The Suburbanization of the United States*. New York: Oxford University Press, 1985.

Jackson, Kenneth T., ed. *The Encyclopedia of New York City*. New Haven: Yale University Press, 1995.

Jackson, Kenneth T., and David S. Dunbar, eds. *Empire City: New York through the Centuries*. New York: Columbia University Press, 2002.

Jackson, Kenneth T., and Fred Kameny, eds. *The Almanac of New York City*. New York: Columbia University Press, 2009.

Jenkins, Philip. *Cold War at Home: The Red Scare in Pennsylvania, 1945–1960*. Chapel Hill: University of North Carolina Press, 1999.

Johnston, Robert D. *The Radical Middle Class: Populist Democracy and the Question of Capitalism in Progressive Era Portland, Oregon*. Princeton: Princeton University Press, 2003.

Kaplan, Amy, and Donald E. Pease, eds. *Cultures of United States Imperialism*. Durham: Duke University Press, 1993.

Katzman, Kenneth. *Congressional Research Service Report: RS21968; Iraq: Elections, Government, and Constitution*. Washington, DC: Library of Congress, 2006.

Kazin, Michael. *The Populist Persuasion: An American History*. New York: Basic Books, 1995.

———. "The Grass-Roots Right: New Histories of U.S. Conservatism in the Twentieth Century." *American Historical Review* 97 (February 1992): 136–155.

Keller, Lisa. *Triumph of Order: Democracy and Public Space in New York and London*. New York: Columbia University Press, 2009.

Kelley, Robin D. G. *Hammer and Hoe: Alabama Communists during the Great Depression*. Chapel Hill: University of North Carolina Press, 1990.

Kerber, Linda K. *No Constitutional Right to Be Ladies: Women and the Obligations of Citizenship*. New York: Hill and Wang, 1998.

Kerber, Linda K., Alice Kessler-Harris, and Kish Kathryn Sklar, eds. *U.S. History as Women's History: New Feminist Essays*. Chapel Hill: University of North Carolina Press, 1995.

Kessner, Thomas. *Fiorello H. La Guardia and the Making of Modern New York*. New York: McGraw-Hill, 1989.

Keyssar, Alexander. *The Right to Vote: The Contested History of Democracy in the United States*. New York: Basic Books, 2000.

King, Moses. *King's Handbook of New York City, 1892, An Outline History and Description of the American Metropolis*. Reprint, New York: Barnes & Noble Books, 2001.

Kofsky, Frank. *Harry S. Truman and the War Scare of 1948: A Successful Campaign to Deceive the Nation*. New York: St. Martin's Press, 1993.

Korstad, Robert, and Nelson Lichtenstein. "Opportunities Found and Lost: Labor, Radicals, and the Early Civil Rights Movement." *Journal of American History* 75 (December 1988): 786–811.

Kruse, Kevin M. *White Flight: Atlanta and the Making of Modern Conservatism*. Princeton: Princeton University Press, 2005.

Kurzman, Charles. *Democracy Denied, 1905–1915: Intellectuals and the Fate of Democracy*. Cambridge, MA: Harvard University Press, 2008.

LaCerra, Charles. *Franklin Delano Roosevelt and Tammany Hall of New York*. Lanham, MD: University Press of America, 1997.

Lagumina, Salvatore J. *New York at Mid-Century: The Impellitteri Years.* Edited by Jon L. Wakelyn. Westport, CT: Greenwood, 1992.

Lears, T. J. Jackson. *No Place of Grace: Antimodernism and the Transformation of American Culture, 1880–1920.* Chicago: University of Chicago Press, 1981.

Leffler, Melvyn P. *A Preponderance of Power: National Security, the Truman Administration, and the Cold War.* Stanford: Stanford University Press, 1992.

———. *The Specter of Communism: The United States and the Origins of the Cold War, 1917–1953.* New York: Hill and Wang, 1994.

Leinwand, Gerald. *Mackerels in the Moonlight: Four Corrupt American Mayors.* Jefferson, NC: McFarland, 2004.

Lerner, Michael A. *Dry Manhattan: Prohibition in New York City.* Cambridge, MA: Harvard University Press, 2007.

Lewis, David Levering. *W. E. B. Du Bois: The Fight for Equality and the American Century, 1919–1963.* New York: Henry Holt, 2000.

Link, Daniel J. "'Every Day Was a Battle': Liberal Anticommunism in Cold War New York, 1944–1956." PhD diss., New York University, 2006.

Lipsitz, George. *Rainbow at Midnight: Labor and Culture in the 1940s.* Urbana: University of Illinois Press, 1994.

Marable, Manning. *Race, Reform, and Rebellion: The Second Reconstruction in Black America, 1945–1990.* Jackson: University of Mississippi Press, 1991.

Mattson, Kevin. *Creating a Democratic Public: The Struggle for Urban Participatory Democracy during the Progressive Era.* University Park: Pennsylvania State University Press, 1998.

May, Elaine Tyler. *Homeward Bound: American Families in the Cold War Era.* New York: Basic Books, 1988.

McAuliffe, Mary Sperling. "The Red Scare and the Crisis in American Liberalism, 1947–1954." PhD diss., University of Maryland, 1972.

McBain, Howard Lee. "Proportional Representation in American Cities." *Political Science Quarterly* 37 (June 1922): 281–298.

McCormick, Richard L. *From Realignment to Reform: Political Change in New York State, 1893–1910.* Ithaca: Cornell University Press, 1981.

McCormick, Thomas J. *America's Half-Century: United States Foreign Policy in the Cold War and After,* 2d ed. Baltimore: Johns Hopkins University Press, 1995.

McEnaney, Laura. *"Civil Defense Begins at Home": Militarization Meets Everyday Life in the Fifties.* Princeton: Princeton University Press, 2000.

McGerr, Michael. *A Fierce Discontent: The Rise and Fall of the Progressive Movement in America, 1870–1920.* New York: Oxford University Press, 2003.

McNickle, Chris. *To Be Mayor of New York: Ethnic Politics in the City.* New York: Columbia University Press, 1993.

Meyerowitz, Joanne, ed. *Not June Cleaver: Women and Gender in Postwar America, 1945–1960.* Philadelphia: Temple University Press, 1994.

Mickenberg, Julia L. *Learning from the Left: Children's Literature, the Cold War, and Radical Politics in the United States.* New York: Oxford University Press, 2006.

Minear, Richard H. *Dr. Seuss Goes to War: The World War II Editorial Cartoons of Theodor Seuss Geisel.* New York: New Press, 1999.

"Minority or Proportional Representation," *Columbia Law Review* 21:2 (February 1921): 182–186.

Mitgang, Herbert. *The Man Who Rode the Tiger: The Life and Times of Judge Samuel Seabury.* 2nd ed. New York: Fordham University Press, 1996.

———. *Once Upon a Time in New York: Jimmy Walker, Franklin Roosevelt, and the Last Great Battle of the Jazz Age.* New York: Free Press, 2000.

Moody, Kim. *From Welfare State to Real Estate: Regime Change in New York City, 1974 to the Present.* New York: New Press, 2007.

Moore, Leonard J. "Good Old-Fashioned New Social History and the Twentieth-Century American Right." *Reviews in American History* 24:4 (1996): 555–573.

Morris, Newbold, with Dana Lee Thomas. *Let the Chips Fall: My Battles against Corruption.* New York: Appleton-Century-Crofts, 1955.

Mumford, Kevin. *Newark: A History of Race, Rights, and Riots in America.* New York: New York University Press, 2007.

Muncy, Robyn. *Creating a Female Dominion in American Reform, 1890–1935.* New York: Oxford University Press, 1991.

Murphy, Kevin P. *Political Manhood: Red Bloods, Mollycoddles, and the Politics of Progressive Era Reform.* New York: Columbia University Press, 2008.

Naison, Mark. *Communists in Harlem during the Depression.* New York: Grove, 1983.

Page, Max. *The City's End: Two Centuries of Fantasies, Fears, and Premonitions of New York's Destruction.* New Haven: Yale University Press, 2008.

Painter, Nell Irvin. *Standing at Armageddon: The United States, 1877–1919.* New York: W. W. Norton, 1987.

Peretti, Burton W. *Nightclub City: Politics and Amusement in Manhattan.* Philadelphia: University of Pennsylvania Press, 2007.

Powers, Richard Gid. *Not Without Honor: The History of American Anticommunism.* New Haven: Yale University Press, 1995.

Quigley, David. *Second Founding: New York City, Reconstruction, and the Making of American Democracy.* New York: Hill and Wang, 2004.

Recchiuti, John Louis. *Civic Engagement: Social Science and Progressive-Era Reform in New York City.* Philadelphia: University of Pennsylvania Press, 2007.

Reeves, Thomas C. *The Life and Times of Joe McCarthy.* Lanham, MD: Madison, 1997.

Ribuffo, Leo P. "AHR Forum: Why Is There So Much Conservatism in the United States and Why Do So Few Historians Know Anything about It?" *American Historical Review* 99 (April 1994): 438–449.

Rogin, Michael Paul. *The Intellectuals and McCarthy: The Radical Specter.* Cambridge, MA: MIT Press, 1967.

Rose, Lisle A. *The Cold War Comes to Main Street: America in 1950.* Lawrence: Kansas University Press, 1999.

Rosenburg, Emily S. "Foreign Affairs after World War II: Connecting Sexual and International Politics." *Diplomatic History* 18 (Winter 1994): 59–70.

Ruderman, Terry S. "Stanley M. Isaacs: The Conscience of New York." PhD diss., City University of New York, 1977.

Ryan, Mary P. *Civic Wars: Democracy and Public Life in the American City during the Nineteenth Century*. Berkeley: University of California Press, 1997.

Savage, Barbara Dianne. *Broadcasting Freedom: Radio, War, and the Politics of Race*. Chapel Hill: University of North Carolina Press, 1999.

Savage, Sean. *Truman and the Democratic Party*. Lexington: University of Kentucky Press, 1997.

Schrecker, Ellen. *Many Are the Crimes: McCarthyism in America*. Princeton: Princeton University Press, 1998.

Scott, James C. *Domination and the Arts of Resistance: Hidden Transcripts*. New Haven: Yale University Press, 1990.

Scott, Joan W. "Gender: A Useful Category of Historical Analysis." *American Historical Review* 91 (December 1986): 1053–1075.

Selcraig, James Truett. *The Red Scare in the Midwest, 1945–1955*. Ann Arbor: UMI Research, 1982.

Self, Robert O. *American Babylon: Race and the Struggle for Postwar Oakland*. Princeton: Princeton University Press, 2003.

Selverstone, Marc J. *Constructing the Monolith: The United States, Great Britain, and International Communism, 1945–1950*. Cambridge, MA: Harvard University Press, 2009.

Shaw, Frederick. *The History of the New York Legislature*. New York: Columbia University Press, 1954.

Sherry, Michael S. *In the Shadow of War: The United States since the 1930s*. New Haven: Yale University Press, 1995.

Sinha, Manisha, and Penny M. Von Eschen, eds. *Contested Democracy: Freedom, Race, and Power in American History*. New York: Columbia University Press, 2007.

Sneider, Allison L. *Suffragists in an Imperial Age: U.S. Expansion and the Woman Question, 1870–1929*. New York: Oxford University Press, 2008.

Solomon, Mark. *The Cry Was Unity: Communists and African Americans, 1917–1936*. Jackson: University of Mississippi Press, 1998.

Steinberg, Peter L. *The Great "Red Menace": United States Prosecution of American Communists, 1947–1952*. Westport, CT: Greenwood, 1984.

Stephanson, Anders. *Manifest Destiny: American Expansion and the Empire of Right*. New York: Hill and Wang, 1995.

Storch, Randi. *Red Chicago: American Communism at Its Grassroots, 1928–35*. Urbana: University of Illinois Press, 2007.

Straetz, Ralph A. *PR Politics in Cincinnati: Thirty-two Years of City Government through Proportional Representation*. New York: New York University, 1958.

Stromquist, Shelton, ed. *Labor's Cold War: Local Politics in a Global Context*. Urbana: University of Illinois Press, 2008.

Sugrue, Thomas J. "Crabgrass-Roots Politics: Race, Rights, and the Reaction against Liberalism in the Urban North, 1940–1964." *Journal of American History* 82 (September 1995): 551–586.

———. *The Origins of the Urban Crisis: Race and Inequality in Postwar Detroit.* Princeton: Princeton University Press, 1996.

Sullivan, Patricia. *Days of Hope: Race and Democracy in the New Deal Era.* Chapel Hill: University of North Carolina Press, 1996.

Terkel, Studs. *Hard Times: An Oral History of the Great Depression.* New York: New Press, 1970.

Thomas, Lorrin. *Puerto Rican Citizen: History and Identity in Twentieth-Century New York City.* Chicago: University of Chicago Press, 2010.

Tichenor, Daniel J. *Dividing Lines: The Politics of Immigration Control in America.* Princeton: Princeton University Press, 2002.

Von Eschen, Penny M. *Race against Empire: Black Americans and Anticolonialism, 1937–1957.* Ithaca: Cornell University Press, 1997.

Walker, George E. *The Afro-American in New York City, 1827–1860.* New York: Garland, 1993.

Waltzer, Kenneth. "The American Labor Party: Third Party Politics in New Deal-Cold War New York, 1936–1954." PhD diss., Harvard University, 1977.

Weigand, Kate. *Red Feminism: American Communism and the Making of Women's Liberation.* Baltimore: Johns Hopkins University Press, 2001.

Weil, François. *A History of New York.* Translated by Gladding Jody. New York: Columbia University Press, 2004.

Westad, Odd Arne. *The Global Cold War.* New York: Cambridge University Press, 2007.

Whitfield, Stephen J. *The Culture of the Cold War.* Baltimore: Johns Hopkins University Press, 1991.

Widmer, Edward L. *Young America: The Flowering of Democracy in New York City.* New York: Oxford University Press, 1999.

Wilentz, Sean. *Chants Democratic: New York City and the Rise of the American Working Class, 1788–1850.* New York: Oxford University Press, 1984.

———. *The Rise of American Democracy: Jefferson to Lincoln.* New York: W. W. Norton, 2005.

Young, Louise M. *In the Public Interest: The League of Women Voters, 1920–1970.* New York: Greenwood, 1989.

Zeitz, Joshua M. *White Ethnic New York: Jews, Catholics, and the Shaping of Postwar Politics.* Chapel Hill: University of North Carolina Press, 2007.

Zeller, Belle, and Hugh A. Bone. "American Government and Politics: The Repeal of PR in New York City—Ten Years in Retrospect." *American Political Science Review* 42 (December 1948): 1127–1148.

Zipp, Samuel. *Manhattan Projects: The Rise and Fall of Urban Renewal in Cold War New York.* New York: Oxford University Press, 2010.

INDEX

corruption in, 38
FBI surveillance of Communist Party
in, 155–156
and New York City consolidation,
26, 28
and New York City Council elections
in 1937, 84–85, 87–98, 108, 135
in 1939, 136–139
in 1941, 147–152, 158, 220n39
in 1943, 160–161
in 1945, 168, 173–174
and proportional representation
referenda
in 1938, 116, 118–122
in 1940, 147
in 1947, 193, 196, 198–199
and Cacchione's replacement on
council, 202–203
See also Cacchione, Peter V.;
county reorganization; Earle,
Genevieve B.
Brooklyn Citizen, 196
Brooklyn Daily Eagle, 28, 196
criticism of proportional
representation, 139, 147–151
and Gerson-Isaacs controversy, 130
opposition to 1938 repeal referendum,
116, 118
Brotherhood of Sleeping Car
Porters, 171
Buffalo, New York, 115
Burke, James A., 90–91, 101–102,
123–124, 138, 221n56

Cacchione, Peter V.
biography of, 119
death of, 199–200, 202–203
FBI surveillance of, 155–157
New York City Council campaigns of,
157–159
in 1937, 89, 108, 135–136,
223n77

in 1939, 136–137
in 1941, 147–152, 220n39
in 1943, 157, 159–162
in 1945, 167–168, 172–175
and service in legislature,
163–166
and proportional representation,
advocacy of, 120–121, 184–186
repeal movement against,
148–153, 161–162, 175–176, 180,
195, 197
California, 32, 34–35, 73
Cambridge, Massachusetts. *See under*
Massachusetts
Carberry, James, 238n61
Caro, Robert, 141–142
Carroll, William A., 90, 138, 148,
160, 174
Carver, George Washington. *See* George
Washington Carver Day
Casey, Rita, 148–152
Cashmore, John, 90, 101–102, 124, 138
Catholic Americans, 37–38, 60
nativist opposition to, 13–14, 17,
19–20
support for Tammany Hall/
Democratic Party, 16, 22–23, 192
Catholic War Veterans, 192
Catt, Carrie Chapman, 55, 142
Central Trades and Labor Council, 56
Chamberlain, Joseph P., 51
Chanler, William C., 87
charter reform in New York, 3–4, 8–9,
123–124
in 1850s, 16
in 1870s, 21–24
in 1890s, 25–28
in 1920s, 31–32, 35, 142
in 1932–1934, 39–49
1935–1936 Charter Revision
Commission (*see* New York City
Charter Revision Commission)